MORDECAI M. KAPLAN:

AN EVALUATION

MORDECAI M. KAPLAN:

AN EVALUATION

Edited by

IRA EISENSTEIN

AND

EUGENE KOHN

———◆———

JEWISH RECONSTRUCTIONIST FOUNDATION, INC.
NEW YORK, 1952

Copyright, 1952
by
JEWISH RECONSTRUCTIONIST FOUNDATION, INC.

PRINTED IN THE UNITED STATES OF AMERICA
PRESS OF *Maurice Jacobs* INC.
224 N. 15th ST., PHILADELPHIA 2, PENNA.

With gratitude

TO

MR. LEWIS S. ROSENSTIEL

WHOSE GENEROSITY MADE
THE PUBLICATION OF THIS
VOLUME POSSIBLE.

PREFACE

On June 11, 1951 Mordecai M. Kaplan was seventy. But already in April, fifteen hundred people had gathered at the Waldorf-Astoria Hotel in New York to extend their affectionate greetings to him; and for months thereafter, Jewish organizations and institutions vied with one another to do him honor. These events will live long in the memory of those who attended them.

Some of his students and disciples felt that a volume in honor of Mordecai Kaplan would serve to signalize the occasion of his seventieth birthday in a manner most appropriate to his distinguished career. The Jewish Reconstructionist Foundation, which has been the main instrument for the dissemination of Dr. Kaplan's views, took up the idea, and commissioned the undersigned to edit such a volume. We hope that this work will enable readers to get a rounded view of Dr. Kaplan's philosophy and program for Jewish life.

Our heartiest thanks go to the contributors to this volume, who so graciously consented to accept the assignments made to them. All of them wrote as a labor of love. Our thanks to Dr. Kaplan for adding his own concluding chapter.

Ira Eisenstein
Eugene Kohn

MORDECAI M. KAPLAN

An Evaluation

Preface.. vii

As Teacher	Mortimer J. Cohen p. 3
His Teachers	Ira Eisenstein p. 15
Peoplehood	Jack J. Cohen p. 27
Organic Jewish Community	Samuel Dinin p. 45
Jewish Social Work	Samuel C. Kohs p. 65
Jewish Education	Israel S. Chipkin p. 85
The Jewish Center Movement	Louis Kraft p. 119
As Exegete	Eugene Kohn p. 137
Theory of Religion	Harold C. Weisberg p. 155
Idea of God	Henry N. Wieman p. 193
Jewish Liturgy	David Polish p. 211
Conservative Judaism	Alexander J. Burnstein p. 223
Reform Judaism	Roland B. Gittelsohn p. 233
Philosopher of Democracy	Joseph L. Blau p. 243
Theory of Soterics	Harold Schulweis p. 263
The Way I Have Come	Mordecai M. Kaplan p. 283

Contributors to This Volume .... p. 323

MORDECAI M. KAPLAN:

AN EVALUATION

MORDECAI M. KAPLAN AS TEACHER
By Mortimer J. Cohen

To evaluate Dr. Mordecai M. Kaplan's influence on the generation of which we are a part requires us to present him essentially as a teacher. Like Maimonides, Dr. Kaplan is best described as "a guide to the perplexed" of the times. Whether we contemplate his life as rabbi, as philosopher of religion, or as servant of the Jewish people and Judaism, it is as teacher that he finds his true niche and meaning in our lives.

In his latest volume, *The Future of the American Jew*, Dr. Kaplan describes the life mission of the Jewish teacher. It is "to give the pupil an awareness of the reality of his people," and "a consciousness of his destiny as a member of the Jewish people."[1] He further defines the teacher's task as that of imbuing his pupils "with the spirit of holiness, humility, gratitude and faith. He could not very well carry out that task efficiently, without communicating to the pupil a vivid sense of the reality of God."[2]

"Vital" versus "Vivid"

A simple incident out of one's student days at the Jewish Theological Seminary will make crystal clear Dr. Kaplan's interpretation of his task as Jewish teacher and, indeed, his attitude towards the whole problem of the reconstruction of Jewish life and values today. In those far-off, ancient days, Wednesday afternoon was the period of homiletic torture for the young aspirants to the rabbinate. Before the drowsy student body and in the presence of Dr. Kaplan, who sat with pencil poised upon his little pad of note paper to jot down errors of thought, quotation, or development of theme, the student delivered his sermon. The particular incident that so illumines the attitude and spirit of Dr. Kaplan arose after a student's sermon on Hanukkah. The student had explored minutely the life and times of Judas Maccabeus, the conflict of the Hellenistic and Jewish cultures. He described the wars and the Syrian-Greek soldiers from helmet down to shoe-latchets. He enlarged upon the religious significance of the Hanukkah story.

When he sat down the speaker must have been convinced that he had preached a good sermon. Many of the students who were asked their opinions thought so. Then came Dr. Kaplan's turn. In his usual courteous manner — and he was always thoughtful and courteous towards his students — he praised the efforts of the young preacher and complimented him upon his diligent research in preparing for his sermon. Then Dr. Kaplan rolled out his big guns into firing position.

He began his criticism by discussing the meaning of two words — "vivid" and "vital." To make a thing "vivid" is to recreate it in the imagination of the audience; but it is a process that merely summons up the past. To make something "vital" is to make the past relevant to the present. It is a life-giving, a life-dealing process; it is life-sustaining and life-illuminating. The preacher's task, in which this young man had failed, was to make Hanukkah's story vital to our times. What does Hanukkah (or for that matter, Judaism) mean to the individual today in his determination to be a Jew in the face of modern American civilization, and in the modern world given to values so hostile to the Hanukkah spirit and to the values of Judaism? What light does it cast upon our thinking, our doubts and fears, our conflicts and confusions? The preacher had made Hanukkah a "vivid" incident in the history of the Jewish people and ultimately in the history of Western civilization. But he had failed to make it a "vital" experience in the lives of men and women today, in the twentieth century, in this vast, bustling, materialistic colossus of America.

The sermon had no relevance to their needs; it offered them no insights for their living as Jews, no significances for their facing the American civilization in which they wanted to live full and complete Jewish lives. The sermon, in a word, was "vivid" but it was not "vital." It was dead, as all history is dead when unrelated to the present.

In this example we find the key to Dr. Kaplan's varied activities as teacher. And we realize his attitude towards Jewish scholarship, his philosophy of communal living, his appreciation of Jewish law, custom and ceremony, his approach to the study of the Bible, the Talmud, the Midrash. Always, his emphasis was on the vital. That did not mean that he did not appreciate Jewish scholarship. On the contrary, time and again he urged the young rabbis-to-be to know their Bible and all the sources of Jewish culture and the treasures of the Jewish spirit. They should know everything within the vast reaches of modern scholarship. But, if they were to be true teachers, preachers, leaders and guides of the American Jewish community, they had to relate all that knowledge to the lives, strivings and aspirations of the Jews of today. Dr. Kaplan's decisive question was: What should Judaism mean in the life of the common man in the American Jewish scene? Unless it has meaning and worth for him, Jewish scholarship is simply antiquarianism, display-goods for dusty museums and archeological exhibits of a dead civilization.

Dr. Kaplan's Method of Teaching

One readily sees how this emphasis on "the vital" affected his approach to the study of the Bible. I first studied under Dr. Kaplan at the Teachers' Institute in New York City. Having come from the usual Jewish home of Orthodox outlook, I held the accepted views of the Bible, as other Jewish youths in a similar environment. I was also sorely perplexed and ofttimes much confused about the Holy Scriptures. So long as I live I shall recall the excitement of those evenings of Bible study with Dr. Kaplan when, beginning with Genesis and moving slowly through its magnificent pages, a new Bible, indeed a new and thrilling world, was revealed to me. It was not a strange and distant world; it was the world of my people; it was the habitat of my ancestors. It was my world.

Dr. Kaplan's methodology in teaching was simple and direct. It was Socratic in the finer sense. His intention, unlike that of the original Socrates, was not merely to undermine current beliefs and notions, nor even to arouse in men a skeptical attitude towards the accepted, current ways. Dr. Kaplan knew, of course, that the old had to be cleared away to make room for the new. But, he had something better with which to replace the old. He built upon or used the old in revitalizing the ancient faith through new and alluring significances. For Dr. Kaplan was not a ruthless destroyer of the past; he plundered the past to enrich the present. He sought to show how the present grew out of the past. His fundamental rule of growth he summed up thus: "The essence of growth is continuity in change."[3] The past had to be reworked into living and vital spiritual values for today.

He began each session with a series of questions to the class. He did not spend much time on the contents of the chapters; he assumed that the students had read them at home. He asked questions that challenged the minds of the students, that often caused them to become perplexed, that made them poignantly aware of the difficulties in the text under discussion. Having explored each strand of thought with his students, he gathered together at the end of each lesson the material that had been contributed, and the answers, and he then reconstructed the backgrounds, the experiences, the human motivations of the people, their beliefs about God and man and the world, and related them to our own needs and our ever increasing questionings of the spirit.

Thus, he opened up the Bible as a vast world of Jewish experience in which Jewish men and women, and mankind as a whole, were discovered as seeking for the meaning of existence in terms of God; but more than merely in the word "God," rather in the spiritual and moral values that the God of the Bible represented.

The second step in Dr. Kaplan's methodology as teacher then came into play. He sought always to place the ancient text back into the life of the times. He dipped the old, dry words into the renewing waters of living reality. The Bible words were thus transformed from book into vital experience. Passages that had seemed utterly devoid of significance sprang into new life. The very genealogies, that so many readers skip over as dull and useless reading, became surcharged with meaning. We came to understand better why these names and places were set properly at their special stations; why some names dropped out; why others cropped up. The dullest texts surged with life and struggle, with power and spirit.

The final step in Dr. Kaplan's methodology, perhaps the most crucial step, certainly the culminating step in his process of making Jewish tradition a dynamic, vital and effective force in our lives, came in universalizing the Bible experience.[4] He would explore and, indeed, expose the basic elements of human nature, the fundamental human needs out of which Jewish experience in the Bible grew, became involved in the evils within and about it, matured, and finally found literary expression. The finest common denominator between ourselves and Noah, ourselves and Abraham, Moses and Isaiah, ourselves and the Jewish past, is to be found in the bond that makes all centuries and all people one — our continuous and common human life and human destiny. The moment affinity was established between the humanness of the Bible and our own humanness, the channel had been hewed through which past and present became contemporaries, wrestling with kingdoms and powers and spirits for the mastery of life and the world, and for the attainment of life's meaning and worth. The past was no longer the "dead" past. It was a living past teeming with everquesting life, with our fathers and mothers, our people struggling desperately for the ethical and spiritual meanings that would give all life and all struggle true significance and worth.

Well do I recall Dr. Kaplan's homely but beloved description of the Bible as "Our Family Album." Abraham was not just a name or a strange and foreign character who lived centuries ago in a far away distant land. No! Abraham was our ancestor; he was our father, blood of our blood, spirit of our spirit. And so with all the characters and happenings in the Bible. They belonged to us; they happened to us. We do not have photographs of our ancestors, unfortunately; but fortunately, we have vignettes of them tipped in golden words that make them alive to our inner sight. Indeed, he explained to us the reason why we recite blessings before and after the reading of the Torah. They help us to identify ourselves in mind and heart and spirit with the Divine that came to full and lively expression in Our Family Album — our Torah, our Bible.

Did Dr. Kaplan's, shall we say humanistic, approach to the Bible, rob it of its mystery and authority for us? Did it undermine our faith in its message and in its sanctity as God's living word? Did he destroy in us that reverence that we imbibed at our father's hand when, in true orthodox fashion, we regarded the whole Bible as the direct dictation of God to Moses on Mount Sinai? Not at all! The Bible became for us a record and a document of living and vital experience in which we were privileged to share the struggles, the strivings and the defeats of our ancestors, and to ascend with them to the golden, starry heights where we looked upon God's face with our eyes. The Divine emerged not out of the swirling fogs and clouds of a mountain's heights, but out of the inner wrestlings of individuals with their own human natures, with their shortcomings and evil tendencies, with their infinite possibilities for good, and out of the desperate conflicts of nation against nation for survival and mastery and place in a crowded world.

These methodological steps that were part of Dr. Kaplan's process of teaching were applied similarly to Midrash and Talmud. What a revelation came to us in ancient texts that otherwise were so barren of meaning and vitality! In bits of folklore, in slivers of ancient customs, in obscure and recondite allusions, worlds of significant human experience were found to be embedded. To sit at Dr. Kaplan's feet and absorb his interpretations of Midrash and Talmud was an unforgettable experience. As with the Bible, he awakened us to the fact that these great treasuries of the Jewish past were not dead documents of a bygone age. They were in truth the very essence of ongoing Jewish life. They needed only to be unlocked, and their rich stores of human and Divine experience would present themselves to us to be understood and then made our own.

The Setting of Dr. Kaplan's Teaching

In evaluating Dr. Kaplan as teacher, one must ever keep in mind the creative, pioneering task he faced. The early 1900's were years of intellectual and spiritual ferment for all religions and all peoples. The accumulated power of new ideas, discoveries and philosophies burst full force on the Jewish youth of those years. Walter Lippman, one of the intellectual interpreters of that age, wrote a book whose introductory chapter he named "The Acids of Modernity." Just as acids eat into metals and dissolve them away, so intellectual acids were eating into and wasting away ancient traditions and ancient faiths. Especially did Jewish youths of Orthodox backgrounds find their spiritual and intellectual moorings slipping away and disappearing. Ofttimes they went through school and college bewildered, and shorn of their ancestral beliefs and faith.

The new biological sciences, best typified in Darwin and Spencer, with the great theory of evolution, challenged the centrality of man in the universe. The new knowledge about the Bible, usually associated with such names as Wellhausen, shook the comfortable beliefs that Jewish youth at the time held of the sacred Scriptures of their people. The new psychology of religion, which, under the guiding hands of William James, Starbuck and Coe, sought naturalistic explanations of religious experience, helped to arouse questionings concerning the objective validity of religion itself. Add to this the writings of Freud and G. Stanley Hall, and the full blow can be better understood. The social sciences gave birth to comparative religion, which in turn robbed so many religious customs and ceremonies of vaunted uniqueness. Frazer and Durkheim, King, Cooley and Ellwood, all discovered religion to be an integral part of a tribe's or people's struggle to survive economically and politically, as well as ethically and spiritually. Karl Marx's doctrine that "religion is the opiate of the masses" set the challenge to religion squarely face to face. It was no easy time for a Jewish youth to go through college, washed by these acids of the mind and heart, and yet try to keep unstained his Jewish religion and his Jewish traditions.

It was at this time that we who were so privileged came under the influence of Dr. Kaplan. Of all the instructors at the Seminary, he alone seemed to be part of the world in which we lived and in which we suffered. Though he had been born in Europe, he came here young enough to receive his college education here. Consequently, he had had to face the new knowledge and the new age in precisely the way we young theological students had to face it. He knew our agonies of mind and heart, for he had experienced them. As one who was almost indigenous to the American environment, possessed of a rich Jewish heritage of knowledge and feeling, aware of the revolutionary changes implied in the new learning and the new knowledge, and blessed with a profound desire to harmonize the new and the old, to reconstruct the Judaism of the past to make it a vital force in the modern age, Dr. Kaplan helped his students to face courageously and hopefully the troubled world of today with all its bitter realities.

Dr. Kaplan opened to us the vast realms of scientific literature that dealt with religion in its psychological and sociological bearings. He helped us to develop a philosophy of Jewish life and religion in terms of the social nexus between religion and group life. Out of this came his strong emphasis on the reality of "community" and "the group" as the mother-womb in which personality and the individuality of people are nurtured and matured. Tirelessly, he pointed out to us the nature of Judaism as a social product of group life through the long ages of Jewish history, and he directed our minds towards the evolving nature of that Jewish heritage.

Preaching as a Means of Making Judaism Relevant

In teaching his students the nature of Judaism, Dr. Kaplan appealed to them time and again to study the facts, and grasp the realities. What social facts entered into the birth and development of ceremonies and rituals? What were people trying to attain through such spiritual exercises? Again, dipping these religious customs, ceremonies, institutions, laws and practices into the living stream of once living waters, they gained fresh and new meaning for today. Ever did he apply the rule of relevancy. He asked of each: How did it function in the past? What satisfactions and benefits did the Jewish group gain through its beliefs and practices? Can these institutions, customs, ceremonies and practices give us the same satisfactions and benefits?

As teacher, Dr. Kaplan used well-tried psychological devices and pedagogical techniques on his students. He liked to "shock" them by some broad statement or judgment and then await the reaction. He liked to "pose problems" for them to solve. He abhorred complacency and a ready acceptance of unreality as if it were reality. He continually appealed for realism in thinking about Jewish life and its problems. Dr. Kaplan denounced the hypocrisy of form that had no substance. For him, religion was something that was sincerely of the heart and the spirit. He could not abide those unthinking Jews who flaunted their Orthodoxy in public, but violated almost every commandment of the Torah in their personal lives.

Naturally, young rabbinical students transmitted these attitudes of Dr. Kaplan mostly in their sermonizing, for through the sermon the rabbi seeks to reach the evils of his day to alleviate, or remove, or if possible heal them. Dr. Kaplan urged his students, in preaching, to deal with the realities of Jewish and modern life, for these are the substance of living, but always to remember that they were not preaching themselves but Torah, God's word and God's judgment upon the people and their actions. Thus, his sermons were always based upon the Sidra of the Sabbath or the portion of the Torah and Prophets read on the Holydays. From them the rabbi gained his authority as teacher and preacher of ethical and spiritual truth. Furthermore, he used to say, "The Bible text is the touchstone of Jewish spiritual reality."

In preaching, Dr. Kaplan taught the need to express the central theme of the sermon in a proposition. After the proposition had been stated, the remainder of the sermon consisted really of definitions of each term of the proposition. Thus, the sermon grew out of the proposition. Its unity was not the mechanical unity of disparate parts joined together by an outward trellis of numbers — 1, 2, 3, and finally — or by logical divisions — firstly, secondly, thirdly, and finally — but it was an organic unity. Each section grew out of all that had preceded it. The proposition went through a process of exfoliation, just as leaves exfoliate and reveal their beauty when they come to full bloom. So the sermon on reaching its completion revealed a full and complete growth in all its rich bloom. It went from thought seed, the proposition, to full flower, the completed sermon. It was fascinating to watch and sense the growth of an idea from abstract seedling to practical reality incarnated in life's struggles and conflicts.

The Mature Teacher

At thirty-five years of age, Dr. Kaplan presented a vigorous, energetic, tireless personality to the world. Always serious-minded, one must confess that he was not always alert to the humorous side of many situations in the classroom. One never felt that Dr. Kaplan could be light and gay. One regretted the fact that he lacked a poetic sense, both in his written and in his spoken words. But one could also understand that, as pioneer, he had to do the rock-crushing job that made the roadbed possible for those who came after him. Under attack from many quarters, Dr. Kaplan did not have the time or even the desire to be light and gay in his attitude towards the serious problems of Jewish survival; nor, under such conditions, could he look upon humor and laughter as anything more than a grudging concession to human absurdity.

In recent years, having hewn out the massive structure of his thought concerning Judaism as a civilization, Dr. Kaplan has mellowed. He shows greater tolerance of the foibles and lightheartedness of others. His old intolerance of intellectual dishonesty remains strong with him. He cannot abide deviousness of mind and spirit. Against deceit, self-deception and other-deception, he stands adamant, unyielding and unbending. Next to deception, he has hated most stupidity. This he can not accept, and at stupidity he directs his sharpest blows.

As teacher, Dr. Kaplan was a profound and creative force. His searching spirit gave no rest to his students. Until they found lodgment in truth, Dr. Kaplan would keep his students hot upon the chase. To study with him was a stimulating and exciting experience. One became aware of horizons broadening, of vistas hitherto unsuspected opening. In the very process of experiencing new horizons and new vistas of the spirit, his students sensed deep inside them spiritual maturing and religious growth. A great teacher is more than a man; he is an elemental force as powerful as the explosive force within the atom. It is understandable why our sages ordained that when we stand in the presence of a sage and teacher of the Law we are to say: "Blessed art Thou, O Lord our God, King of the Universe, who hast imparted of Thy wisdom to them that revere Thee."

Standing before Dr. Kaplan, who has struggled within his soul for power to serve and save the Jewish people of today, and prepare them for the adventure of living in Israel, in America and in the world of tomorrow, we stand before a great and creative personality who has been the guide and friend of a distraught, harassed and perplexed generation — a teacher who has helped us to attain a positive and fruitful understanding of the Jewish way of life.

NOTES

[1] M. M. Kaplan, *The Future of the American Jew*, Macmillan, New York, 1948 p. 458.
[2] *Ibid.*, p. 459.
[3] *Ibid.*, p. 438.
[4] Compare below, Eugene Kohn, "Mordecai M. Kaplan As Exegete," pp. 137–154.

MORDECAI M. KAPLAN AND HIS TEACHERS
By Ira Eisenstein

Like the foremost thinkers of every generation, Mordecai M. Kaplan represents the convergence of the main streams of thought in his time. He has made himself thoroughly conversant with history, sociology, psychology, economics, theology, literature; indeed, his adventures in the realm of ideas have led him into almost all the by-paths of knowledge. In addition, of course, as a Jew, a rabbi and a scholar, he has mastered the Biblical and Talmudic literatures, the philosophical and ethical writings, and the history of the Jewish people throughout its long career. It is given to very few, in any generation, to fall heir to two heritages of culture, and to make them both part of an integrated personality. Mordecai Kaplan, one of those few, is the product of both Judaism and Western civilization; in himself, they interpenetrate and enrich one another.

This synthesis of cultures, however, is made particularly interesting and fruitful because Mordecai Kaplan happens to have lived through one of the most rapidly changing periods in all human history. The last seventy years have transformed the face of the world. They have witnessed the transition from gas-light and the horse-drawn carriage to electronics and the jet plane; from the concentration of Jewish masses in medieval eastern Europe to the establishment of the State of Israel and the rise of a free and numerous Jewry in a democratic America. The revolutions in the thinking and the manner of life among Jews, and among the peoples in whose midst they live, created unprecedented situations and presented challenges never before faced by the Jewish people. Mordecai Kaplan has not only helped his people to meet those situations and to confront those challenges with courage and intelligence; he has also directed his vast knowledge and his penetrating philosophic power toward the creative survival of Judaism and the happy adjustment of Jews to the new world.

The extent of his contribution in the many areas of Jewish and American life is the subject of the several chapters in this volume. To be discussed here is the question: what are the sources of Dr. Kaplan's inspiration, the mainsprings of his system of thought? Who taught him; from whom did he learn most? What, in other words, were the intellectual influences that shaped his life? The writer sought answers to these questions in a series of conversations with Dr. Kaplan. What follows is, therefore, Dr. Kaplan's own story in brief; he gives a fuller account in the closing chapter.

Intuitions Supported by Teachers

According to Dr. Kaplan, he had no teachers, in the sense of master guides. He studied with many instructors, but none of them gave him that total orientation to life which, shall we say, he is responsible for having given to so many of his own disciples. He learned piecemeal; he had to put the pieces together himself. Step by step, he had to fall back upon his own thinking in order to formulate a consistent and integrated conception of Judaism, and its relation to the rest of Western culture. Often, he arrived, intuitively, at tentative theories; he would then turn to experts to reenforce his convictions, to corroborate what he had already sensed to be valid generalizations.

The entire process of establishing hypotheses, and then verifying them, presupposes a powerful intellectual curiosity, the will to make use of it, and the honesty to go on seeking until genuine answers are found. These qualities Dr. Kaplan traces to his own father, Rabbi Israel Kaplan. "My father," he wrote a decade ago,[1] "although a devout and meticulously observant Jew, did nothing to make me feel that I was a sinner by refusing to accept the teachings of tradition. He would let me vent my protest against some of the most sacred beliefs because, as he put it, he was sure I would ultimately find my way back to Jewish loyalty. His toleration of my outbreaks was in consonance with his emphasis on intellectual honesty." Rabbi Israel Kaplan would frequently pinch young Mordecai's cheek in loving approval of "a good question." At seventy, Mordecai Kaplan is still being praised for asking the "right questions."

He was thus prepared, by an Orthodox father, to weather the shock of his first encounters with heterodox views. Another personality entered upon his horizon at an early age, who not only encouraged questions, but also stimulated doubts. Arnold B. Ehrlich, the brilliant Bible critic, was a frequent visitor at the Kaplan home, a *ben bayit*. He would try out some of his interpretations on the young student. If they seemed sufficiently impressive, they would be incorporated into the ever-growing manuscript which Ehrlich was working on. For approximately twelve years, from 1894 to 1906, the Ehrlich manuscripts were constantly to be found at the Kaplan home, and in the mornings, for a half hour each day, young Mordecai would read from them — with his *tefillin* on.

Anyone familiar with Ehrlich's commentaries may gather their general effect on the developing mind of Mordecai Kaplan. "Ehrlich opened up to me that appreciation of the Bible which has enabled me to read it as the expression of the spiritual genius of Israel, which revealed to me the intrinsic depth and beauty in the original meaning of the text."[2] Ehrlich's naturalistic approach to the Bible provided the groundwork upon which Kaplan later constructed his "pragmatic interpretation" of Torah, one of the basic elements of his philosophy of Judaism.[3]

Religion and Group Experience

The naturalistic approach of Ehrlich was soon supplemented by the similar influences exerted upon Mordecai Kaplan, the college student. At Columbia University, he studied with Nicholas

Murray Butler. There the fields of anthropology and sociology were opened up to him. "Though these studies undermined the conception of religion as supernatural intervention in human life, they prepared the way for evaluating religion as a normal and indispensable expression of human nature."[4] Thus, though Butler's courses dealt harshly with miracles and the literal historicity of sacred texts, they offered, for those who were alert enough to appreciate it, the opportunity to reconstruct, along new lines, the structure which had been shattered. The new sciences demonstrated that, in response to clearly felt human needs, men had established institutions of society; that among them were the institutions of religion, which satisfied the need for believing in a Power that "endorses what we believe ought to be, and that guarantees that it will be";[5] that the conception of what "ought to be" was always a projection of the conception of salvation at any given time, and that this conception of salvation emerged out of the prevailing science, psychology and social consciousness.

Dr. Kaplan's hypothesis concerning the relation of religion to culture was amply borne out for him by the works of the French school of sociologists, particularly Emil Durkheim. LeBon, who wrote on the psychology of the mob, contributed the idea that religious expression grows out of the deep-seated desire to give meaning to group life, and that the basic drive in most people was the drive toward *belonging*, toward feeling and making themselves feel part of the larger entity. In this, suggestion and imitation play a significant role, highly relevant to the whole problem of rituals and traditions. Among Americans, King, Pratt and Ames stand out as scholars whose books cast light upon the function of religion as the expression of man's search for salvation. They confirmed Dr. Kaplan's feeling that sociological conditions must be shared by all who hope to share the religious experience. He formulated this truth in the words, "To have religion in common, people must have other things in common besides religion."

Meaning Always "In Relation To"

What Mordecai Kaplan had come upon, in these sociological and psychological studies, was the larger and more general truth which John Dewey helped him to clarify, namely, that all human experience must be understood in the light of its context. The very meaning of "meaning" had to be rethought, for "meaning" is always "in relation to." Phenomena have their significance insofar as they interact with other phenomena. This fits in with the results of the French sociologists, for, in dealing with human personality, Dewey stressed the place of the individual in society, and recast the whole conception of education in terms of integrating the person into the group.

These were wholesome corrections to what were otherwise stimulating and constructive suggestions emanating from William James. James, in his *Will To Believe*, had strengthened Dr. Kaplan in his belief that Truth could have meaning only in relation to total experience, and that all those doctrines whose "truth" was beyond any possible experience (save through divine revelation or grace) simply by-passed human life and added to the dispensable baggage of dogma. Kaplan found much in Pragmatism, because he was seeking a *Weltanschauung* which was relevant to the kind of salvation that modern men were seeking, namely, this-worldly salvation.

Where James seemed to need correcting, however, was in his failure to recognize sufficiently the group character of religion. In his *Varieties of Religious Experience*, James concentrated to such a degree upon individuals that he missed the opportunity to point out that their various experiences were actually inconceivable without prior conditioning by the groups to which the individuals belonged. The experience out of which each of these "experiences" emerged was always a distinctive culture.[6]

Dewey, with a stronger sense for the reality of social forces, confirmed Dr. Kaplan in his conviction that the "divine" had to be found in "those forces in Nature and Society that generate and support ideals."[7] The commercial, industrial and social revolutions which resulted in the development of the democratic ideal seem to Dr. Kaplan to deserve identification with the "divine," insofar as they make for the maximum of individual personality and the maximum of compatible social cooperation. It is no accident, therefore, that Dr. Kaplan, seeking always the broadest possible context into which to fit his ideas concerning any aspect of human life, raised the idea of democracy to the level of a *religious* ideal. Carrying the logic of Dewey and the sociologists to their conclusions, he recognized that the democratic faith could be expressed — and should be — through the *sancta* of a democratic society, utilizing the significant events, personalities, places and books as the building blocks of a structure of religion closest to the experience of the people whose national history is thus put to use.[8]

The Place of the Individual

The idea of the democratic faith so appealed to Dr. Kaplan that he could never subscribe to Karl Marx's conception of the class struggle — even during those years when so many intellectuals were tempted to accept Marx *in toto*. To be sure, Marx gave vigorous expression to many of Dr. Kaplan's beliefs, especially to his contention that all aspects of culture emerge out of the basic structure of society, with adequate emphasis upon the economic. He went along with Marx in recognizing the retrogressive influence of religious institutions upon society in specific periods of Western history.

But he could never swallow the bitter doctrine of inevitability, both implied and explicit in Marxism. His profound belief in prophetic religion rendered that idea as abhorrent as the Greek notion of Fate. Nor could he find sustenance in the contention that violent and totalitarian methods could ever usher in the Kingdom of God.[9]

He was confirmed in his urge to select the valid in Marx and reject the invalid by the writings of Max Oppenheimer, whose *The State* was based upon many of the fundamental theories of

Marx, but who sought the reconstruction of society in the deliberate attempt to create instruments of cooperative living which would take into consideration the need for group effort, and would at the same time save the individual from becoming completely submerged in the larger whole. Max Oppenheimer's contribution to the idea of the *kibbutz* in Israel (then Palestine) called attention to the fact that the new society need not necessarily emerge out of a struggle between masters and slaves, but might come out of the idealism and intelligence of equals, whose common antagonists are drought and famine.

While Dr. Kaplan learned, with Durkheim, LeBon, Dewey, Marx and Oppenheimer the vital role played in the life of the individual by the social unit of which he is a part, he always kept in mind the role of the individual in moulding society, indeed, in moulding himself. This polarity — the one and the many, the individual and the group, the part and the whole — invests all his thinking. It is therefore not surprising that he should have become so fascinated by the new dimension in human life which Sigmund Freud uncovered. That Man is driven by irrational, unconscious drives was a truth that bore many important implications. Nevertheless, here, too, Dr. Kaplan did not allow himself to go overboard. He was adamant in his refusal to describe in terms of sex alone the manifold impulses that operate below the level of consciousness. The newer schools of depth psychology, particularly that of Sullivan, Horney and Fromm, restored the equilibrium by dealing with the total personality in a total situation. Erich Fromm was studied with additional satisfaction by Dr. Kaplan because he (Fromm) underscored that faith in human nature and in man's ability to overcome his subhuman past without which the moral structure of society is inconceivable.

Meeting the Challenge of Democracy to Judaism

It is almost impossible to trace the growth of a mind, for so many events overlap, and so many influences coalesce. In the instance of Mordecai Kaplan, the difficulty of describing his development chronologically is complicated by the fact that he has been more than a student; he has been a man of action. Modestly, he avers that he has been taken "for a thinker among men of action, and for a man of action among thinkers."[10] The truth is, however, that he was put into a position where he was expected to teach teachers and rabbis, and influence laymen through his synagogue leadership. He faced this responsibility at a time when Judaism was undergoing a crisis of unprecedented proportions and of unique character. Jews were running away from their Judaism, hating their people and themselves. Jewish education was at a low ebb; Jewish religion was rapidly disintegrating; Jewish communal life was disorganized; Jewish culture was suffering from pernicious anemia.

If Dr. Kaplan had not had to meet this challenge, he might never have struggled through to a clarification of his philosophy of Judaism. His role as teacher and rabbi may therefore be listed as one of the most powerful influences of his life. "My education," he writes, "was the product of those I had to teach to a far greater degree than of those who had taught me.... My students.... made me a Reconstructionist."[11] But, without the disciplines of the broader culture he would never have known how to cope with the problem. For these were the essence of the question: history, sociology, anthropology, psychology, economics — these constituted the challenge; these were responsible, directly as they changed society, and indirectly as they influenced thought, for the fact that Jews were running away from Judaism. *Dr. Kaplan resolved the dilemma by appropriating the very factors which created the problem and utilizing them for the purpose of alleviating it.*

In all candor it must be said that he received very little help from Jewish thinkers, past or present. After he had worked out his method, he "discovered" that Maimonides had "reconstructed" Judaism by the same means, and that Mendelssohn had attempted it too. Jewish scholars had been either denying that there was a problem, or had been occupied with the task of investigating the details of past Jewish experience. Only one figure may be said to have helped Dr. Kaplan in his search for a method of interpreting Judaism in such a way that it might become again a potent force in the lives of Jews.

The Influence of Ahad Ha-am

That figure was Ahad Ha-am. He recognized the fact that the constant amid the changing in Jewish history was the *Jewish people*. "The Zionist movement," Dr. Kaplan writes, "and particularly the Ahad Ha-amist's conception of the Jewish people as a living organism animated by an irresistible will to live enabled me to find spiritual anchorage."[12] Throughout the long career of Israel, ideas of God changed; methods of worship changed; ethical standards changed; the very locale of the people's life changed. What never changed was the consciousness that the Jews were the same people throughout. Just as an individual grows, matures, develops, yet retains his sense of identity, so the members of a people at any age look back upon their history and identify themselves with it, and recognize it as their own. Ahad Ha-am was much concerned about that stable factor, the enduring element which made it possible for Jews always to know themselves as Jews. He identified it with language, and with a spirit of justice, the prophetic spirit.

Dr. Kaplan agreed with Ahad Ha-am in his estimate of the effect of language, and placed great stress upon the need for Hebraizing Jewish life. But he was not altogether satisfied with Ahad Ha-am's failure to reckon with the religious element in Judaism. "I have always missed in Ahad Ha-am's conception of Judaism an appreciation of the indefinable religious longings and aspirations."[13] Nevertheless, Dr. Kaplan found in Ahad Ha-am's method of interpretation a close parallel to his own method "by which the God-idea in Jewish tradition might be transformed into a vital element in modern Jewish ideology." Dr. Kaplan divides the method into four propositions, based upon Ahad Ha-am's essay on Moses.[14] In the course of the analysis, it becomes quite clear that Ahad Ha-am came closer than any other Jewish contemporary to Dr. Kaplan's general approach to the reconstruction of the past.

To the extent that Ahad Ha-am dealt at all with the problem of Judaism in the Diaspora, he confirmed Dr. Kaplan's belief that the "Jewish problem" was the result more of the possible success of emancipation, than of its failure. "Slavery in Freedom" was the social and psychological fate which Ahad Ha-am feared more than the ravages of anti-Semitism. While he had no clearly formulated program for Diaspora Jewry, he nevertheless realized that the new community in the Land of Israel could never hope to be an end in itself, that it must be the center of World Jewry. Dr. Kaplan found much inspiration in this so-called "Cultural Zionism," especially when the Herzlian type seemed to engulf the Zionist world. It enabled him to keep his equilibrium here as well, to maintain the polarity between the Zionists who saw no hope for Judaism outside Israel and those who saw in Zionism only the opportunity to create an intellectual elite, but not a fully developed state.

It is an interesting task, to attempt to understand the mysterious process by which an intellectual giant attains his stature. What has been recorded here may, or may not, throw some light upon that process. But in the final analysis, it remains a mystery. Perhaps Mordecai Kaplan himself realized this when he remarked, "The more I look back to the early stages of my career, the more I feel as if I have been lured by a transcendent will — call it the will of the Jewish people, call it the will of God — to work for ends of which I have become only progressively aware."[15]

Notes

[1] "The Influences That Shaped My Life," *The Reconstructionist*, VIII, No. 10.
[2] *Ibid.*
[3] Compare below, Eugene Kohn, "Mordecai M. Kaplan as Exegete," pp. 137–154.

[4] "The Influences That Shaped My Life." Compare below, Harold C. Weisberg, "Mordecai M. Kaplan's Theory of Religion," pp. 155-192.

[5] "Why Humanism Is Not Enough," *The Reconstructionist*, II, No. 7.

[6] The same line of reasoning led Kaplan to reject Whitehead's conception of religion as "what a man does with his solitariness."

[7] John Dewey, *A Common Faith*, Yale University Press, New Haven, 1933, p. 51.

[8] Compare below, Joseph L. Blau, "Mordecai M. Kaplan As a Philosopher of Democracy," pp. 243-261. Note also *The Faith of America*, ed. M. M. Kaplan, Paul Williams and Eugene Kohn, Schuman, New York, 1951.

[9] Compare M. M. Kaplan, "Jewish Religion and the Disinherited," in *Judaism In Transition*, Behrman, New York, 1941.

[10] "A Heart of Wisdom," *The Reconstructionist*, XVII, No. 6.

[11] *Ibid.*

[12] *Ibid.*

[13] M. M. Kaplan, "The Impact of Benderly's Personality," *Jewish Education*, XX, No. 3.

[14] For the complete discussion, see "A Note on the God Idea in Judaism," *The Reconstructionist*, I, No. 14.

[15] "A Heart of Wisdom."

MORDECAI M. KAPLAN'S CONCEPT OF PEOPLEHOOD

By Jack J. Cohen

Among the difficulties facing social scientists in their investigations is the state of flux which characterizes all organized group life. Societies come into being and disappear, while others alter their character fundamentally from one generation to another. Historians and sociologists, in analyzing these societies, must therefore take aim at moving targets. One of the fastest moving targets has been the "wandering Jew," who, it seems, refuses to stand still long enough to facilitate a definitive analysis. As a result, even the most competent social scientists often miss the mark when they aim their critical gaze on the Jews.

The Jews

A notable example of faulty analysis is a statement by two famous scholars, Ruth Benedict and Gene Weltfisch. In a pamphlet[1] written to counteract Nazi propaganda about race, they declared, "Jews are people who practice the Jewish religion.... Whenever Jews are persecuted or discriminated against, they cling to their old ways and keep apart from the rest of the population and develop so-called 'Jewish traits.' But these are not racial or 'Jewish'; they disappear under conditions where assimilation is easy." Exception can be taken to this description of the Jews on a number of counts. Not all Jews who are recognized as Jews and consider themselves such practice the Jewish religion. Not all Jews who are discriminated against cling to their old ways; indeed discrimination often leads to a desperate effort to assimilate. Benedict and Weltfisch can also be taken to task for their cavalier dismissal of "so-called" Jewish traits. There are, after all, distinct cultural traits which have been developed by the Jews in their long history and which are considered by them sufficiently worth retaining even in free surroundings.

Benedict and Weltfisch apparently found it difficult to believe that a minority group which had been hard-pressed for centuries might want to perpetuate its community life when the pressure was removed. In their superficial treatment of the Jewish people, they failed to find any inner creative force compelling Jews to meet the challenge of a free environment to their group survival. But the Jews have not been merely objects of history; they have created history as well and are still doing so.

The thesis of Benedict and Weltfisch is only one example of many which err through the attempt to define the Jews in static terms or in neat sociological categories.

In his efforts to help Jews understand themselves and their group status, Mordecai M. Kaplan has always sought to avoid the trap of one-sided definitions. He has seen the broad sweep of Jewish life in an historical perspective and with a complete awareness of its changing character. He has, therefore, succeeded in cutting through the underbrush of the numerous party-line and short-sighted definitions that have confused the average Jew about himself and his relation to his fellow-Jews.

The Jews Viewed as a Religious Group

To understand Dr. Kaplan's philosophy of the Jewish people, it will help us if we trace his thinking about some of the points of view held by significant segments of Jewry.

On the basis of a cursory study of the Jewish past, it is easy to understand why so many people should define the Jews as a religious communion. Superficially, such a description seems to settle the issue, for there is no question about the central role which religion has played in Jewish life throughout the ages. This fact about the Jewish past enabled most Reform, Orthodox and Conservative thinkers of the nineteenth and early twentieth centuries to agree, with almost complete unanimity, on classifying the Jews as a religious communion. In like vein, the American Council for Judaism today advocates for American Jewry a designation paralleling that of "Germans of the Mosaic faith," which was used by some of the German Reform Jews of the nineteenth century.

It should be obvious, without our having to spell it out, that each of the groups mentioned has its own understanding of the meaning of religion in general, and of the Jewish religion in particular. But they share in common a point of view concerning religion which Dr. Kaplan has shown to be sociologically incorrect and ideologically dangerous to the very quality of Jewish religion itself.[2] As conceived by all of these philosophies and parties, a religion is to be identified by certain ethical doctrines and theological beliefs to which people are expected to assent, and by rituals which they are expected to practice. The "authentic" or "good" Jew thus becomes an adherent of a particular form of "authentic" Judaism, whether that form be the Rabbinic Judaism of the Orthodox, the historical Judaism of the Conservatives, the ethical monotheism of the classic Reformists and the American Council for Judaism, or the existentialist Judaism of some latter-day intellectuals. Dr. Kaplan cuts the ground from under all these "religious" approaches by exposing the necessary implication of the assumption that the Jews can be defined solely in terms of religious ideas or practices. For if adherence to the Jewish group is to be judged by belief in a specific set of principles and/or practice of a uniform set of rituals, then we should have to concede the existence of several Jewish groups, each defined by its principles and rituals.

But a regard for logic is not the only reason for Dr. Kaplan's rejection of the various religious interpretations of the character of the Jewish group. His philosophy, after all, is motivated by a programmatic objective, namely, the advancement of Judaism and the enhancement of its role in furthering the spiritual development of each Jew. It is precisely for this reason that he has rejected the emphasis of the "religionists" on doctrine. For the doctrinal approach almost always causes the development of religion to lag behind the changing conditions of life and to ignore the individual needs and differences of men. Hence this type of religion, if it is to preserve itself, must rely on authority rather than conviction. The attempt to fashion Jewish life along particular religious lines can result only in its sectarianization. How, in a free society, can uniformity of belief or practice be achieved? Freedom of thought inevitably results in diversity of thought. To insist, therefore, that being a Jew means to subscribe to a specified formula of beliefs and practices, is to cause the progressive dissolution of the Jewish group. For what are to be the common ideological criteria which are to determine the designation "Jewish"? Obviously, there are none. The definition of the Jewish group as a religion leads to confusion; it does not enable us to identify the entity we are seeking to define.

The Jews Viewed as a Nation

Others besides Dr. Kaplan have seen the danger of characterizing the Jews in terms of their beliefs rather than of the realities of their group existence. Jewish nationalists of all sorts have perceived that danger. Although Jewish nationalism was largely a response to oppression, its proponents saw clearly that it could succeed in alleviating the condition of the Jews only if their unity could be maintained in the face of the growing diversity of outlook among them. That diversity stemmed from the impact of the Enlightenment and Emancipation. During the nineteenth century, in the process of adjustment by the Jews to the new world outside the ghetto, the doctrinal uniformity of the European Jewish communities began to give way. The traditional beliefs and practices could no longer serve to unite Jews in the new and free environment.

Jewish nationalism, then, in addition to seeking a release for Jews from suffering caused by anti-Semitism, was also an attempt to save Jewish unity without insistence on doctrinal assent. It is significant that before the establishment of the State of Israel, all the competing Zionist parties, despite their differences, united in constituting the *Keneset Yisrael*, the Jewish community of Palestine, and in working for the establishment of the state. It was the sense of common history and destiny which bound all these Jews together, and not their agreement on any theological beliefs or ritual practices.

In Israel, moreover, the necessity for living together and solving the day-to-day problems of human existence now enables the Jewish community to overcome the ideological differences that render Jewish communal institutions in the Diaspora so ineffective for perpetuating Judaism. However bitter the struggle for the soul of the Jewish community in Israel may be, the Jewish group and its culture are there as thriving realities. This is the reason many Zionists have striven for a Jewish state and have often insisted, rightly or wrongly, that only in Israel can the Jewish people survive.

The foregoing is a brief description of Zionist theory as it has been formulated over and over again for the past fifty years. At a time, however, when Zionists ignored the implications of the establishment of a Jewish state for the future structure of World Jewry, Dr. Kaplan was already showing the essential shallowness of much of Zionist thinking. Always a staunch Zionist, he nevertheless refused to adopt any of the party lines. He saw that the Jews could "not go home again," that a Jewish state in the sense of the old theocratic commonwealth could not, or at any rate should not, be reconstituted in Eretz Yisrael. He was clear-sighted enough to realize that the acceptance of a democratic conception of state precluded the erection of a "Jewish" commonwealth in which only Jews could be full-fledged citizens.

Dr. Kaplan has likewise been severely critical of those more moderate Zionists who have worked hard for the Jewish state and have expected that its establishment would by itself solve the problem of Jewish existence in the Diaspora as well. Many American Zionists had assumed that Ahad Ha-am's conception of the "spiritual center" would automatically be proved true once a Jewish state was created. Only a few Zionists understood that Ahad Ha-am's idea set forth an objective that had to be pursued. Consequently, during the whole fifty years of American Zionism, scarcely a thought was given to the status of the American Jew and his preparation to receive "Torah from Zion." For decades now Dr. Kaplan has been demonstrating the inadequacy of both extremist Zionism and the Zionism of those who expect Israel to solve the problem of Jewish status and spiritual and cultural creativity throughout the Diaspora. This latter view, according to Dr. Kaplan, is pure wishful thinking, and is unjust to Ahad Ha-am himself, whose "spiritual center" idea involved an intensive Jewish educational program for the Diaspora.

Dr. Kaplan foresaw that, while the establishment of the state would solve some of the old problems of status for world Jewry, it would create new ones as well. As has been mentioned above, Zionists unthinkingly assumed that the end-product of the Zionist movement would be a reestablished "Jewish" state. But anyone who has followed the Orthodox press in Israel realizes how even the religious parties take as axiomatic the citizenship of non-Jews in the country, although in the ancient commonwealth only Jews could be full-fledged citizens. As a result, the adjustment of Jewish law to make room for non-Jewish participation in its legislation, interpretation and execution has become a dilemma that is confounding the best minds in the Orthodox camp. (There is, of course, the still greater problem facing the Orthodox of convincing the non-Orthodox that Jewish law, based on the traditional hermeneutical principles, should form the law of the land.)

What actually exists in Israel is a Jewish community that

constitutes a majority population in a democratic state. *This status of the Jews in Israel is something entirely new in Jewish history*. It is, therefore, surprising that so few groups have reckoned with this fact. For, strange as it may seem, the mere existence of a Jewish majority in Israel, while it is essential to the well-being and creativity of the Jewish people, does not guarantee the maintenance of Jewish identity. The Orthodox alone seem to have understood this and have therefore insisted upon banning all intermarriages within the State. They would thus preserve the identity, if not the unity, of the Jews on a religious basis. While all persons born as Jews, whether religious or not, would automatically qualify as Jews, converts to the Jewish group could be accepted only by passing a number of religious requirements. Whether the restriction on civil marriage and intermarriage will long continue is one of the key questions of personal status confronting the new State. Even should it remain in effect, however, Israel's Jews would still face the problem of defining the differentiae that distinguish them as a group from non-Jews within the Israeli population, and link them to other Jews throughout the Diaspora.

Meanwhile, here in the United States, the problem of establishing Jewish status clearly in the minds of all Jews remains as one of the chief items on the agenda of American Jewry. Dr. Kaplan has helped to clarify the issue by showing that the status of Jewry has always undergone change in new environments, from the loose tribal union of ancient Israel to the religio-political nation of the kings, down to the national minority of Eastern Europe and the yet-to-be-defined character of the Jewish group in America. In stressing these changes Dr. Kaplan has been careful to distinguish between the will to adjust and the will to assimilate. Adjustment, when it occurs in a free environment and in accordance with an ethical pattern, is a healthy and normal reaction of social groups to local situations. Assimilationism, on the other hand, is a desire for group suicide occasioned by pressures that are usually unethical and irrational. Thus, while adjustment to the American scene is essential for normal living, it must, says Dr. Kaplan, take into account the morally justified elements in Jewish group life without which the Jew would lose his soul.

The Jews Viewed as a People

With this background of the contemporary search for Jewish status, we can now outline the role that Dr. Kaplan is urging upon Jews. His starting point is a basic principle which he would urge upon all peoples, the principle of voluntarism. Group life must no longer be a matter of mere descent or of cultural coercion. It must either be an ethical force, enabling each individual to become more human, or it is not justified. Dr. Kaplan believes with Hans Kohn that nationalism "is first and foremost a state of mind, an act of consciousness . . . ."[3] It is a product of a "living and active corporate will."[4] In other words, the kind of group status which Dr. Kaplan would urge upon Jews is a spiritual enterprise stemming from the will of the people to establish a covenant dedicating them to a common purpose.

In his early thinking, Dr. Kaplan generally applied the term "nation" to describe the Jewish group. In using this designation, he meant to say that the Jews originated in a particular land and developed there a distinctive ethnic character which has persisted throughout the centuries, even after the loss of political independence and the subsequent dispersion. In so characterizing the Jewish group, Dr. Kaplan defined "nation" in a much broader sense than that in current usage, which restricts the term to a group bound together by geography and a common government. In recent years, Dr. Kaplan has come to recognize the ambiguity of the term in current usage and now speaks of the Jews as a "people." Of particular concern to him has been the political and cultural exclusivism with which the concept "nation" has been identified as a result of the events of the past several decades. He also knew that the progress of Zionism in the late 30's and 40's would inevitably create a misunderstanding about a people which was trying, at one and the same time, to create a homeland and to maintain far-flung communities in other parts of the world. How would the term "nation" hold up when applied to such a group? Since "nation" as previously applied by Dr. Kaplan to the Jewish people was essentially a spiritual rather than a political concept, he had to seek another word in popular usage which could apply to the Jews and which would be free from the unwarranted associations that cling to the term "nation."

Dr. Kaplan is not the first to use "people" as a designation for the Jewish group. Among Reconstructionists, Milton Steinberg was, I believe, the first to emphasize the need for substituting "people" for "nation."[5] The word is the nearest English equivalent to the Hebrew *am*, which is used throughout traditional literature when speaking of the "people of Israel," *am yisrael*. *Am*, it has been pointed out, has almost a racial connotation, since it is related to a Semitic root meaning "family." But the family is also a primary cultural unit, and it is this which Dr. Kaplan has sought to emphasize in his discussions about Jewish peoplehood. No term, of course, is perfect, and no one recognizes this fact more clearly than Dr. Kaplan. Yet, at the present stage of his thinking, because he realizes that subtle nuances of meaning do not affect the large mass of Jews, he has chosen a designation which can be explained and amplified without arousing any initial antipathy among Jews of divergent opinions.

Dr. Kaplan's conception of peoplehood or spiritual nationalism involves a description of Jewish life both as it is and as it might be. He prescribes as well as describes. It is apparent that what makes Jews a distinct group is the compound of the following factors: 1) the sense of common history and destiny on the part of the individuals who make up the group; 2) the recognition of, if not the active sharing in, a common language and literature, a common ancestral land which is at the same time the focal point of its future hopes, common folkways, and a common religion; and 3) the actual social cohesiveness imposed by the fact that Jews are recognized as a distinct group by non-Jews who often react toward them with xenophobia. Sometimes Jewish ethnic distinctiveness is defined in terms of the particular content of Jewish behavior or belief, as in the case of those who mistake the possession of a common religion as the be-all and end-all of Jewish group life. A religion may be common to a particular people, but its practice need not necessarily be the criterion by which belonging to the people is determined. That is certainly the case among the Jews who share a common religious heritage, but who are bound by other ties — that sometimes are more significant to individual Jews — than religion. Jewish peoplehood is thus a natural, rather than a supernatural or theological phenomenon, because it is subject to all the stresses and strains of a developing society. Being a developing society, its content must necessarily change. True, there is nothing in the history of human society to parallel the history of the Jewish people. But there is also nothing in that history which guarantees the Jews protection from the pressure of the majority culture that batters against the bulwark of group survival.

Dr. Kaplan has therefore sought a conception of Jewish peoplehood which would render Jewish unity possible despite the fact that Jews are scattered throughout the world. He seeks to preserve Jewish group life, and he is interested, as already stated, not only in description, but in prescription as well. It is by its pragmatic implications that the concept of peoplehood or spiritual nationalism remains to be tested.

Dr. Kaplan long ago took his stand in opposition to any struggle for world political domination. That struggle, despite the growing recognition of the need for world government, is rooted in an assumption that nations can survive only when protected by the power of a sovereign state. But nationhood need not be synonymous with statehood. Chauvinism, which is so commonly a concomitant of statehood, must be eliminated from the national consciousness. Indeed, it is only in such a world that the status of the Jews as a transnational people can become more than a theoretical possibility. As Dr. Kaplan puts it, "If democratic nationalism is to heed fully the claims of justice and reason, it must concede the right of Jews throughout the world to retain their status as a nation, though the retention of such status involves their becoming a new type of nation — an international nation with a national home to give them cultural and spiritual unity . . . . ."[6]

This sentiment became crystallized in his latest book, in the suggestion that "World Jewry should unite as a people, and apply to the United Nations Assembly for recognition of its claim to peoplehood. A bill of individual rights is not enough. What is needed is a bill to legitimize Jewish association and cooperation for all purposes that would secure for the Jew freedom of worship and freedom from fear."[7] Dr. Kaplan, of course, is well aware that the world will not readily accept spiritual nationhood as a basis for representation in the United Nations, but his apparent lack of realism is in keeping with the great prophetic tradition in its insistence on the practicability of the idea. Moreover, the willingness of United Nations bodies to accept the counsel of many non-political associations, such as the World Jewish Congress and the World Council of Churches, suggests that Dr. Kaplan's dream has possibilities, however distant may be its achievement. But, whether or not the United Nations recognizes Jewish peoplehood, it should be obvious that only some internationally organized polity of world Jewry can insure the continued identity of the Jewish people both in Israel and in the Diaspora. Without that polity, each community of Jews will go its separate way until all semblance of common history and sense of common destiny are lost. It is apparent that the experience of the past cannot be conjured up to dispute the need for an international community of Jews. In the past, when religious doctrines filled every nook and cranny of the human mind, Jewish unity could survive the cutting off of each community of Jews from other segments of Jewry, because all Jews based their lives on the same code of practice and belief. That uniformity is no longer possible and must be replaced by shared experience — that is, if Jews want to survive as a people. Dr. Kaplan therefore proposes, as I have mentioned above, that the Jews formulate a new covenant among themselves.

The Need for a New Covenant

The idea of covenantship is not a new one in world history, and certainly not in the history of the Jews. Yet, in the philosophy of Mordecai Kaplan, it takes on new significance. In the ancient past, the covenant of Israel with God was considered to be an exclusive arrangement, for which God was altogether responsible. It was He who caused Abraham to leave his home and set off on a journey that was to change the course of his own life and that of his descendants. God selected Israel to carry out His plan for humanity. Therefore, He made a covenant with this people. Israel's acceptance of its mission was a necessary factor in the covenant; but that acceptance, at least initially, was a foregone conclusion, since God's purpose required it. The burden of the covenant often proved later to be too great for the mere mortals who constituted the Jewish group. They therefore sometimes sought to escape it. But, according to the traditional view, the covenant continued to operate, constantly restoring the Jews to a recognition of their responsibility.

Dr. Kaplan has preserved what is essentially true in this age-old doctrine of Judaism by declaring that the dedication of a people to God's purposes is the highest vocation to which any group can aspire. He rejects, of course, the assumption that the Jews alone are capable of such dedication, or were chosen by God for that function. He refuses also to consider his ancestors the divinely inspired formulators of a program for human conduct that cannot be amended or abrogated. Any such "ancestor worship" renders the covenant an altogether one-sided affair, in which the younger party simply abdicates the right to criticize fundamental premises, and therefore dares say nothing about the terms of agreement.

Dr. Kaplan's idea of a covenant among Jews is close to that which is increasingly motivating free nations to work together for peace and human betterment. There is little in the "nature of things" to impel peoples to accept their brotherhood. They do so when conditions seem to point to the desirability of such action. Among Jews, a covenant would assume the desire by men and women of widely diversified philosophies of life, cultural background and economic, social and political status to live for one another and for a common purpose. It implies that the Jew of Central Park West in New York or Lake Shore Drive in Chicago will look upon the dark-skinned Yemenite Jew as his partner in the enterprise of enhancing the spiritual quality of the Jewish group. It means that the hard-headed Jewish business man who goes to Israel to invest his money will give considerable thought to the benefits which his fellow-Jews will derive from his capital. It means, therefore, that Jews really want one another, and, through their mutual love, strive to create a social entity that will prove to be a blessing to mankind. In this sense, says Dr. Kaplan, a covenant among Jews would be serving God's purpose.

Dr. Kaplan's sociology is thus not an effort to construct an artificial system capable of classifying and explaining all social phenomena. Sociology for him is empty if it is conceived as an isolated discipline having no bearing on social psychology. Consequently, the very status of the Jews in the world is largely subjective. In this way, he avoids the mistakes of the classifiers. In his hands a sociological category becomes a program of Jewish living, a tool for social planning. It remains to be seen whether that program is sufficiently rooted in the realities of Jewish life, and whether Jews really want to live as Jews in the spirit implied in the concept of Jewish peoplehood.

Regarding the Chosen People

No discussion of Dr. Kaplan's thesis of Jewish peoplehood would be complete without some comment on the "chosen people" idea, particularly since his conception of the Jews as a people, or a spiritual nation, requires the adoption by the Jewish group of an ethical and spiritual vocation. Dr. Kaplan must, therefore, react to the traditional belief that the Jews are divinely *chosen* for a particular career as a people.

He rejects the doctrine of chosenness. He does so with a full awareness of the metamorphosis which the doctrine has undergone. His attack is directed at the best in the tradition of chosenness, not simply at the elements of racialism which crept into the doctrine from time to time.

What is the history of this belief which so many Jews are reluctant to abandon? And what does Dr. Kaplan say about each stage of its growth? Its roots are in the ancient covenant which we have described above. God chose Israel to be His messenger among mankind. What did this choice imply? As far as we can tell, it was the Jewish counterpart of similar covenants between ancient peoples and their gods, except that the Jews believed their God to be the only Lord of the universe. Thus, the choice of the Jews meant that they were in possession of an exclusive mandate. Dr. Kaplan's first criticism of chosenness is therefore his assertion that it is a theory incapable of proof, which the ancient Jews, like other peoples, held about themselves. It cannot, therefore, be accepted as a fact.

From the assumption that they were in possession of God's truth, it was possible for the Jews to draw several inferences, more or less logical. They could, in the first place, have assumed that their own special merit as human beings warranted their choice. This inference was actually drawn by Judah Halevi in the *Kuzari*, when he declared that the Jews had a unique gift for religion. It is still held as a private opinion by some Jews who seek comfort from the ignominy visited upon their people by the non-Jewish world, in a compensatory belief in the moral superiority of the Jewish group. But mere assertion is no proof; and as a matter of fact, the overwhelming burden of Jewish tradition is opposed to any assumptions of Jewish racial superiority. Dr. Kaplan has had many supporters in rejecting this inference from chosenness.

Another possible inference from the belief that the Jews were "chosen" is that the choice of the Jews necessarily resulted in their possession of a superior tradition. From that viewpoint, the Jews developed a feeling both about the superiority of their religious heritage and its completeness, with the ethical features receiving special emphasis.[8] Dr. Kaplan, by drawing upon many different cultures and showing the inadequacies of certain facets of Jewish tradition, refutes this inference. Those Jews, for example, who insist that the Jews are ethically self-sufficient, in that their Torah gives them the right to teach others but does not impose the duty to learn from others, are themselves illustrating the moral bankruptcy of this inference from chosenness. No people which has lived through this modern period of cataclysmic change can afford to claim the absolute worth of its own tradition.

It was possible to infer — as was first inferred by Amos and subsequently by other great religious teachers throughout Jewish history — that the meaning of chosenness is to be found in the ethical responsibility which election imposed upon the Jews. Since God gave His Torah to the people of Israel, they would have to raise the level of their own moral behavior. They were expected to set an example for the rest of the world. This interpretation of chosenness is highly respected in some Jewish circles today since it appears to have ethical validity. Dr. Kaplan, however, points out that every group has the *same* responsibility so to organize its polity as to elicit the best in the character of each of its members and of the group as a whole.

When apologists for the chosen people idea began to sense its logical and ethical weaknesses, they drew an altogether new inference from the original conception of the covenant. God *did* choose the Jews, they insisted, but He chooses other people also, each for a special function. Dr. Kaplan believes this reinterpretation to be an unwarranted inference from the biblical conception of chosenness. When the Bible speaks of Assyria as an instrument of God's wrath, it does not in any way seek to draw a parallel between the choice of Assyria to punish Israel and the choice of Israel to be a light to the nations. Whatever functions were assigned to the nations were solely in reference to instructing Israel itself in the meaning of its own career.

But the apologists for chosenness go far beyond this biblical teaching. They assert that Israel was chosen to teach ethics or religion, the Greeks were chosen to teach art or philosophy, the Romans to teach law and the Americans to practice democracy or develop their unique "know-how." In the strictest sense of the term, this is not chosenness. For when one chooses, the choice involves a selection among alternatives and, necessarily, the elimination of all but the chosen one. Hence, according to this theory, every people would be destined by the will of God to be selected and rejected at the same time. If the Greeks, were selected for art, no other people could contribute in this field. By the same token, if the Jews are the ethical teachers of mankind, the Quakers can have nothing new to say. Need one consider further the absurdity of this assumption? Dr. Kaplan, however, relentlessly pursues the argument by indicating that, even if the Jews were chosen for a particular career, there is no evidence that they have lived up to it consistently; nor is there any proof that they can continue to do so in the future. And even if it were possible for them to act always as God's chosen children who are destined to teach religion to the world, by what right do they glory in this favored position? Was it not poor taste on the part of Joseph, who was indeed his father's favorite son, to boast about this fact to his brothers? Shall an entire people continue to be guilty of such lack of tact?

Dr. Kaplan is aware of the psychological power of the chosen people doctrine. He understands its role in having enabled

Jews throughout the ages to maintain their morale in the face of their detractors. But morale which is based on an illusion is bound to be destroyed when the illusion is exposed. The doctrine of chosenness has emerged, in the modern universe of discourse, as a well-meaning but grandiose illusion. Those who hold on to it do so because they think belief in Jewish chosenness necessary to sustain the morale of Jews or the validity of the revealed tradition, and thus to insure the survival of the Jewish people and of Judaism. Dr. Kaplan, however, has shown that another alternative is available, the alternative of spiritual vocation.

The chosen people doctrine always selects one element in the historical experience of a people and confers upon it theological significance. The character of that chosenness depends, of course, on the quality of the element selected. Among the Jews chosenness always involved an ethical purpose. That purpose is worth preserving. In order to do so we must know the historical conditions which went into the making of the Jewish heritage, and we must then decide what portion of that heritage is worth emulating or developing as a means of serving God. Then, Dr. Kaplan tells us, we can examine our position in the modern world and explore the possibilities open to us as a people for raising the level of human civilization. When we dedicate ourselves to this ethical task, we can feel that we are acting in accord with a call, a vocation, which has come to us, in great measure, by virtue of our belonging to a distinct group. Whether we achieve any worthwhile end, however, will depend on our own behavior from generation to generation.

There is nothing inevitable about the role of the Jewish people in the world. We have existed for a long time, as the history of societies is measured, but no man or group of men has ever proved to be immortal. We have risen to great ethical heights; but we have also fallen to the depths of human degradation. Dr. Kaplan has urged us at least to see ourselves as we are and to strive to become the kind of people whom God can use for the improvement of human life. In setting before ourselves this purpose in life, we should only be doing with our civilization what it devolves equally upon all the other peoples of the world to do with theirs.

NOTES

[1] *The Races of Mankind*, Public Affairs Committee, New York, 1943, pp. 12, 13.

[2] Compare below, Harold Weisberg, "Mordecai M. Kaplan's Theory of Religion," pp. 155–192.

[3] *The Idea of Nationalism*, Macmillan, New York, 1944, p. 10.

[4] *Ibid.*, p. 15.

[5] Cf. *A Partisan Guide to the Jewish Problem*, Bobbs-Merrill, New York, 1945, p. 151.

[6] *Judaism as a Civilization*, Macmillan, New York, 1934, p. 232.

[7] *The Future of the American Jew*, Macmillan, New York, 1948, p. 80.

[8] Cf. Hayim Greenberg's carefully documented study in *The Jewish Frontier*, XII, nos. 10–12, in which he shows how the doctrine of chosenness definitely emphasizes the superiority of the Torah.

MORDECAI M. KAPLAN'S CONCEPT OF ORGANIC JEWISH COMMUNITY

By Samuel Dinin

In the pre-emancipation era Jewish life was characterized by a general uniformity of belief and practice. Jews lived in self-contained and self-containing Jewish communities which in certain periods and in some lands were statewide in character. For the individual Jew there was no escape from the life and hegemony of the Jewish community except through acceptance of the dominant faith.

Self-government was imposed upon the Jew, in part by the needs and the requirements of the Jewish way of life and in part by the exclusionist attitude of the outside world. "The sense of mutual dependence was the sustaining force of organized community among Jews everywhere."[1] The Jew needed the social heritage of his people for his basic literacy and culture,[2] as well as for his Jewish cultural, religious and communal needs.

The Jewish community was a legal corporate entity recognized and backed up by the state or ruling power, and used for its own fiscal and economic purposes. "Jewish communal evolution," says Baron, "can be explained only by the state's self-interest in the fiscal and ecclesiastical organization of Jewish subjects; the influence of political and economic struggles between the organized Jewish group and similar groups among their neighbors, especially the burghers; the general evolution of corporate bodies in a particular society; the forces of imitation of institutional and legal patterns developed by the non-Jewish nations; and generally by that subtle and often indiscernible interplay of social and cultural influences between Jews and their environment."[3]

As Baron further points out, this recognition of the organized Jewish community by public law and the placing in its hands of compulsory powers of taxation, and the backing of the state's executive organs, served to reinforce the peculiarly Jewish means of law enforcement and to strengthen the hands of the leaders of the Jewish community.

The Beginning of a New Era

In modern times the Jewish community as it existed in the pre-emancipation period and the uniformity of belief and practice which characterized it are no more. The Jewish community, too, has been affected by the secularization of the western world and by everything which the word modern connotes — the rise of capitalism and its concomitant industrialization and urbanization; the emergence of democratic nationalism and scientific rationalism; and Jewish as well as general emancipation.

We can see all of these forces conjoining in a particular environment and in a particular community like that of New York, and we can study in detail the process by means of which Jewish communal life disintegrated.

"The early separation of Church and State gave each man the right to worship or not, as he chose. No group could force an individual to remain within its fold, or dictate to others how to act in matters of conscience. Secession after secession was a natural development among the synagogues of New York. Jewish organization of a purely cultural or social nature, having no connections with the synagogue or with religion as such, soon came into being. Individual Jews lived outside or inside of the Jewish community without molestation. It became equally impossible for the community to control ritual, dietary and reform tendencies."[4]

Until 1825 there was a more or less united Jewish community in New York. (In that year B'nai Jeshurun broke away from Shearith Israel.) There was one synagogue, one set of officials and one mode of accepted behavior. The Synagogue and the community were coextensive — each synagogue that came into being called itself Kahal. But secession after secession brought about a multiplicity of synagogues and of Kahals, and soon the term Kahal itself became obsolete. A state of anarchy ensued: men performed marriage ceremonies and gave divorces and set themselves up as oracles of Jewish law without the sanction of existing synagogues. Not only new synagogues sprang up, but a host of extra-synagogal organizations and activities catering to the fraternal, philanthropic, social, recreational and even literary interests of individual Jews and Jewish groups.

The Jewish community has long ceased to be a legal corporate entity and a vehicle of fiscal or economic control. The state enacted its own laws on burial and marriage, on incorporation of religious societies, and later on other matters once the province of the Jewish community. The Jewish community ceased to be a self-containing and self-governing body, not only in relation to those legal and fiscal areas which once were under its jurisdiction but as regards purely Jewish affairs as well. The *herem*, once a potent disciplinary instrument of the Jewish community, fell into decay. Its decay was symbolic of the total disintegration of the Jewish community as a self-governing entity.

The Jews of New York made many attempts to set up a super-Kahal and to restore to Jewish communal life some of its former cohesiveness, but every attempt met with failure. Jewish life, nationally and locally, witnessed the rise and growth of a multiplicity of divergent and competitive groups and organizations expressing the religious, synagogal, fraternal, recreational, Zionist, philanthropic, defense, social and other needs of the growing Jewish population. Many decades were to pass before limited success was registered in unifying and coordinating Jewish communal endeavors in specific areas.

(Though the general disintegration of Jewish communal life is characteristic of modern Jewish life in the western world, the pace, the character, the extent and the time of the disintegration differ with different sections of the world. All sorts of adjustments were made in communal organization, and in some East European and central European countries many of the characteristic powers of the pre-emancipation communal organization were carried over into the twentieth century. But since we are primarily interested in the United States we need not go into the specific variants of the problem.)

The Need to Rebuild the Community

Dr. Kaplan has always been concerned with the problem of community and community organization, even in his pre-Reconstructionist days. He was the first, as far as is known, to use the term "community center;" the first Jewish Center, which he established, survives to this day. The Community Center movement owes a great deal to his thinking. Though the center movement as a national movement and some Community Centers in some of the smaller communities exercise a unifying influence in certain aspects of Jewish life, the Jewish Center as an institution has not assumed the place in Jewish life once occupied by the Synagogue, nor even of the Synagogue as it exists today.[5]

Dr. Kaplan was also involved in the organization of the New York Kehillah prior to World War I, the most ambitious of the attempts at communal self-organization in American Jewish life. Like similar previous attempts, this too proved abortive, though out of it came the first organized Bureau of Jewish Education under Dr. Samson Benderly, which survives to this day in one of its *gilgulim* ("reincarnations").

Contemplating the chaos that was Jewish life, Dr. Kaplan long ago realized that, if the Jewish people were to survive in the modern world, it would be necessary not only to get "a new heart and a new spirit," but also to re-establish the conditions under which the Jews could once again begin to function as a healthy social organism. For the Jewish people as a whole he saw no future without a Jewish homeland in Eretz Yisrael and without self-governing communities in the Diaspora capable of cohesive and coherent thought and action.

Such self-governing communities he saw not only as a need of the Jewish group, but also as a necessity for the modern democratic state itself. The existence of such self-governing, religious-ethnic communities would be a guarantee, in a sense, that modern democratic, national states would not lose their democratic character and become totalitarian.

The Jew today lives in a perpetual state of quandary. He receives few benefits from the Jewish community. He is both accepted and rejected by the general community, and may as an individual Jew suffer from discrimination and indignities of one kind or another, whether or not he identifies himself with his group.

To give the Jew status and dignity, to help him overcome the political, economic and social disadvantages which he suffers by virtue of his being a member of a minority group, the Jew needs an organized community. "Without an enduring social structure, such as only a well-organized community can provide, being a Jew is like trying to live as a disembodied soul."[6]

Such a community, in the Diaspora at least, will never have the scope and functions of the pre-emancipation community. Adherence to it can no longer be, for the modern Jew, an alternative to adherence to the general community, but an additive factor in his life.[7] On the other hand, it cannot have the loose-structured, tepid form of organization which is characteristic of most of our Jewish community councils today. What Dr. Kaplan wants is an *organic Jewish community*.

The Concept of Organic Community

Now what is an organic community? The first ambiguity in dealing with this question is the confusion between community and some form of community organization. The Jews obviously live in communities, if we accept any standard definition of the term "community." They may even live in organic communities. The trouble is that they do not have an organic community organization to match the reality of their communal existence.

The dictionary defines "community" in many ways: as the people who reside in one locality and are subject to the same laws, *or* have the same interests; as a society having common interests, privileges, etc., *or* sharing many or all things in common; as a corporation (in law) having common ownership, possession or enjoyment; as a sharing or participation. Samuel C. Kohs defines it as "an association of people with similar backgrounds and objectives, whose aim is to satisfy common social, economic, physical and spiritual needs."[8]

The Jews are obviously a community, but how much of a community or how good a community they are depends on what they share in *common* and how much unity there is among the different parts and entities. Some Jews have very little in common with other Jews except the accident of birth and the appellation Jew (though these often are enough in the eyes of the "outside" world to identify even these Jews as subject to the same fate or destiny as other Jews). At the other extreme we have some Jews who have much in common. In between we have the vast majority who share one interest with one group of Jews, another interest with another group, and very few interests in common with all of these Jews. There has been a loss in modern times in the quality as well as in the quantity (the number of shared interests) of Jewish community life.

However, as poor as is the quality of our community life, our community organization is even worse. It does not even mirror or reflect the extent of the shared interests already existing in the Jewish community. For, strange as it may seem, the Jewish community is over-organized, with many competing, overlapping organizations in practically every area of Jewish life. What the community needs is an effective organization of its activities, associations, institutions, organizations, which will be selectively inclusive, in short an *organic* community organization.

The dictionary defines organic in one sense as pertaining to, or of the nature of, organisms. Let us discard this use of the term because it means getting into the problem of the vitalism of social organisms. Let us rather take one of the other definitions — forming or belonging to a system, an organized whole; characterized by correlation and cooperation of parts; organized; systematized. In philosophy, "organic" refers to a thing or a system of things regarded as a unity in itself, made up of inter-related and inter-acting parts, after the analogy of living beings. In law, it means acting as a means or instrument of formation; constitutive; regulative.

It is in these senses that we should seek an *organic* community — an organization of community in which there will be systematic correlation and co-operation of parts, which will be regulative in some way or ways. Thus Dr. Kaplan defines an organic community as one in which "all matters of Jewish interest would in some way deeply affect the lives of all who desire to remain Jews."[9]

Progress Toward Organic Community on the National Level

During the past few decades American Jewry has made tremendous strides along organizational lines, locally and nationally. Except for the brief existence of the original American Jewish Congress, American Jews have not succeeded in establishing an over-all, inclusive community organization even on as limited a basis as the late lamented American Jewish Conference. Under stress of great emergencies organizations functioning in one particular area of Jewish life have effected coordination of one kind or another. When the fate of the Jewish homeland was in peril, shortly before and during World War II, Zionist groups of various ideologies worked together along political lines in an American Zionist Emergency Council; but it was always a precarious kind of partnership which courted dissolution with every resolution. The Federations and Welfare Funds organized a national Council of Federations and Welfare Funds, which, though a *conference* for the most part, exercises actual influence, if not control, in areas of fund-raising, allocation of funds and community organization. This Council was organized in part because of the restiveness of local community councils and welfare funds, due to the multiplicity, size and character of the many competing fund-raising campaigns for overseas, national, and local needs.

Under the aegis of the Council, a National Advisory Community Relations Council has been set up (after prolonged negotiations and after many unsuccessful attempts), which acts mostly as a clearing house and umpire for the national defense agencies and local Community Council Relations Committees. The reception given to the MacIver report is only a slight indication of the difficulties which would be encountered in any attempt to achieve integration and coordination of program and activities, even in this one functional field of defense.

There is a Synagogue Council in which are represented the major religious groupings in American Jewish life. But though this body has on occasion issued significant resolutions, it is at best an innocuous organization which can pass resolutions, but even then, only when there is substantial unanimity of opinion, and then only on limited questions.

All of these are signs of an awareness of a need for collective action, but are still a far cry from the organic community (on a national scale) which is the desideratum of the Reconstructionist movement.

Progress on the Local Level

Locally there has been more substantial progress towards an organic Jewish community. Long before the emergence of community councils on the American Jewish scene, considerable integration and coordination had been achieved along functional lines, particularly in the field of philanthropy and social service. In Jewish education, in Jewish center work, and occasionally in other areas, as well as in the social service field, the trend for some time has been toward a more inclusive community setup, prompted by the need for greater economy and efficiency, for more democratic representation, and for wider community service. All of these were partial solutions (from the point of view of the organic community) along strictly functional lines.

The Jewish Community Council, a recent arrival on the American scene, represents the first successful attempt on a local level to establish an all-inclusive organization of all Jews and all Jewish groups in a community. Its rise is also due, in large part, to the stress and pressure of great crises and emergencies in Jewish life — the need to take common counsel and action in the face of the spread of Nazism and Fascism which imperiled the security and life of Jews everywhere; the need for centralizing and reducing the campaigns for funds in the face of the staggering sums needed to help the Jews in Europe, Israel, and other regions.

These community councils, however, are not all of one piece. Some are oligarchic in character, others more democratic. Some exist primarily for the sake of conducting a united welfare fund campaign, and do little else as a collective community council. Others engage in various communal activities. They may have central bureaus or committees on Jewish education, community relations committees which act as a clearing house for defense agencies on a local level; émigré committees, and the like. In some cities, the community council is under the direct control of, or gets its subsidy from, a Federation; in others the Federation is a constituent agency of the Jewish Community Council. But only a few approach the organic community organization which alone can begin to give that status and belongingness which Jews can get in no other way.

The Inadequacies of the Community Councils

In what way do even the best of our community councils fall short of the criteria set up for the organic Jewish community?

Dr. Kaplan sets up three principles of Jewish community organization:

1. All who definitely desire to see Jewish life fostered, regardless of how they conceive the form and content of that life, shall be eligible for membership.

2. Those institutions whose main function it is to foster Jewish consciousness shall occupy a position of primacy — synagogues, communal centers, institutions of elementary and higher learning, etc.

3. All organizations engaged in specific tasks should continue what they are doing, but in addition should be represented in the community councils. This applies as well to organizations and agencies that are national in scope.

A number of community councils are well on their way to the realization of the first and third of these principles. Some of them have made a beginning towards the incorporation of some of the objectives set forth by Dr. Kaplan as immediate aims, such as the coordination of all efforts in behalf of health and social welfare, maintenance of a complete register and vital statistics, etc. (Of the specific objectives, the one that will be most difficult of realization is the second — to activate the high ethical standards transmitted in the Jewish tradition, by the formulation of specific codes and sanctions for various social and economic relationships.)

The outstanding omission is the second principle — the primacy of the religious and educational institutions in the communal structure. Although synagogues are represented on community councils, they are in no case beneficiaries of community funds allocated by community councils; the principle of separation of church and state is at work in Jewish community life too. Nor are educational and cultural institutions and community centers at the heart of the nuclear pattern of community organization. To what extent is such expectation naive utopianism? Can we really expect American Jews to move toward an organic community in the foreseeable future?

The Postulates Underlying Organic Community

Before engaging in speculation or prophecy about the future, however, it would be well to examine some of the problems of Jewish community organization and reexamine some of the premises underlying the concept of organic community. All I can do is to pose those problems which will have to be resolved before we can make further progress toward an organic Jewish community; a discussion of solutions is something which should engage all men actively concerned in the administration of Jewish communal life.

Is World Jewry a Living Organism?

The concept of peoplehood promulgated by the Reconstructionist statement of principles and the notion of an organic community rest on the postulate that "world Jewry constitutes an indivisible people which has a living continuing organism and it is legitimate for Jews in a democratic *society* to be part of that organism."[10] Now it is true that Jews in a democratic society have a right to belong to an international people, but it is questionable whether they are an *indivisible* people. To apply to them the term a "living organism" is to resort to a bit of sociological mystique. It may be, as was pointed out above, that the outside world, or more realistically some states or certain types of government in period of stress, make every Jew by definition and treatment members of a unitary group. But the facts of the situation are quite different. There are many Jews who in lesser or greater degree are or consider themselves to be part of this "living social organism," and many who do not and are not. I doubt whether it would even be wise to go ahead on the principle of "as if" — to organize Jewish life as if world Jewry were that kind of living organism, or even to make that a goal of Jewish community life on the assumption that potentially world Jewry can be that kind of organism. It would be better to deal with the realities of the situation and to organize the Jewish community locally, nationally, and internationally in the light of these realities.

Who Shall Belong to the Jewish Community?

The question of who shall belong to the organized Jewish community will in great measure determine whether we shall ever get an organic community. On the one hand, there is a desire to make the Jewish community all-inclusive; membership in it would be determined by "regional propinquity rather than by interest in particular objectives."[11] The only membership requirement for groups and individuals would be a broad, general interest in the survival and growth of Jewish life.

On the other hand, a real community involves an active sharing of common interests, "the presence of a *common* goal, of an inclusive common interest, in which all the differences share and to which they all may contribute. The basis, in other words, is not a mere live-and-let-live. There must be much more, there must be *community* before differences can be welcomed, or even admitted at all. Community does not consist of distinct enclaves, self-centered, self-fulfilling."[12] MacIver made these remarks in connection with the democratic state and the general community; but they can be applied equally to the Jewish community.

In many communities every one who contributes to the welfare fund is automatically considered a member of the Jewish community and entitled to vote for representatives to the Jewish Community Council. The act of contributing to the welfare fund may be due to social coercion of a kind, rather than to a real interest in the survival and growth of the Jewish community. Nevertheless, such contributors, if their contributions are substantial, can exert tremendous influence on the distribution of funds and on the nature of the organized Jewish life encouraged and supported by the community. The admission of all groups on a broad, survivalist democratic basis often serves to perpetuate, and occasionally to strengthen, "the self-contained enclaves" rather than to promote the common good.

There are many who feel that under present conditions it will take a long time for an organic community to emerge and that it would be better to build a Jewish community around those groups and individuals who have, for want of a better term, an affirmative philosophy of Jewish life, and have more in common than philanthropy, fund-raising and defense. Whether this is wise or democratic is a pertinent question. Certainly no move of this kind should be contemplated without a great deal of soul-searching discussion. In the meantime it would be best to begin with those elements in the community program in which there is already a great deal of common interest, to strengthen this interest, to build upon it, and to extend it to those aspects of Jewish community life which for the Reconstructionist are primary and central.

Religion and the Synagogue

As we saw above, a synagogue, under present conditions of community organization, may be affiliated with a community council but is not a beneficiary of its funds. The concept of organic community calls for the reintegration of the Synagogue into the community structure and for placing it in one of the positions of centrality, if not in the central position. Synagogue groups are particularly restive under the present community structure, and many synagogue representatives openly talk about the organization of the American Jewish community around the congregation and the national congregational bodies.

The position of the Reconstructionist movement on this question is slightly ambiguous and needs further exploration. On the one hand, there is a recognition that, under conditions of modern Jewish life, the Synagogue can no longer be made coextensive with the Kahal or the Jewish community, and that the community organization must include all Jews, even those who are not religious; that at best the Synagogue can be one of the central institutions and the congregation one of the central agencies of the Jewish community, but not *the* central agency, and certainly not the sole institution, nor even the sole cultural-educational institution.

On the other hand, the postulates of the Reconstructionist platform and the conditions of American Jewish life may lead inexorably to a congregational community structure. There is first the emphasis on Judaism as a *religious* civilization. There is further the placing of the Jewish group in a position in American life analogous to that of the Catholic Church. "It is essential to accept for American Jewry the status of a religio-cultural group analogous to that of the Roman Catholic church, minus its authoritarianism."[13]

The climate of America is more favorable to the survival of religious minority groups than to ethnic groups. Baron points out that, despite the fact that the Synagogue has lost its position of centrality in modern Jewish life, the religious factor in western Europe and America "has retained its preeminent position on the scale of communal values."[14] The congregations are the mainstay of all organized Jewish life, and in membership, activities and cooperation far outdistance the federations and philanthropic agencies, and all the communal and super-communal defense agencies.

As against this, it must be admitted that the various synagogue groups have not displayed any marked ability to work together in community, either locally or nationally, and that religious Jewish life still suffers from factionalism, competitiveness and institutional rivalry. It is difficult for orthodox fundamentalists of any kind to work with those who deviate from them in matters affecting the "true faith," except on their own terms.

In the light of these questions the Reconstructionist movement must study more carefully what kind of Jewish religious civilization it desires for America, what kind of community structure is needed to give strength to such a program, and, above all, what is possible for American Jewish life in view of the realities now existing.

The Problem of Leadership and Control

The problem of leadership complicates the realization of the ideal of an organic community in which primacy will be given to cultural, religious and educational needs. For one thing there are very few persons in positions of leadership in the local Jewish communities who have the requisite Jewish literacy for positions of leadership. The primary requisite for leadership today is wealth and influence. Too often leaders are selected on the basis of how much they contribute to the welfare funds or the influence they wield over those who contribute. It is difficult to interest such leaders in intensive Jewish education or Hebraic culture, for example, when they themselves do not have the equivalent of an intensive elementary Jewish school training and evidently did not need it to rise to positions of leadership. To tell young people to study at an adult Jewish school in order to qualify for informed leadership in Jewish life (among other things) is merely to invite cynicism on their part.

By the same token, control of allocation of funds is vested in the hands of the large contributors. In some communities, even where community councils are democratic in character, it is difficult to cross the large contributors. There have been any number of cases where large contributors have threatened to cut off or reduce their contributions to the welfare fund, unless the particular agency in which they were interested got the allocation they thought it should get. Even where councils are, in large measure democratic, the committee on allocations, which determines the distribution of funds raised, is composed of the large contributors and of the people wielding influence in the community.

The Battle of Funds[15]

The problem of organic community is further complicated by the competing demands and requirements of local, national and overseas needs on the one hand, and by the presence of many small, supplementary campaigns for special causes which are beginning to encroach upon and challenge the central, united fund. The conflict has arisen first, because the Jewish community as a whole, though its total contributions are magnificent in scale, still does not contribute all that is needed by all the agencies included in the category of local, national and overseas causes. Then again, the staggering needs of the government of Israel make it necessary to keep allocations to local and national agencies to a minimum, particularly in those communities where not enough money is raised to meet all these requirements. The proponents of the United Jewish Appeal claim that the communities use Israel and its wants as the means of appealing to Jews for contributions to the welfare fund as a whole, and that therefore the larger part of the funds raised should go to the United Jewish Appeal for the needs of Israel.

It is true that the best selling point in a campaign for funds is Israel and its needs. But as important as it is to raise the maximum sums necessary to help the state of Israel, it is doubtful whether an appeal based solely on funds for Israel is wise from the point of view of the future growth of the Jewish community in America. Unless due attention will be given to the needs and activities of local and national agencies on the American scene, there may come a time when these needs will not be properly appreciated and supported. There are those who are suggesting that it might be best to conduct two separate campaigns — one for overseas needs and one for local and national needs. This suggestion is not one which the fund-raising leaders want to adopt, knowing the terrific work that has to go into a campaign for raising funds. However, unless some solution is found whereby due consideration will be given to the growing needs of the local Jewish community, there will be some communities which will begin resorting to this plan.

In this conflict over the allocation of funds to local, national and overseas needs, it is always the cultural and educational agencies, which from the Reconstructionist point of view should be of primary concern to the community, that are squeezed out or receive reductions in allotment. Both the protagonists of Israel and the leaders of the federations of philanthropy and social agencies are the ones who have the power in the community, and in the battle for position and allocation of funds compromises are reached usually at the expense of the local and national cultural and educational agencies.

According to Dr. Kohs[16] there were in 1935, 4035 agencies spending $48,157,038. Of these 3909 were local and regional agencies which spent $41,227,377 or 85.6% of the total, and 126 national, overseas and other agencies which spent $6,929,661 or 14.4%. It is interesting to note that of the 3909 local and regional agencies, 2200 were Jewish educational organizations spending $5,825,000, but there were 67 health agencies which spent $18,786,222 — 39% against 12.1%.

In 1944, however, the percentage spent for overseas agencies alone was 40.8%; if one includes national agencies and others—administration of community councils, welfare funds, and fund-raising agencies, the grand total is 54.7%. (This is for 133 cities.) This shows in a dramatic way the transformation which has taken place in the proportion of money spent on local as against overseas needs in this decade; this at a time when, in communities like Los Angeles in particular, there has been a tremendous increase in population and thus in the need for new schools, new centers, new local institutions, religious and cultural, to meet the requirements of the increased population.

Even those interested in the future of Israel should study with great concern this neglect of local Jewish needs. The weakening of the local Jewish communities will, in the long run, have an adverse effect on the support which American Jewry will give to the state of Israel. It is true that in many communities individual congregations and agencies, not beneficiaries of the welfare funds, have gone out on campaigns of their own, and some have even put up beautiful structures at great cost at a time when such building could be postponed. These individual campaigns undoubtedly hurt the united welfare funds and gave those interested in Israel the impression that the local community was spending a disproportionate amount of money for luxuries at a time when the needs of Israel were so pressing. This is only another indication of the need for organic community which will be all-inclusive and which might be able to prevent unnecessary building and too many campaigns.

National vs. Local

Finally, the problem of organic community is complicated by the relations between national and super-national agencies and local agencies. Each of the religious groups has a national structure; so do some of the fraternal organizations, such as the Workmen's Circle and Jewish National Workers Alliance, which conduct schools as well. The local communities that have bureaus or committees of education attempt to coordinate the work of all the schools and try to proceed on the basis of what is best for the community as a whole. Each national religious and educational body, however, is anxious to retain its position of control, and is loath to give up that position even when the schools are small and in the process of decline, and should be merged with other schools in the community in the best interests of Jewish education. The incursion of national bodies into local communities holds true for a great many other problems, the problem of congregational dues and tuition fees, the problem of the differences between curricula worked out by a local bureau and those worked out by the national bodies, etc.

This is characteristic of other areas of Jewish life as well. The Council of Jewish Federations and Welfare Funds gives budgeting advice to local communities, which in some cases is resented because it is often slanted in a certain direction, although from the point of view of information it is an excellent service. There is the problem of national agencies dealing with defense and their counterparts in the local communities; of the national religious bodies and the local congregations. It would take us too far afield to go into all the ramifications of the problem. What is intended is merely to state the areas of conflict. There is no intention of implying that the problems here posed are insoluble. All that is meant is merely to indicate that these problems exist, and that we will not achieve organic community unless and until we make systematic and careful attempts to resolve the conflicts and to reach an amicable understanding regarding a division of responsibility and control between national bodies and local community agencies.

The thinking of Dr. Kaplan and the Reconstructionist movement has had a tremendous influence on the growth of Jewish community life and organization. It would take a long investigation involving hundreds of interviews with influential people in hundreds of communities to assess the ways in which the Reconstructionist thinking on community organization has influenced the development of the Jewish community in America. In making one of the foci of the Reconstructionist movement the need for organic Jewish community, the Reconstructionist movement is pointing in the direction which American Jewish life must take if American Jewry is to survive as a creative force in the life of America and of world Jewry. To propose an idea, however, without a full awareness of the problems involved, is an empty and gratuitous gesture. What has been attempted here is to indicate what are the problems which must be faced and met if we are to achieve an organic Jewish community, locally and nationally.

NOTES

[1] M. M. Kaplan, *The Future of the American Jew*, Macmillan, New York, 1948, p. 107.

[2] *Ibid.*, p. 106.

[3] Salo W. Baron, *The Jewish Community*, Jewish Publication Society, Philadelphia, 1942, Vol. I, pp. 22–3.

[4] Hyman B. Grinstein, *The Rise of the Jewish Community of New York, 1654–1860*, Jewish Publication Society, Philadelphia, 1945, p. 5.

[5] Compare below, Louis Kraft, "Mordecai M. Kaplan's Contribution to the Jewish Center Movement," pp. 119–135.

[6] M. M. Kaplan, *The Future of the American Jew*, p. 111.

[7] *Ibid.*

[8] *The Jews*, ed. Louis Finkelstein, Harper & Bros., New York, 1950, p. 1267.

[9] M. M. Kaplan, *The Future of the American Jew*, p. 114.

[10] Kaplan, *ibid.*, p. 121. Compare above, Jack J. Cohen, "Mordecai M. Kaplan's Concept of Peoplehood," pp. 27–44.

[11] Kaplan, *ibid.*, p. 114.

[12] R. M. MacIver, *Report on the Jewish Community Relations Agencies*, National Community Relations Advisory Council, New York, 1951, p. 41.

[13] M. M. Kaplan, *The Future of the American Jew*, p. 121.

[14] S. W. Baron, *The Jewish Community*, Vol. I, p. 4.

[15] Compare below, Samuel C. Kohs, "Mordecai M. Kaplan's Contribution to Jewish Social Work," pp. 65–83.

[16] *The Jews*, pp. 1286, 1288.

MORDECAI M. KAPLAN'S CONTRIBUTION TO JEWISH SOCIAL WORK

By Samuel C. Kohs

Dr. Mordecai Kaplan's contribution to an understanding of Jewish social service activities in the United States divide themselves into two categories. The one category provides material through which we may comprehend more clearly the various social, economic, political, and religious forces, both positive and negative, which are currently operating, and through which we may more clearly understand the present scene. The other involves a variety of suggestions and recommendations for strengthening, advancing and enriching Jewish life, in order to make it more meaningful to the individual Jew, more significant to each community of Jews, and to the general society of which Jews are a part.

The material in this essay, dealing with Mordecai Kaplan's contribution to social work thinking, has been divided into three segments: Jewish community organization, the functional social services, and the Jewish social worker. A fourth area of social work, touching upon the Jewish content agencies, has been covered in other sections of this volume.

Present Structure of Jewish Communal Life

Individuals and families organize themselves into "communities" in order, collectively, to meet more satisfactorily their individual and group needs of a social, economic, political and religious character. In the case of Jews, not only these influences are operative, but in addition, there is the tradition and momentum of centuries which tend to bring Jews together, in a sort of automatic social behavior pattern, without the apparent force of any obvious need. This results in what appear to be anomalies, seeming contradictions and inconsistencies in the ways that Jews live and function together.

In the early period of Jewish settlement in this country the pioneer conditions under which all Americans had to live forced the few centers of Jewish population in this country to form close-knit ties. Religion and the synagogue played a much more important part in maintaining the unity and the integrity of the Jewish group than they do today. Through the period of almost three centuries of Jewish residence in this country, various forces have been in operation tending toward group disintegration rather than integration.

As we examine the structure of Jewish communities throughout the country we find divisions within it based upon religious differences — Orthodoxy, Conservatism, and Reform; differences due to national origin — German Jews, Russian Jews, Polish Jews, Hungarians, etc.; differences due to economic status — the rich, poor, the middle class; differences in attitudes to Zionism — Zionists, anti-Zionists, non-Zionists, — and even within each group variations and diversity of opinion; diversities due to differences in occupational interests — the merchants, the professionals, the "rank and file" workers; divisions due to differences in attitude to Jewish survival — assimilationists, and survivalists; divergencies due to political ideologies — conservative, liberal, radical; fragmentations due to differences in education — religious and secular. Just as the United States represents an association or a congregation of people from all points on the world's compass, with wide variations in background and interest, so, also, does the Jewish group represent a great diversity among its members in terms of background, current interests and loyalties. In its reaction to many problems that face Jewish life today, Jewish communities quite generally manifest a diversity of attitudes and practices to deal constructively with these questions. Occasional unity occurs only when an outside threat is directed universally against the entire group, thus stimulating a kind of emergency "get-togetherness" which dissolves once the threat is diminished or reduced.

Perhaps no other group in this country, numbering some four to five million, and scattered over every portion of the United States, presents such an array of divisions within its ranks, and divisions representing such deep-seated antagonisms, as does the Jewish group. How it manages to survive under these circumstances is indeed miraculous. Yet we do have Federations, Welfare Funds, Jewish social agencies, and a large variety of Jewish organizations: men's, women's, youth, and quite a wealth of Jewish communal establishments and institutions. We do get together from time to time to discuss common needs, common problems, and ways and means of acting jointly on important questions and issues.

Factors Making for the Breakdown of the Jewish Community

Apart from the influences already listed which tend to divide and fragmentize the Jewish community, there are a number of other forces which tend to weaken, if not destroy, unity within Jewish life.

One of these is the absence of a universally acceptable philosophy underlying Jewish life and its survival. Many Jews look upon themselves as different from all other peoples only by accident of birth. They see no relation to the whole stream of Jewish life in the past, and have no conception of their involvement in the current stream leading to an ongoing Jewish life of the future. They have no comprehension of the contributions that the Jewish group has made to civilization. They are overwhelmed with the conviction that there is no hope for Jewish life in the Diaspora. They feel they have much more to gain by becoming members of a "world brotherhood of mankind" than by being too closely identified with any separate or limited group. They see no point in any social benefits that may come through the survival of the Jewish group, and are convinced that individual human beings can make as great a contribution to civilization as "citizens of the world" as they can through identification with any specific group, especially with a Jewish group.

Another factor tending to weaken and fragmentize Jewish life is the tremendous force making for the assimilation and absorption of Jews in the general population. Although no exact figures are available, it is known that the rate of intermarriage, among Jews throughout the country, is taking on amazing proportions. Jews involved in mixed marriages frequently develop defensive mechanisms, protective coloration, rationalizations and other varieties of behavior patterns to make it possible for them to live in a "new world," although their birth roots and their background are anchored elsewhere. There are many who labor under the delusion that renunciation of all affiliation with Jewish institutions and associations will provide them with greater opportunities for advancement, recognition and material gain.

Still another influence which attacks the vigor and vitality of a constructively organized Jewish life is the large incidence of self-hate and self-depreciation which characterize the attitude of so many Jews toward themselves and their fellows. A great deal is said and done with reference to the anti-Semitism manifested by non-Jews. Unfortunately too little is said and done with reference to the anti-Semitism that some Jews themselves manifest. Those who have studied this phenomenon have been led to the conviction that ignorance of one's background and one's self breeds self-hate and self-depreciation. If a person is possessed of normal mental capacities, and his emotional life is normally constituted, a sound Jewish education will serve as the best antidote against hatred of one's self as a Jew. One then is sufficiently aware of what being a Jew represents, what the Jew has represented in the stream of civilization, and what he has stood for in terms of eternal religious and ethical values. He sees clearly that one of the greatest contributions that the Jew can make to accelerate the progress of civilization is to continue functioning through his group, and advancing the ideals for which it has always fought.

Another factor helping the disintegrative forces of American Jewish life is the non-Jewishness of many Jewish social workers. There are occasions when the professional men and women associated with national and local Jewish organizations exercise a greater influence in determining the quality and direction of Jewish life in the United States than the rabbis. The position of many Jewish social workers, as important Jewish communal leaders, gives them an outstanding opportunity to mould Jewish opinion and to influence the pattern of Jewish life for the present and the future. Regrettably, many Jewish social workers are utterly unequipped, in terms of Jewish background, Jewish idealism, and dedication and devotion to basic Jewish values, to recognize the forces that have given meaning and significance to Jewish life in the past. Efforts that are being currently made to provide this background to Jewish social workers who lack it are amateurish, superficial, and quite inadequate.

Last, but not least, in the alignment of forces making for the disintegration and disruption of Jewish life are the continual struggles between Jewish organizations to secure the maximum of recognition and financial support for their individual enterprises. They appear to have no regard for the losses that this will cause other Jewish organizations that have an equal or superior right to the financial resources of the American Jewish population. This war of vested interests may be of temporary advantage to the victorious organization, but in the long run it spells inestimable damage to the future strength and vitality of Jewish life, not only here in our own country but throughout the world as well.

Factors Making for Jewish Life

On the other hand, the picture is not entirely black. Centripetal forces do exist which, to an extent, are helping to counteract the negative and destructive forces just mentioned.

We do have the men and organizations that are attempting to bring to the American Jewish people a positive and constructive philosophy of Jewish life which aims to conserve all the wealth of our past, in religion and in history, and to point out in what ways our present thinking and community programs may be enriched and motivated by them. Dr. Kaplan's *The Future of the American Jew* and Milton Steinberg's *A Partisan Guide to the Jewish Problem* are excellent examples of this effort to provide a positive and constructive philosophy for Jewish life today.

Few people realize how colossal is the ignorance of the average American Jew with reference to his religion, his history, his contributions to science, art and literature, his influence in bringing to realization some of the finer aspects of modern civilization. There are quite a few who point with pride to the increasing amount of Jewish education being provided, as a communal responsibility, by the Jewish communities of this country. Looking at it realistically, however, the quantity and quality of Jewish education received by the average American Jew is pitifully inadequate in its failure, not only to transmit to him his social and cultural heritage in full, but to help him to build that sense of inner security, inner strength and self-regard, that only a sound and complete Jewish education can provide. The kind of *ersatz* that goes for Jewish education in this country cannot begin to lay the foundation upon which a strong Jewish community life can be developed.

It is interesting to note that the young people that are now coming into leadership in American Jewish life are the product of communities where Jewish education is recognized as one of the primary obligations of the Jewish community, and where

Jewish education is available on a very high qualitative level. A community leader, whose motivations are rooted in ignorance, may do some good; but a community leader, who possesses a rich reservoir of knowledge and Jewish background, is much more likely to make the contributions to American Jewish life that will give it inspiration and vitality. So too, communities whose members operate out of ignorance may, occasionally, largely by the example of others, engage in constructive efforts. On the other hand, a Jewish community whose members have been provided with the best that Jewish education can afford not only will be acting most constructively on the various issues confronting it, but will set the pace for others to follow. This generality applies regardless of whether it is a question of building the right kind of local Jewish institution, taking a position on an important issue, or whether it involves extending local co-operation and assistance to some remote Jewish group that needs the sympathetic understanding of a "Big Brother" community. It is a fact that those communities whose Jewish members have received a higher grade of Jewish education will be able better and more effectively to relate themselves in their integration with the general life of the community of which they are a part.

The establishment of the State of Israel is going to be another factor which will undoubtedly exercise a great influence in strengthening Jewish communal life in America and help counteract those negative and destructive forces that are gnawing at its vitals and aiding in its destruction. No other incident in the life of any generation of Jews in this country is going to have the kind of positive and constructive influence that developments in Israel are going to exercise. There is no question here of a divided loyalty. What is involved is the basic concept of the unity of the Jewish people all over the world regardless of what political regime they may live under. This unity is not a political unity. It is rather a unity of the spirit, and the kind of unity that grows out of a common religious and cultural heritage. Already there are ample signs of an exchange of cultural influences between the Jews of Israel and Jews living in other parts of the world. This exchange of religious and cultural stimulation is bound to give increased strength to those forces that are making for the integration of Jewish life in the Diaspora, and that are giving it increased richness and greater meaning.

It has been said, and correctly so, that anti-Semitism has been an integrative force in American Jewish life. This cannot be gainsaid. There is no question that, when Jews are threatened, they will unite against the aggressor, as best they can. However, it does not take a very analytic mind to discern the difference between the kind of unity that is stimulated by anti-Semitic attacks and the kind that can grow out of an understanding and general acceptance of a positive and constructive philosophy of Jewish life, and a well-financed communal system of Jewish education. It is the second kind of unity that is developing and will continue to develop as a result of the interchange of contacts and influences with Israel.

Were we in possession of instruments to measure the strength of the forces in American Jewish life tending toward its weakening and ultimate disappearance, as against those forces that operate in the opposite direction, we might be inclined to find that the negative and destructive forces now exceed the positive and constructive ones. However, to be forewarned is to be forearmed. No matter what happens, "a remnant shall be saved." How large that remnant is going to be will depend very largely upon the understanding and the will of American Jewish communities to strengthen those forces which will make for a secure, sound and constructive Jewish life in America.

The Functional Social Services

It must be recognized that the social service activities which Jewish communities support at present have had their roots in the patterns of philanthropic activities going back hundreds of years. However, in view of the fact that American Jewish life operates in a predominantly Protestant Christian environment, many Jewish social services have lost contact with the basic philosophy underlying Jewish social service practices, and have taken on the coloration and the techniques which are characteristic of so-called non-sectarian organizations and those established by city, county, state and federal administrations.

(a) *Basic Philosophy*

The test of whether a Jewish social service activity should be supported by a Jewish Federation, a Jewish Community Council, or a Jewish Welfare Fund is the question: does this particular social service agency have a positive outlook upon Jewish life and serve constructively Jewish community purposes? Where such rationale does not exist, there is legitimate question whether that agency and its function can properly be regarded as a responsibility of the Jewish community. It is a question whether the Jewish Family Service agency that has a predominantly Christian staff, or non-Jewish staff, (whether the social workers are Jewish by birth nor not), and where the clients may be Jewish or not, and where the "Jewish component" is neither visible nor significant, has a place as one of the organizations supported by the Jewish community. Whether agencies render religious service, Jewish education, or social service in all its varieties, unless these serve to enrich and advance Jewish life, they have no place among the organizations and enterprises supported by the Jewish community.

(b) *Family Welfare and Child Care*

In many Jewish social service agencies, a "permissive" or "functional" approach is utilized in determining how or whether a Jewish family applying for service can be helped. There are Jewish Family Agencies, supported by Jewish community funds, which accept Christian families as clients, and who are serviced by a Christian or a "Jewish" case worker, under the major auspices of a *Jewish* social service agency. The situation is not so striking in the case of child care, since there is a legal requirement that a Jewish social agency is under compulsion to provide a Jewish child with religious and moral training that has some relation to Judaism. However, in the case of the placement of children in private foster homes, this requirement is not always observed to the letter. This is not the case, however, for children placed in Jewish institutions. In the latter instance, the directors or superintendents of these institutions invariably provide not only for religious services, but for religious training and for Jewish education.

Complicating these difficulties is the previously mentioned fact that many Jewish social workers have a very inadequate, if any, Jewish background and Jewish orientation to the problems of Jewish life. Many of them are not affiliated with any Jewish organizations, religious or secular, and service to the Jewish community and Jewish agencies is on the same detached level as it would be if these Jewish social service workers were on the staff of a public or a so-called non-sectarian agency.

Dr. Kaplan has frequently drawn community attention to this condition, for it has always appeared to him inconsistent with the sound organization of Jewish life, and with an intelligent and effective advancement of its interests and its needs. Unless Jewish Social service agencies serve specific Jewish needs and objectives, there appears to be no reason why such social service activities should be carried on under Jewish auspices. If the service is of a non-sectarian character and has no relationship to the structure and functioning of Jewish community life, then it should either be tax-supported or be operated and financed by a private group, on a non-sectarian basis.

(c) Fund Raising

Fund raising for philanthropic purposes has gone through a most interesting evolution during the past 50 years in this country. Abandoning reliance upon charity balls, theatre benefits, bazaars, ticket selling for all kinds of enterprises, dinners, synagogue *shnudering*, etc., fund-raising in the Jewish philanthropic field has become "big business." Regrettably, the measure of a social worker's competence as head of a central Jewish community organization has become, "Is he a good money raiser?" His competence in other fields may be extraordinarily high, but a disproportionately great value is placed upon his ability to organize and conduct fund-raising campaigns. Also to be regretted is the fact that the successful fund-raisers can command salaries far beyond the level achieved by most competent and outstanding social service workers in other important areas of Jewish communal service.

This makes for the wielding of extraordinary power by those who control the dollar, either in its collection or in its distribution. This condition is not always in harmony with the kind of balance that should be maintained between local, national and overseas enterprises, nor between the various enterprises within each of these categories.

The greatest challenge to democracy in community organization derives from the differentials in the contributions between various contributors. The person who contributes $10,000 to a campaign is inclined to demand ten times as much influence in determining a decision as the person who gives only $1,000. Since membership and participation in Jewish community life and affairs today is entirely on a voluntary basis, it is quite apparent that, unless the $10,000 contributor is satisfied that his voice counts to the extent of the dollars he contributes, he is entirely free to withdraw his contribution and to separate himself entirely from any participation in the affairs of the Jewish community. This is a real problem; only community education can solve it.

What is greatly needed at this time is the development of the necessary perspective and machinery to place fund-raising in its proper relation in the affairs of the community, and to reduce the power and the authority of the "big giver" in determining community policy and program, if that authority is based solely on the size of his contribution.

It is to be regretted that we are raising a generation of Jews in America today, who are primarily and almost exclusively "fund-raising specialists". They are so busy with fund-raising activities throughout the year that they have very little opportunity to develop an interest in or understanding of those areas of much greater importance for the enrichment and advancement of Jewish life.

The Jewish Social Worker

We may speak about a philosophy of Jewish social work and Jewish social work objectives from now until doomsday, but those words will be wasted unless we take into consideration the agent through whom those objectives and values can be achieved.

(a) *His background and attitudes*

Perhaps a few thousand Jewish social workers are now employed by Jewish community agencies throughout the country, and also in overseas activities on behalf of American Jewish organizations. It is to be regretted that we have no statistics on the types and varieties of Jewish social workers that are active in Jewish social agencies, their general background of education and training, their Jewish education, their attitudes with reference to Jews, Jewish life and Jewish survival. Whatever can be said is, therefore, based primarily on general impressions and on contacts with various branches of Jewish social work during the past thirty-five years.

Increasingly, Jewish social workers are receiving their training in graduate schools of social work throughout the country. The proportion of Jewish social workers employed who have no certification of graduation from a school of social work is rapidly declining.

For some fifteen years, there existed a Graduate School for Jewish Social Work. For reasons that we need not go into here, the School ceased to exist some ten years ago, (around 1940). At this School, some substantial effort was made to provide the beginning Jewish social worker with something of a Jewish orientation and Jewish background, in order to relate his own activity to the stream of Jewish life whose existence for some four thousand years gave it direction and content. Dr. Kaplan was a member of the Faculty of this School.

Following the closing of the Jewish School for Social Work, there was established a Bureau for Jewish Communal Training which lasted some four years, and which has also ceased to exist.

Currently, there is not a single facility, supported nationally by Jewish communities throughout the country, interested in training Jewish young people for Jewish social service, or interested in providing supplementary courses, at community cost, in order that those social workers who receive training in existing schools of social work should receive the kind of orientation to Jews and Jewish life necessary for adequate functioning as social workers in Jewish communities.

However, the need is recognized, and such agencies as The National Jewish Welfare Board, Yeshiva University, and the Yiddish Scientific Institute are making efforts to fill the gap. But none of these are recognized by the American Association of Schools of Social Work, which is the validating organization for establishing competence for professional training for social service. During the period of its existence, the Graduate School of Jewish Social Work was a member of that Association. (Some four or five Catholic Schools of Social Work are currently members of the Association.)

It should also be pointed out that, in acquiring social work skills, Jewish students attending schools of social work are inevitably indoctrinated with principles and philosophy that grow out of Christian values and Christian ethics. The inference here is not that Christian philosophy and Christian ethics are inferior to Jewish philosophy and Jewish ethics; but, at some very essential points, they *are* different. In many respects, they are the same or overlap. But the differentials, what the Yiddish writers have come to call "*dos pintele yid*", are extremely important and too frequently overlooked.

Therein lie the hazard and the dangers inherent in Jewish social work as it is practiced by Jewish social workers today.

(b) *His preparation*

If we could locate and examine that mythical "average" Jewish social worker, we would find that he has come from something of a religious home, he has had few if any Jewish interests or contacts, but has maintained a sort of passing interest in Jews and Jewish life. At times he has had a curiosity about certain aspects of Jewish life which appear rather ancient and alien. But on the whole, he seems to maintain a queer sort of detachment, which he may pass off as representing "objectivity", as against "sentimentality".

In determining the selection of a career, he figured that social work might offer inducements and emoluments superior to what he might find in medicine, law, merchandising, teaching or the like. Quite probably he was animated by a desire to be helpful to human beings.

So, he decided upon social work as a career. Even if he has an interest in serving the Jewish community through its social service agencies, he learns quickly that there is no Jewish school which prepares Jewish social workers for Jewish community work, but that there are some thirty so-called "non-sectarian" schools of social work throughout the country, all of them associated with state or privately endowed higher educational institutions. He may also discover in his investigation that some four or five schools of social work are supported by the Catholic Church and prepare students for work in Catholic agencies and in the public welfare field. They do not turn away Jewish students who wish to receive training in a Catholic school. The other schools of social work, although presumably non-sectarian, inevitably provide a base of principles and philosophy that have their roots in Protestant ideology and Protestant values.

Our average young person interested in social work as a career has selected one of the non-sectarian schools of social work, and during his two year course, may, if he or she has been particularly fortunate, have been placed for field service training in a Jewish social agency. But that is not always the case. There is practically no Jewish content in case work. In Jewish Center work, he is more likely to face challenges leading to the development of greater knowledge and understanding of the Jewish group. In some instances, these may stimulate a real awakening.

When the Jewish social worker is through with his training, there is a question of placement. Certainly the opportunity for placement in Christian agencies is extremely limited. He now has a choice between public welfare agencies and the Jewish field. Public welfare agencies are known to pay notoriously lower salaries. The natural tendency, then, is to make oneself available for the Jewish field. The two major agencies that help place personnel are the National Jewish Welfare Board for the Jewish Community Center field, and the Council of Jewish Federations and Welfare Funds, for persons in the community organization field (Federations, Welfare Fund, Community Councils) and also for the functional fields. In the latter categories, it will cooperate with such non-sectarian agencies as the Family Welfare Association of America for family case workers, and other specialized agencies in the other specialized fields. Although the Jewish Welfare Board is particularly concerned with reference to the Jewish background of a person recommended, and is on record as not referring people for placement unless they have an adequate Jewish background, this is not necessarily the case for the Council of Jewish Federations and Welfare Funds, as far as the various functional fields are concerned. The Council of Jewish Federations and Welfare Funds is much more "realistic" and provides the communities with social workers according to the community's own specifications. The Council does not impose any standards upon local communities. It may advise or suggest, but the decision is ultimately that of the community itself.

Unfortunately, there are very few opportunities provided by the local Jewish community organization agencies for institutes, in-service training programs, or leaves of absence, to develop a better Jewish orientation or to acquire the kind of Jewish knowledge essential for effective performance in the Jewish social service field.

The result of all this is that we have much of our Jewish social service work carried on and directed by Jewish social workers who have a limited Jewish background. That may be one of the reasons why so few Jewish social workers exercise positions of Jewish leadership, not only in their own local communities, but regionally and nationally as well.

(c) *His activities and influence*

Because of the peculiar way in which national Jewish life in the United States is organized (or unorganized), the role of the Jewish social service worker in formulating plans and proposals for the conduct of Jewish affairs and his participation in leadership, are peculiar. There is no doubt that the top executive leadership in the social work agencies of a local community exercises great influence upon the top lay leadership in each locality. These professionals are expected to have information, views, experiences and other assets which give them particular qualifications to advise community "elders" on the kind of local policy to be pursued. In many instances this advice also covers policy on matters of national and international Jewish concern.

As far as the rank and file of Jewish social workers is concerned, they exercise very little if any influence upon local Jewish life or upon the thinking of the Jewish leadership. In many instances, local Jewish lay leadership looks with disdain upon the quality of participation that local rank and file Jewish social workers may offer, when they do.

At one time, the National Conference of Jewish Social Service was an effective instrument in determining national policy on Jewish affairs, especially concerning philanthropy. It was then a conference of outstanding lay and professional leaders throughout the country. For reasons that need not be elaborated here, the National Conference of Jewish Social Service (now the National Conference of Jewish Social Welfare) has become a "forum" primarily of rank and file workers. Professional top Jewish community leadership participates in the Assemblies of the National Council of Jewish Federations and Welfare Funds, together with the top lay leadership of the Jewish communities throughout the country. In that regard, the Council of Jewish Federations and Welfare Funds is supposed to be predominantly a layman's council and their Assemblies a layman's assembly. However, increasingly the Council and the Assembly have represented a partnership between lay and professional leadership.

From time to time, the annual meetings of the National Conference of Jewish Social Welfare have discussed the subject of Jewish content and Jewish social work. However, nothing has come out of the thinking of that group which is particularly helpful in terms of any program that can make Jewish life in America much more significant.

It would be very helpful if, once a year, an assembly of all Jewish community functionaries could be brought together under capable lay leadership, so that all those engaged in Jewish community service, of one kind or another, religious and secular, could get together and discuss their common problems and needs. Undoubtedly, a cross-fertilization of ideas would thus be made possible, which would yield great benefits in terms of constructive Jewish community work. As it is, the rabbinical groups meet by themselves, the Jewish social workers meet by themselves, the lay leaders in Jewish community work, presumably, meet by themselves, the Jewish educators meet by themselves, except in so far as they meet biennially with the National Conference of Jewish Social Welfare and the Jewish Center Workers. This division or divisiveness in American Jewish life, as far as the professional community workers are concerned, is not conducive to the best kind of ongoing program that will advance Jewish life most satisfactorily.

As far as the rank and file Jewish social workers are concerned, a great deal will have to be done to get them to recognize that, when they serve a Jewish social agency, they are serving the Jewish community, and that in serving the Jewish community, they are obligated to advance those objectives and ideals for which the Jewish community exists and functions.

How to relate and integrate the Christian social workers, who are increasingly becoming part of the Jewish social work staff of Jewish agencies, is another problem that should be faced realistically. It may be surprising to some to learn that many Christian social workers associated with Jewish organizations are much more in sympathy with and more cooperative in advancing Jewish community values and Jewish community objectives than are some of the Jewish social workers themselves.

Summary and Conclusion

The material just presented provides a brief overview of the status of Jewish social service in this country today, and some of the forces that are operating to strengthen Jewish life, and to weaken it. Dr. Mordecai M. Kaplan, who has given serious study to this phase of Jewish life in our country, has, over the years, offered many constructive proposals which have been incorporated in the summaries and discussions above. An attempt has been made to introduce the kind of recommendations that Dr. Kaplan has made to remedy some of the shortcomings that now exist in this area of community work.

Whatever else may be said with reference to the reconstruction of Jewish life in the field of religion or any other field, if we are to pass beyond mere academic discussions, it is tremendously important to bring our influence to bear upon those lay and professional persons active in Jewish community affairs who exercise a great influence on its direction and its content.

Let us hope that the kind of thinking that Dr. Kaplan has done, and has stimulated, will provoke a review of the current status of Jewish social work and of Jewish social workers, so that, as the years progress, we will train a better qualified group of Jewish social service functionaries. For they can be a real asset toward making Jewish life, for the community and for our country, a richer and much more meaningful experience.

DR. MORDECAI M. KAPLAN AND JEWISH EDUCATION

By Israel S. Chipkin

The fundamental contributions of Mordecai M. Kaplan to Jewish education are his call for a philosophy to direct and to vitalize Jewish life, and his formulation of principles and criteria for the evolution of this philosophy.

These contributions are the product of his own profound experiences in the synagogue and in the classroom, where, through the original sources of Judaism, he endeavored to inspire and to teach the Jewish way of life to nearly three generations of Jewish parents and youth in America. His formulation of principles and criteria is the analytic summation of his own critical thinking based on intensive, continued and reverential study of the classic Jewish traditional sources, of world literature and of modern science. This formulation is offered by him as a response to the challenge of American Jewish youth who, turning to him as guide to the perplexed, have sought inspiration and knowledge to live as Jews and as Americans, or who have come to him for guidance and encouragement to serve Judaism and the Jewish community as lay leaders, or as rabbis, Jewish teachers, Jewish communal workers, Jewish scholars and Jewish artists.

This personal challenge he records with characteristic concern in the Preface to *Judaism as a Civilization*:[1] "Judaism is a problem to those who have to teach it, and what Jew is exempt from teaching it? ... So difficult indeed has it become to teach Judaism that only those undertake the task who are too naive to realize what they have to cope with, or too much committed to Judaism to escape responsibility of envisaging in concrete forms the future they contemplate for it."

This call for a philosophy of Jewish living must not be interpreted as his desire to create another philosophical system. Quite the contrary, his primary and fundamental desire is to preserve the Jewish way of life in America, to make "young and old thrill to the beauty of meaning of the Jewish heritage." He is much more concerned with creating a Jewish milieu which will reflect Jewish ideals than with developing a new ideology.

It is apathy which he fears as the greatest threat to Judaism in America. In examining the underlying causes for this apathy, he discovers a "spiritual crisis in American Judaism, which seemingly is brought about by maladjustment between the old and the new, between Jewish traditionalism and modernism." He attempts to resolve this spiritual crisis by urging a revitalization of the spiritual assets of Jewish tradition and a restatement of this tradition in the modern idiom. He therefore offers his own restatement of Judaism as an evolving religious civilization in the high hope that, thereby, he will help to restore its vitalizing creative spirit in the modern American scene. As one of the chief requisites for the successful attainment of this hope, he calls specifically for the formulation of a philosophy of Jewish education. "Jewish education," he says, "has suffered long enough from the lack of any guiding philosophy ... the time has come for the formulation of a philosophy of Jewish education which holds the greatest promise of a worthwhile future for Jewish life in this country."[2]

Why A Philosophy for Jewish Education in America

Why does he regard the formulation of a philosophy of Jewish education so important? Because he feels that radical changes have taken place in the life of the American Jew, which cannot "but be reflected in equally radical changes in the historic functions of Jewish education." What were these functions and what are these changes?

Formerly the Jewish educational process offered both inner motivation and outer compulsion.[3] It helped to prepare the child for life in this world and in the next. In this world it helped him to overcome illiteracy, to adjust to his group life, to achieve a sense of belonging to an eternal and God-chosen people, and to find self-fulfillment or meaning in his earthly existence. Knowledge of and adherence to the prescriptions of the sacred Scriptures as interpreted by the Rabbis brought not only community approval but also a guarantee of salvation in the world to come. Incidentally, "achieving salvation through one's own merit apart from the Jewish people and its traditions was unthinkable." Since all peoples in whose midst they lived believed in the world to come and in their own supernatural selection, it was easier for our ancestors to adhere to their own beliefs. Jewish education was, therefore, not only an effective process but a categorical imperative for every Jew and every Jewish community. For it helped the individual to find his place in the world and to share in preserving the Jews as a people and in protecting its special status in the universe. Pedagogically, this educational process needed only to rely on authority and verbal memory to achieve its purpose. Study of the Holy Writings and prayer became a daily activity of the Jew, and religious law became the way of life of the individual, the home, the school, the synagogue, the marketplace, and the community as a whole.

Today, in this country, the Jewish educational process lacks inner motivation as well as outer compulsion. Why? Because radical changes have taken place in our environment, in the knowledge of the world and its natural forces, in the knowledge of the human being and his behavior, in the structure of our society, in the values of life, in the estimate of the supreme good in life, in the way we acquire knowledge and faith, in the way we study the Scriptures, in the way we worship and believe in God. These changes have caused so radical a revolution in

Jewish life that its social and spiritual existence will disintegrate unless it is reconstructed through a new Jewish educational approach. Hence the need for a philosophy of Jewish education in America.

Why a Philosophy for American Education

It is interesting to note that these changes from traditionalism to modernism, which have caused so much concern to Dr. Kaplan for the future of Jewish life in America as to press him to ask for a reconstruction of its social and spiritual structure, are also the reasons which have caused American educators to call for a reformulation of the philosophy of American education. In his book, *Education For A Changing Civilization,*[4] William H. Kilpatrick states that "up to recently the rate of change has been so slow that philosophy and morals could in essential degree affect to ignore change ... Today change has become too obvious and too inclusive to be able to ignore it ... We must have a philosophy of education that not only takes positive recognition of the fact of change but one that includes within it change as an essential element."

A philosophy of education must not only reflect change; it must also reflect the social structure and cultural standards of the group. These thoughts are expressed in a declaration contained in a *Report by the Commission of Social Studies of the American Historical Association,*[5] part of which reads as follows:

"Education is a form of action on the part of some particular social group; it is not a species of contemplation removed from social life and relationships. Education always expresses some social philosophy, either large or small, involves some choices with respect to social and individual action and well-being, and rests upon some moral conception. Conceived in the large and clarified frame of reference, education is one of the highest forms of statesmanship: a positive and creative attack upon the problems generated by the movement of ideas and interests in society. Finding its immediate expression in individuals, education so conceived is concerned with the development of rich and many-sided personalities capable of cooperating in a social order... Being a form of social action, education always has a geographical and cultural location; it is therefore specific, local and dynamic, not general, universal and unchanging; it is a function of a particular society at a particular time and place in history; it is rooted in some actual culture and expresses the philosophy and recognized needs of that culture... Since culture plays a dominant role in giving form and substance to education, the formulation of a relevant and effective educational philosophy for a particular society at a particular time and place in history must rest in a large measure upon the findings of the social sciences, findings pertaining to nature, trends and thoughts of that society in its regional and world setting."

These thoughts are stated even more specifically by I. B. Berkson in *Preface To an Educational Philosophy*.[6] He writes, "Some organized way of living must be assumed as a basis for an educational philosophy... Conceivably it might be a religious system, a philosophic school, a socio-economic order... Lines of history, heritage of language, political and social institutions, common struggles in the past, common problems today, and above all, the common territory and the common government make of America a definite and distinct cultural order... It is the American nation that gives the tangible base for a unified educational philosophy."

Thus we see that American educators are as troubled about changing forms and values in American life as Dr. Kaplan is concerning the form, content and direction of Jewish life in America.

Essential Considerations for a Philosophy of Jewish Education

What, specifically, are the essential considerations for a philosophy of Jewish education in America as suggested by Dr. Kaplan?[7] To him, Jewish education is essentially the process by which the individual Jew and the Jewish people grow morally and spiritually. The individual and the group are merely the counterparts of each other. For him, the main function of the Jewish school is the development of the spiritual character of the child; and the main purpose of Jewish community organization is the maintenance of moral and spiritual standards whereby the individual and the group may find self-fulfillment, social or world status and continued creative existence in this world. He offers special reasons why, today in this country, explicit stress must be laid on moral and spiritual values in Jewish education. One reason is the fact that the public school may not engage in religious education, which is the prerogative of the religious school. Moral and spiritual values in Judaism are best expressed through religious practices and ideals and through group participation. Since Judaism is a religious civilization, it includes all aspects of life — the secular and the sacred. There is no dichotomy between them. It is the Jewish educational process which can best help to spiritualize all individual and group values.

A second reason is "the truth," as he puts it, "that ethical character as a conscious objective of education is of comparatively recent date. This fact is the result of the changes which differentiate the modern from the medieval world." Until recently obedience and conformity were the ideals of the school, and still are in all totalitarian systems. Today in democratic countries the ideal is the development of self-determining, integrated personality. In these latter countries the historic religious groups have as their distinct function to contribute to and to help evaluate the moral and spiritual standards of their respective environments.

Talmud Torah and Jewish Education

Does this function of Jewish education differ radically from the traditional function of Talmud Torah? Yes and no. There may be few differences in motivation, but there are many differences in conception, procedure, and expression due to changes involved in the transition from traditionalism to modernism.

Jewish education as here conceived is, in many respects, wider in scope and responsibility, more complicated in procedure, more inclusive of knowledge, more varied in expression than Talmud Torah. The latter was limited to its literal meaning. It stressed the study of Torah, which, while it included the Biblical texts, was primarily preoccupied with the study of Talmudic and Rabbinic literature. Verbal memorization of text, or of Talmudic discussion, accompanied by the practice of piety, represented high social status. Higher distinction could possibly be attained through the ability to propound an original discourse involving Talmudic text or, in extreme situations, through martyrdom for *Kiddush Hashem*. It was expected that learning could help attain a higher level of piety, and thus assure bliss in the hereafter. These standards were actually set by community approval and were handed down from generation to generation. No individual could violate the community standards without suffering exclusion in this as well as in the next world. High standards of learning were actually open to the mentally elect, including, of course, the children of the poor. Proper or even pious behavior was not, however, completely dependent upon high learning. Every home and the community as a whole, through its social institutions, set the standards for individual and group behavior. In other words, Jewish tradition and the Jewish community (environment) were as effective in the educational process as the school or Talmud Torah, if not more so.

The Jewish school in America, by contrast, must not only teach Scriptural texts; it must also help to guide the individual and the group toward moral and spiritual self-realization. It is expected to keep alive Jewish tradition, Jewish learning, the Jewish way of life, the Jewish people, its institutions, hopes and ideals. And, in order to do so, it must relate all of them creatively to the American environment and to modern science. Its immediate responsibility is even more concrete. It must help actively to build in America the Jewish home, the Jewish community and its social institutions, and to set up community standards. It must, moreover, help to recreate a motivation for those who can no longer believe in the world to come. Obviously, these added burdens of the American Jewish school cannot be the sole responsibility of an individual institution in American Jewish life. They must become the educational and voluntarily accepted responsibility of all social institutions organically related within a democratically organized Jewish community.

These, then, are some of the essentials which underlie Dr. Kaplan's search for guiding principles and selective criteria for the development of a system of Jewish education in America.

Guiding Principles and Selective Criteria

What are these guiding principles and selective criteria? In his opinion, they must be such as will help the individual Jew and the Jewish group to reconstruct Jewish experience, or the way of Jewish life, in this country so as to relate it to the great Jewish historic past and help it to evolve into an attractive, virile creative Jewish future. To achieve these ends, a philosophy of Jewish education will have to (1) draw on the inspiration and sustaining powers of Jewish tradition, (2) re-interpret the facts and values, the history and literature of this tradition in terms of modern scientific concepts, (3) view Judaism as an evolving religious civilization, removing the false modern dichotomy between the secular and the sacred, (4) lay the social and spiritual foundations for an organic, democratically functioning Jewish community and its several related institutions, (5) charge Jewish group life with a new creative vitality so as to advance the standards of Jewish learning, Jewish moral and esthetic values, (6) give spiritual meaning and motivation to the life of the individual as well as of the group, and (7) relate Jewish group life to American society and to world interests.

How are these guiding principles and selective criteria to be translated into a program of Jewish education? Let us consider first Jewish tradition. That tradition [8] is indispensable for the life of the individual Jew, of the Jewish group and of Judaism itself. None of them can continue to exist without it. Jewish tradition, Dr. Kaplan emphasizes, is not "dead wood but a civilizing agency." It enlarges the horizon of the individual Jew and gives him social purpose. It helps to elicit in him traits of loyalty, social responsibility and self-sacrifice, loyalty to God and to humanity generally. Hence, it is an important part of character training. It helps to initiate him into the Jewish group where he finds dignity in a fellowship of his own, which may be a minority surrounded by a friendly or a hostile majority. Tradition offers the standards of fellowship, and helps the individual achieve ethical personality and harmonious self-fulfillment, or salvation, via the group. Traditions are not just abstract ideas. They are crystallized facts, standards, habits, usages and beliefs handed down from generation to generation. They belong historically to a specific group. The one thing we must remember about tradition, however, is that while its intrinsic spirit may continue through time, the forms and content through which they are expressed may change in the process of transmission. Dr. Kaplan cites many instances in Jewish historical experience and in rabbinic literature when new practices and new concepts were introduced in the spirit of Jewish tradition. If we, in our generation, he urges, wish to be loyal to Jewish tradition and to preserve it, we must recognize this historical, evolutionary process. We must so restate it and reconstruct its manner of expression as to make it better understood and appreciated by our generation, in order that our people will want to live by it and, if necessary, to die for it.

It is here that he calls attention to the paradoxical position of those who blindly contribute toward the abandonment of Jewish traditions only because they regard these traditions as static and insist that they must be retained in exactly the same conceptual or behavior patterns as those held by our ancestors in former times and in other climes. It is at this point that Dr. Kaplan expresses with greatest emphasis the need for making Jewish tradition the vehicle of *ethical integrity* for the life of the individual and of the group. Character and ethical personality, he insists, cannot be produced in a modern democratic society, unless the individual can accept goals and purposes in life which bear intrinsic rationality and social value. Tradition, unevaluated, cannot be accepted as a final criterion for what is ethical. It must be modified to conform to modern intellectual and social ideals evolved from reasoning about human experience.

Israel, Torah and God in Jewish Tradition

To enable Jewish tradition to serve as a source of moral and spiritual strength for the individual Jew and for the Jewish people, Dr. Kaplan suggests the revaluation of the three main aspects of Jewish life, namely, the Jews as a people, the Torah as a Jewish way of life, and God as the source of all Jewish values. This triad of supreme values in Jewish existence is itself the core of Jewish tradition as declared by the Rabbis, who said that "Israel, the Torah and the Holy One, Blessed be He" are all one. To the preservation of these values he devotes all his energy, his thought and his erudition. These values constitute the motivation and the content of his presentation of Judaism as an evolving religious civilization. They also constitute the purpose and program of his philosophy of Jewish education in America.

In discussing the principles of method involved in this philosophy, he points out that by method he does not refer particularly to modern pedagogic techniques, much as he values them. By method he means the reinterpretation, the revaluation, the reconstruction of the content and the concepts of Jewish historic experience. These principles of method are so basic to this philosophy that without them, he feels, neither Jewish education nor Judaism has much of a future in this country. Just how are they to be applied to the aforementioned supreme values of Jewish tradition and existence?

He uses these words, — reinterpretation, revaluation and reconstruction, — to describe a process of evolving the new meanings, forms and practices without necessarily destroying the original sources. He wants the history of Jewish experience, its classic literature and its spiritual motivation to become a part of the consciousness of the individual and of the group. This does not mean studying history or sacred literature or participating in worship merely by translating or explaining words and phrases. It means helping the individual to study and to understand the facts, the concepts, the practices and the values of each generation of Jews in accordance with its own knowledge and understanding. It does not mean following the method of the great expositor, Rashi, who could have felt quite at home in the world of the *Tannaim*. It means recognizing that "the transition from man's medieval to modern outlook on life is so great that it has no equal in all of Jewish history." Therefore, more than a difference in language is involved; there is a difference also in idiom of thought and of comprehension. Without understanding wherein our knowledge of and outlook on life differ from those of our forefathers, "we cannot recover a feeling of kinship with them, nor can we understand their ideals and strivings and what they meant for our well-being today." This means revaluating their values. But it means more than that. It means acknowledging the fact that Jewish tradition is a record of our evolving expression of Jewish life over the ages, and that change is a natural phenomenon in Jewish tradition as reported by Jewish historians. Such presentation of Jewish tradition may even stimulate our generation towards further creative expression of this tradition.[9]

Implied further in this discussion of method and the transmission of the content of Jewish tradition is Dr. Kaplan's reminder that no program of Jewish education in America can be implemented without a functioning group life.[10] Hence, he calls for the establishment of an organic, democratic Jewish community, in which all related institutions, and not the school alone, will contribute towards making Jewish tradition an effective influence in the development of ethical personality. Equally significant is his caution against reliance on the elementary school for the effective transmission of the content of Jewish tradition. Most of the subject matter studied in the elementary Jewish school, he comments, is too advanced for the age of its pupils. To develop a reconstructed program of Jewish education, more attention should be given to youth and adults. It is they who could help to create a home and community environment favorable to Jewish education and to the preservation of moral and spiritual standards within Jewish community life.

Having examined some of the implications of Dr. Kaplan's guiding principles and selective criteria as applied to the general content and development of Jewish tradition, how can we apply them more specifically to each of the trinity of supreme values in Judaism, namely, Israel, Torah and God, so that they may continue to be organically unified, bring self-fulfillment to the individual Jew and contribute to the moral and spiritual welfare of America and of mankind, generally.

The Concept of the Peoplehood of Israel[11]

Israel represents the concept of Jewish peoplehood and of Jewish group life. This group life, as has been stated, is indispensable to the preservation of Torah and to the worship of God. How can Jewish peoplehood express itself in the American environment, and how shall Jewish group life be reconstructed in this country? What is the function of Jewish education in the solution of these problems? To answer these questions we must first understand them.

As individual Jews, we have accepted citizenship within the nations among whom we dwell. We want equal status with all our neighbors; yet, together with other Jews in the same country and in other countries, we want to preserve our status as an historic people with a recognition of special cultural rights. This creates a problem not only in the matter of loyalty, but, even more, in psychological and social adjustment and in the matter of the preservation of Jewish culture. In the totalitarian countries of our generation, the Jewish problem is solved either by complete annihilation of the Jewish group or by the enforced assimilation of its individuals through the destruction of Jewish cultural institutions, especially the Jewish school. Only in democratic countries can Jews enjoy large measures of Jewish group life and Jewish cultural expression. In democratic countries these rights are constitutionally guaranteed to all religio-cultural groups who want to exercise them, provided they can contribute to the general moral and cultural welfare of these countries. This places the burden of Jewish group life and Jewish religious and cultural expression completely upon the Jews themselves. This freedom creates for them a complexity of new problems.

Since the state offers the individual Jew equal opportunities with all others towards self-fulfillment politically, economically and culturally, what specifically can the Jewish group offer him? In other words, is there any further need for the existence of a Jewish group? The answer is that most individual Jews in democratic countries feel a psychological need for Jewish group life in order to achieve complete social status and spiritual security. There is a sense of kinship with world Jewry and with historic Judaism which they cannot escape, and of which they are reminded by the non-Jew who belongs to another historic religio-group. That social and spiritual kinship calls for group activity and group responsibility. This accounts in large measure for the many existing religious, philanthropic, cultural, social and fraternal agencies which the Jews in America and in other democratic countries have developed. But their meaning and functions are disappearing gradually as the democratic governments assume added responsibilities for the economic welfare of their citizens, and as the State of Israel assumes greater international responsibilities, assures complete social status to individual Jews and fosters continued creative expression of historic Judaism. These agencies also suffer from an inherent weakness. They lack a unifying spiritual purpose and an organic democratic function, says Dr. Kaplan. In other words, there is need for the establishment of a democratically organized and organically functioning Jewish community. Through this kind of community, not only the school and the synagogue but all agencies and institutions, the Jewish home included, will be charged with an educational and spiritual function. A social environment influenced by group standards will give new meaning and vitality to the Jewish educational process.

"No tradition," Dr. Kaplan reminds us, "that ceases growing can continue to live, and the impetus for this must come from a living body, which is the carrier of this tradition and without which it cannot live... It was the social structure of the Jewish people which gave the Torah its potency throughout the centuries, otherwise it would have remained esoteric doctrine... By the same token that we need to reinterpret the Jewish tradition properly in order to live in the modern universe of thought, we need also to reorganize the social structure of the Jewish people properly, if we want to have a place in the frame of modern society."[12] All reinterpretation and revaluation will be carried on in a vacuum so long as we are without an organic Jewish community that possesses the educational machinery to put into circulation the results of such efforts.

These considerations raise two more problems. If American Jewry can succeed in establishing an organic and spiritually creative Jewish community, and if Judaism is a religious civilization, what are the relationships between American Jewry and the State of Israel, on the one hand, and between Judaism and Americanism on the other? Obviously these are not questions concerning political loyalty. For American Jewry and for any other Jewry in the Diaspora there exists but one political loyalty, and that is to the country in which they live as full-fledged citizens, bearing all privileges and obligations of such citizenship. Anything which affects the welfare of that country affects them personally and as a community. On the other hand, it is equally obvious that so far as historic Judaism is concerned, its greatest potentialities for continuous creative expression and for making a contribution to the spiritual welfare of all mankind is to be found in the State of Israel. The interest of American Jewry in that State is fraternal and spiritual in character. American Jewry has, at this juncture in history, a fraternal and historical obligation to help set up that State and to contribute to its welfare, so long as it needs outside help. That State, on the other hand, holds a promise for American and world Jewry in terms of spiritual and cultural values. Thus, there is a kinship and a cultural interrelationship between the American Jewish community and the State of Israel.

These facts raise still another question. If Judaism is a religious civilization with a spiritual center in the State of Israel, will it not conflict with the American civilization? Definitely not. Far from conflicting with it, Judaism as an evolving religious civilization, because of its spiritual purposes, will tend to strengthen the democratic foundations of the American civilization. The American form of democracy expects the American Jewish community to provide its members with that spiritual sustenance, security and striving which the State cannot supply because of the historic separation of Church and State in the founding and development of the American government. Genuine democracy, we are reminded, does not permit the state to monopolize the lives of its citizens and control their consciences. "It leaves place in their lives for ideals and loyalty that transcend the state ... Whatever prevents individuals or a group from achieving salvation cannot be ascribed to the democratic process. As Jews, we cannot achieve salvation unless the democratic process permits us to retain our identity as an indivisible people." The destiny of

Jewish life is therefore bound up with genuine democracy in the Diaspora, and for that matter, in Israel as well.

From the Jewish point of view these thoughts imply faith on the part of the American Jewish community in its own creative powers. It implies a philosophy and a program of Jewish education which make it possible for the individual to find spiritual self-fulfillment in the American environment through Jewish group life, through historical and spiritual bonds with Israel and through participation in the cultural assets and spiritual welfare of the American democracy. Thus, "Jews in America live by a twofold norm." They achieve social security in the general community and spiritual security in the Jewish community.

The Concept of Torah as a Way of Life

How do Dr. Kaplan's guiding principles and selective criteria apply to the concept of Torah?

Torah has been variously defined. Sometimes it refers to a set of laws and prescriptions, sometimes only to the Pentateuch, sometimes to all the accumulated sacred writings over the ages, sometimes to Jewish learning and culture generally; and sometimes Torah describes a way of life. In Dr. Kaplan's treatment of this concept, Torah constitutes in large measure the content of Jewish tradition, and the substance of Judaism as an evolving religious civilization. He includes within the concept Torah the knowledge of the classic religious literature, the function of study as a daily religious obligation, and the behavior of the individual or of the group in accordance with the spiritual imperative of its teachings. "So long as there is any room in the contemporary scene for Jewish life, the knowledge of Torah must figure in it," he says, "or that life will be anything but Jewish."[13] He, too, wants *mitzvot* to be observed as obligations and as privileges. But he believes that they will be more faithfully observed and generate inspiration if they are better understood. Hence, he is concerned always with the functional values, the evolutionary process, the historical setting, the spiritual significance and the creative potentialities of the text studied and the *mitzvot* performed.

Because the content of Torah is so rich in its variety, this kind of study and observance can offer opportunities to individuals and groups with diversified temperament, calling, experience and belief to find Jewish self-expression. "To make Torah or tradition function for us today, as Jews and as Americans," he states, "we must make it speak to us in terms relevant to the ethical and spiritual problems of our day ... We must become accustomed to the idea of growth in experience and meaning ... to do so, it is necessary to discover the latent and permanent ethical and spiritual urges beneath such elements in the tradition as miracles and the supernatural, through research in the historical background of the tradition as developed during life in Eretz Yisrael or in contact with cultures in other lands. The results of such research should be evaluated in the light of the new human sciences in order to discover the extent of Jewish tradition's verification of the higher trends in human nature and to relate these findings to the social and spiritual problems of our day ... There is need for evolving in our day something akin to the Talmud and Midrash. Since they have become so vital a part of Torah, they too should be reinterpreted and revaluated and be made available to the layman and not only the scholar." The new method of studying and interpreting Torah should help to save Judaism in our times, even as the *Tannaim* saved Judaism in their times. Incidentally, we might also learn another lesson from them. They offered their teachings first to adults, and then brought these teachings down to the level of children.

In former times, when a child studied Torah, he was introduced to all facets of Jewish life simultaneously. Today, he must study a variety of subjects to understand Judaism, and frequently fails to experience their interrelationship. In *Judaism As a Civilization*, the emphasis is again placed on experiencing in their organic relationship all manifestations of the life of the Jewish people who possess a common history, a common literature, common folkways, mores, ethical standards, spiritual goals and a distinct social structure, and whose spiritual center is rooted in Israel. This organic relationship is strengthened by the religious purpose which permeates all these manifestations and, in that measure, helps to spiritualize the life of the group and, through it, that of the individual.

How To Study the Bible

Chief among the studies underlying Judaism as a religious civilization, as advocated by Dr. Kaplan, is the Bible. To derive the utmost from such study, it must be accompanied with proper interpretation. Even in Rabbinic times, the child was introduced to the Biblical text together with commentaries. To Dr. Kaplan it is the purpose of such study and commentaries which constitutes his primary concern. "The purpose," he says, "must be derived from what we believe to be the actual nature of the Bible and must have a bearing on the mental and moral growth of the child."[14] Nor is the esthetic, historical and philological approach of the moderns all-important in the study of the Bible; rather is the Bible's all-pervasive influence which it exercised when it was conceived as supernatural in origin. In the past, it served as a means of giving continuity to the life of the Jewish people, despite variation in time, place and points of view. "Its legends, histories, laws, exhortations, reflections and prayers are motivated by three definite purposes: (1) to arouse in the Jew an awareness of God, (2) to fortify his collective consciousness and (3) to direct him in the proper way of life."

How to achieve these purposes depends upon the spirit of the times and upon the most urgent social and spiritual needs of those who study and interpret the contents of the Bible. To our forefathers, interpretation was a *sine qua non* in the study of the Bible. They developed four ways of interpreting the written law, the literal, the homiletical (Talmudic), the metaphorical (esoteric) and the mystical. We, in our day, are in need of another approach. It may employ scientific method but its purpose must always be moral and spiritual. "The contents of the Bible itself reflect a period of spiritual gestation which is truly miraculous." To evolve this new method of interpretation so that it may achieve its purposes, it will have to reckon with three main sources of challenge to modern Jewish life, namely: modern nationalism which is threatening it from without, modern scientism which is threatening it from within, and the acceptance of force as the arbiter of human affairs, which is always a threat to minorities and the physically weak.

We must so study the Bible as to derive from it moral support for our status as a people. This means acknowledgement of Eretz Yisrael as our spiritual homeland and of democratic rights as vital to our organic Jewish group life in the Diaspora. Bible study should help us also to acquire an awareness of God with which the better to appreciate the spirit of man and with which the firmer to combat false theories of naturalism and materialism. Even though it may not be possible to suggest nowadays a universally acceptable affirmation of God, it is possible to indicate what a difference an active belief in God frequently makes in the life of a person, and how that belief expresses itself in the spirit of holiness, humility, gratitude and faith. A person in whose character these qualities of mind and spirit do not find a place is ill-equipped to achieve self-fulfillment in life. And finally, this manner of studying the Bible should make it possible for the student to find a rationale for the Jewish struggle for existence. From it, he will learn that the Jewish way of life would substitute justice and righteousness for force as an arbiter in human affairs, and that Judaism and genuine democracy, which have these ideals in common, join in their opposition to totalitarianism, fascism or communism.

Discussing the modern approach to the textual study of the Bible, Dr. Kaplan seeks to preserve another traditional value, namely: the reinstatement of the Pentateuch to its position of primacy in the curriculum of the school. It contains, in his opinion, the very core of Judaism and can serve as a foundation for subsequent studies. He asks teachers to stress three aspects of Pentateuch study, the narrative which leads the child to a consciousness of his destiny as a member of the Jewish people, Eretz Yisrael which helps to stress the reality of the Jewish people, the laws and the moral teachings which help to stress the awareness of God and His moral purpose.

Customs, Ceremonies, Social Institutions

Important as he regards the study of the sacred texts for the reordering of Jewish life, Dr. Kaplan feels that that purpose cannot be achieved unless the Jewish community fosters a mode of life that is animated by whatever in the traditional attitude toward Torah is of incontestable worth.[15] Our forefathers were not as book-minded as we are, although in the course of time the Book became the symbol of Judaism. The study of Torah was and always must be accompanied by the practice of *mitzvot* and *minhagim*, because Torah is not just book study or a philosophy of religion.[16] Torah is a way of life, a civilization, therefore it requires social institutions and social practices by which to express its ideals. The difference in character between one civilization and another is not so much in the ideals they profess as in the social institutions they evolve to express their ideals. "Social institutions are to the forces of human nature what machines are to the forces of physical nature."

The customs and ceremonies, the mores and the folkways are the social practices by which a people externalizes the reality of its collective being. They help to give individuality and character to a civilization. The religious folkways or customs and ceremonies, like the Sabbaths and festivals, *kashrut* and prayer, are spiritualizing experiences, if entered into properly and wholeheartedly. Customs may lose their original meaning, but they can be revised so as to retain the sense of historic continuity. In addition to the specific religious ceremonies which help to enrich the social content of the life of the individual and the community, there are of course the cultural bonds and folkways, such as the Hebrew language, Jewish names, the Jewish calendar or the Jewish arts.

These social practices find their best expression within the historic social institutions which the Jewish people has developed. First among them, of course, is the home. There the child receives his first impressions of Judaism; there the foundation for his Jewish cultural and spiritual life is laid. The family constitutes the miniature Jewish community and has historically constituted the spiritual fortress of Jewish living. In the American democratic state the historic religious groups are depended upon for maintaining the integrity of the family institution. If Judaism is to uphold the social and spiritual conception of marriage among Jews, the Jewish community must help its young people to build Jewish home life.

Here the synagogue can play its part. The synagogue can serve as the extension of the Jewish home or family life. It can help to solemnize many of the family experiences, and can offer its members wider-scope, social, recreational, cultural and spiritualizing experiences. But the synagogue in America, whatever its ideological affiliation, if it is to function effectively, must become a neighborhood center or representative of the organic Jewish community of its city or state. It should be conducted under joint local and general community auspices. For the synagogue is the link between the Jewish home and the Jewish community. It should help to solidify and spiritualize both.

American Jews have developed another social institution which resembles the synagogue in many ways. It is called the Jewish Center. It is in a sense a new *Bet Haknesset* and *Bet Hamidrash*. It corresponds to the *Bet Am* in Israel. It is a manifestation of Judaism as a civilization. It offers individuals and families opportunities for physical recreation, cultural activity and spiritual renewal. The center, like the synagogue, can help to direct the leisure time of its participants towards the service of Judaism and the Jewish community.[17]

Torah for Adults

One of the most important contributions to the discussion of Jewish education in America is Dr. Kaplan's emphasis on the role which adult education must play in it. All the social institutions and social practices, the Torah as a way of life, Jewish community life, the reinterpretation of Jewish tradition, creative Jewish living in America are practically meaningless and almost impossible if the advanced youth and the adult will not assume responsibility for them and set the example for the children. The adults and the student youth, even more than the child, need to study and practice Torah. They can profit most from an approach to Judaism as an evolving religious civilization. The American program for Jewish education should therefore be better planned and balanced if it is to be effective. It should make greater provision for and place greater dependency on the adult branch of its activities. In providing study activities, it must be remembered that curricular studies and methodology can communicate knowledge, but they do not produce character and conduct. The only way to learn is by doing. The main purpose of adult Jewish study should therefore be not merely to learn about Judaism and the Jewish people but to afford an opportunity for Jewish experience.[18] The adult should get to know what a "good Jew" is, not only from his studies, but from his participation in Jewish group life and its social institutions. Adult Jewish education should also help the layman understand and appreciate the *religious* aspirations and expressions of life. He must discover through study and experience that Judaism sees in human history the inevitability of a process which makes for righteousness. He should be encouraged to participate in general community activities which help to advance the standards of justice and righteousness, peace and democracy. A new social order is possible through the recognition of the role played by creative intelligence and by the divine will. "Religion can charge the zeal and free the will of men for ethical purpose, social justice and economic abundance."[19]

The Concept of God

We have quoted previously a Rabbinic statement that Israel, the Torah and the Holy One, Blessed be He, are one. If the writer may be permitted a privileged observation, he would equate the word "one" in this quotation with the word "civilization" in Dr. Kaplan's description of Judaism as an evolving religious civilization. By means of this modern word he seeks to describe the organic and unified character of the three aspects of Judaism, the people, its way of life and its spiritual essence. This observation also covers the fact that the Rabbis refer to God as the Holy One, who evokes their immediate blessing. Dr. Kaplan, in attempting to discuss the God concept in the light of his critical analysis and constructive reformulation, also dwells on the essence of holiness which, if sought, can evoke a blessing on Israel and on all humanity.

It is in this search for holiness and for the presence of God in human affairs, that Dr. Kaplan has made his supreme contribution to a philosophy of Jewish education. Without this search for holiness and an honest belief in God, he cannot find any reason or possibility for the existence of the Jewish people or of a Jewish way of life, and hence any purpose to a program of Jewish education. To understand the essentials of Dr. Kaplan's theory of Judaism and of all his writings, one should read his book, entitled *The Meaning of God In Modern Jewish Religion.*"[20] It is the most fundamental, the most illuminating and the most courageous of his writings. His constant search for an understanding of God and for ways to affirm His presence deserves his own quotation from the Psalms, "My soul thirsteth for God, for the living God." (Psalms, 42:3) Because of this fact and also because the teaching of the God-concept underlies all study of and experience with Torah, it becomes necessary to present here some inkling of the spirit and the manner with which Dr. Kaplan attempts to present the God-concept. This can best be done, perhaps, through direct quotations of passages from the book mentioned above.

"The ardent and strenuous search of God in all that we know and feel and do is the true equivalent of the behest, 'Thou shalt love the Lord thy God with all thy heart, all thy soul and all thy might' ... We cannot expect to understand the nature of God. Who of us even knows the nature of man, or for that matter, his own nature? ... But we must be prepared to state what experiences or phenomena we identify as manifestations of God and why we do so. There can be no single definition that can answer once and for all what is meant by God. The intrinsic character of the God concept calls for constant restatement in a variety of ways. In fact, it should be remembered that religion calls for a progressive unlearning of false ideas concerning God as it calls for learning of new ones ... The divine is no less real, no less dependable for our personal salvation or self-realization, if we think of it as a quality than if we think of it as an entity or a being ... To the modern man, the name of God will have to stand for a truth about reality, not in terms of division between the natural and the supernatural, but in terms of normal human experience ... Without faith that the world is a cosmos, and not chaos, there can be no scientific theorizing ... Religion must help to identify as divine or holy whatever in human nature or in the world about him enhances life ... We shall not come to experience the reality of God unless we go in search of Him. To be seekers of God, we have to depend more upon our thinking and less upon tradition ... To seek God, to try to discern His reality is religion in action ... When we believe in God, we believe that reality — the world of inner and outer being, the world of society and nature — is so constituted as to enable man to achieve salvation. If human beings are frustrated, it is not because there is no God, but because they do not deal with reality as it is actually and potentially constituted ... God must not merely be held as an idea. He must be felt as a presence, if we are not only to know about God, but to know God. The purpose in the various attempts to reinterpret the God idea is not to dissolve it to ethics. It is to identify it with experience which would identify for us the reality of God ... It is only as the sum of everything in the world renders life significant and worthwhile — holy — that God can be worshipped by man. Godhood can have no meaning for us apart from human ideals of truth, goodness and beauty interwoven in a pattern of holiness. To believe in God is to reckon with life's creative forces, tendencies and potentialities as forming an organic unity and giving meaning to life by virtue of that unity ... We must not adopt the attitude of the philistine who departmentalizes life into secular and holy ... We may have to revise our liturgy to express with greater truth the sincerity of our thoughts and feelings, but we cannot dispense with worship ... There will always be need of prayer, which voices a yearning for those abilities of mind and body, or for that change of heart and character which would enable us to avail ourselves of such aspects of life as in their totality spell God ... Study and work as well as prayer and praise must express our faith in God ... The feeling of togetherness is indispensable to the realization of God.

"The unique element in the Jewish religion consisted in this unconscious recognition, that the chief function of the belief in God was to affirm and to fortify the moral law, which was his principal self-revelation ... The prophets were not concerned with the conception of God but with the manifestations of His presence and with human behavior consistent with the acceptance of Him ... The Jewish religion selects those purposes and possibilities in the life of the Jewish people in which there is most promise of good and makes God sponsor for them ... God symbolically represents their highest ideals or maximum good for which they strive. Jews have manifested in their civilization certain characteristic attitudes toward reality which have made for a more adquate conception of Godhood than that evolved in any other civilization."

It is this conclusion which evidently gives him confidence in the further revelation of Godhood and holiness in Jewish experience if developed in the tradition of Torah. It is with this conviction that he challenges Jewish education in America.

In attempting to simplify some of these thoughts and values for the benefit of children in the classroom, Dr. Kaplan suggests that the teacher try to clear the children's minds of psychological and theological illusions and to fill them instead with such ideas about God and self as will eliminate inner conflict. The teacher must "accustom the child to sense reality in those tendencies in the world which deserve appreciation. Conceived as belonging to an organically interrelated world, those tendencies will come to spell for him the reality of God."[21] Only properly prepared teachers can teach religion. Its teaching should culminate in religious practice. "The spirit of thankfulness whereby a child first experiences the sense of life's inherent worth, should be expressed through religious services participated in by a large number of children. Through such services Jewish education can bring to bear upon the child all those factors in Jewish life which have an emotional appeal. All artistic skills of children should be enlisted in rendering the religious service an occasion of joyous self-expression. Worship of God should bring with it the desire to serve mankind ... The entire range of things true, good and beautiful will be appreciated by the child in a spirit that will impel him to augment them in accordance with his abilities." His capacity for thankfulness can be reinforced by his studies and social contacts. His capacity for esthetic creativity can be encouraged by helping to focus his feelings upon Jewish values and to express them through art, music, the drama, arts and crafts. These will constitute part of his religious experience and will relate his Jewish heritage to his environment.

Application of Theory to the School and to the Child

Dr. Kaplan attempts to restate the aims of Judaism as an evolving religious civilization in terms of the educational process as they apply particularly to the school and the child. His presentation of the subject is still, of course, addressed to the teacher and to the trained adult. He presents the aims of Jewish education first in terms of the needs of the Jewish community, or the perpetuation of its culture, and then in terms of the needs and expectations of the child.[22] In all his discussions he recognizes the individual's wellbeing and self-fulfillment as the ultimate goal of the educational process. But he cannot see how this process can be successful without the community's participation and cultural growth. With Prof. R. B. Raup, he holds that "the educator is vitally concerned with the direction which the culture is taking ... If that be so, he will strive better to understand what he is doing and make his selections with the largest vision of which he is capable ... Of course, the educator's chief concern is the individual, but not in any way isolated from the common culture. The person is socially made. It is not enough to ask the adjustment of the individual to the culture; the culture itself may call for change. Adjusting personalities and seeking harmony among the common traditions which are the heart of our culture, are phases of the same total process. To neglect either is to misdirect the program of education."[23] The educator not only transmits but helps to remake the culture. It is in this spirit that Dr. Kaplan keeps repeating the demand on the Jewish educational process, not only to transmit the Jewish social heritage, but also to reconstruct it in the process of transmission.

In terms of the child's needs he expects Jewish education to help him enlarge his mental scope, socialize his attitude towards his fellow-man, and inculcate in him an appreciation of life's worth and sanctity. In more specific terms, as applied to the curriculum of the Jewish school, he expects the child's Jewish training to help him 1) gain an insight into the meaning of spiritual values and their application to various kinds and levels of experience, Jewish and general; 2) develop an attitude of respect toward human personality as such, cultivate the habits of intellectual honesty, of international-mindedness, foster loyalty to and participation in Jewish life in America and elsewhere; 3) gain an appreciation of individual and group creativity, general and Jewish, in religion, ethics, language, literature, mores, laws, folkways and the arts; 4) seek peace and ideals of justice and kindness in our economic relationships; seek a creative Jewish life in Israel as well as in America; 5) cultivate his habits of reflective thinking, purposive experiencing, spiritual use of leisure time; 6) find his place in the synagogue or Jewish center, celebrate the Sabbath and Jewish festivals, observe the Jewish customs and ceremonies, read Jewish books in English, Hebrew or Yiddish, attend Jewish concerts and the Jewish theatre, and patronize Jewish artistic endeavor; 7) acquire a knowledge of the Hebrew language, Jewish history, selections from the Bible, Talmud and other classic Jewish writings, the history and meanings of Jewish customs and ceremonies, religious beliefs, ethical ideals; a knowledge of current Jewish problems and institutions, Jewish arts and crafts, Jewish home building and its domestic arts.

This listing of the Jewish school's aims for the child will strike us as too idealistic or even utopian when one considers them in the light of the curricular and schedule limitations of the existing Jewish schools in the United States. Most of these schools would probably feel happy if they could achieve the last two numbered aims in this list. Yet the listing of all seven of them here helps to illustrate concretely Dr. Kaplan's emphasis on the moral, the spiritual and creative aspects of Judaism. It is in this same spirit, and in keeping with all modern educational standards, that Dr. Kaplan asks the Jewish school to stress experience rather than memorization of text and formal studies. "The Jewish educative process," he says, "must start with the actual experiences of the child as he lives them in the present, and lead him constantly so to reorganize and interpret his experiences that he comes to identify his own good with the good of society in general, and to do so in a manner as will indicate personal growth in mind and character. To achieve this aim the child must be given increasing control over his own experiences towards aims freely and intelligently chosen."

In the counterpart to these aims and methods as they apply to Jewish community needs and the development of Jewish culture, Dr. Kaplan assigns similar educational functions to the home, the synagogue and center, and to all communal agencies or institutions. "The Jewish community cannot rely solely upon the Jewish school to achieve these aims," he says. "Education is not a process distinct from life in general and confined to the class-room ... Every element in a person's environment is potentially educative making for growth in knowledge and character ... The survival of Judaism as a civilization depends upon having all the activities that constitute Jewish life contribute to the educative process.... All Jewish organized effort must be made consciously and purposely educative through participation in the Jewish training of the young ... The child must be reached through all possible angles."

Specifically, these are the communal and cultural aims of Jewish education:

1) To integrate the child into Jewish communal life so as to make him feel himself a member of the Jewish community. The club-room and the qualified club leader can perform a special function in this respect. Children can be involved in all functions and responsibilities of the synagogue. They can also be related to Federation activities, to activities on behalf of Israel and world Jewry, and they can participate in the city-wide cultural activities directed by Bureaus of Jewish Education.

2) So to transmit the Hebrew language as to make the child feel that through this knowledge he will be able to commune with the past of his people and to participate more intelligently and creatively in their present. This knowledge should help make his contacts with the State of Israel practical and meaningful. In this effort to transmit the knowledge of Hebrew, the community should encourage the opening of Hebrew kindergartens, of day-schools for those who wish to receive an intensive Hebrew training, of Hebrew summer camps and Hebrew clubs. It should also seek to encourage

public high schools and colleges to teach Hebrew and Jewish history.

3) To mold Jewish character and personality by fostering patterns of Jewish living and maintaining group standards and ideals for Jewish behavior. Here the school needs the cooperation of the home, the synagogue, the center, the camp and all other Jewish agencies. Here the example of the adult becomes exceptionally important. Here, too, the function of the Jewish teacher must be widened. He must be able not only to teach subject matter, but to help the child in all his recreational and cultural activites. He must also establish contact with the home of the child and its parents, and assume functions akin to the pastoral duties of a rabbi. The main function of the Jewish teacher is to furnish inspiration for living a Jewish life. The fact that Judaism is undergoing a metamorphosis makes his task particularly difficult.

4) To transmit Jewish values, those derived from the past and those drawn from contemporary Jewish life. In doing this the teacher must "seek to free the cultural content of Judaism from its antiquated elements and from outward authority, so that it can cultivate the individual conscience and be effective without the aid of outside or supernatural reward and punishment." The teaching of religion must henceforth be conducted on rational lines. The Jewish teacher must have an affirmative orientation toward the Jewish religion and reconstruct the curriculum of the school accordingly. "Jewish education is inconceivable without reference to God ... Sanctions and aspirations of any civilization, when objectives in education, furnish the subject-matter of history and religion." The teacher should revise the curriculum so as to help the child realize the difference between Jewish religion, Jewish history and Jewish folklore. Rather than teach children traditions about God, tradition should be used to help them experience God in their personal reaction to life, to help their personalities grow and develop in them a capacity for wholesome adjustment to life. Jewish values must so be transmitted to the child that they

will fully arouse his senses, emotions, imaginative intelligence and will and elicit creative capacities. "If Jewish living can satisfy the emotional, intellectual and social demands of human existence, it will awaken the creative capacities of the artist first and the creative appreciation of his audience, secondly ... When Judaism will have acquired the potency of multiple appeal, not even extreme diversity of belief will threaten its integrity."

Application of Theory to Church and State in Education

What is the function of the Jewish school in relationship to the public school?[24] In Judaism as a civilization there is an affinity between the secular and the sacred. "The churches," says Dr. Kaplan, "should not permit the term 'secular' to become an antonym of the term 'religious'; they should utilize men's secular interests for achieving religious objectives." In Judaism as a civilization there is also an affinity for American democracy. "Torah study in our day should be associated with meaning for the social, economic, political problems of our day, so that we may so behave as to leave a better world than we found." "The real trouble with American education," he says, "is that it lacks an all-absorbing and inspiring purpose to motivate it, something that will call forth the maximum self-sacrifice of its people." There is too much individualism and isolationism in America. Faith in democracy must be strengthened and given the sanction of religion. "Some religious faith must underlie all normative teaching, even of secular subjects ... Loyalty to the state must be supplemented with loyalty to God." He acknowledges that with the advent of modernism, religions have been secularized to the extent that they touch upon social, economic and political problems, and nationhood has been religionized to the extent that it touches upon loyalty to ideals and individual self-realization. American democracy recognizes the sacredness and dignity of the human being.

Does this mean that the American public schools must now begin to teach religion? This notion is categorically rejected by Dr. Kaplan, if such teaching implies the teaching within these schools of historical religions, either under the auspices of the state or of the church. Religious teaching cannot be in the abstract. It must be specific. It must draw on the content, collective experiences, sancta and interpretations of a particular historical group. This means the teaching of sectarian religion. The majority groups have, through pressure, already penetrated the public schools with their particular customs and ceremonies. On the other hand, if historic religions cannot be taught in the public schools, should the latter be abandoned and all children turned over to state-supported church schools? That plan would destroy the very foundations of American democracy and all the advance in human progress it represents. All that Dr. Kaplan proposes is that we regard American democracy itself as a divine manifestation. Since it offers a means of salvation to the individual and to society, it has the attributes of a religious experience. The history and culture of American democracy should therefore be taught in the public schools in a religious spirit. "Loyalty to American religion does not involve disloyalty to the religious traditions of the historical churches," he asserts, "so long as they can be reconciled with democracy." The historic religious groups have a special function to perform. They can correct the abuses of modern national religion, since they can view life with longer historical perspective. From this point of view, Judaism and American democracy are mutually acceptable and have a cooperative role to play.

Under the circumstances, the Jewish school in particular must assume a special responsibility on behalf of Judaism. It must help make Judaism's contribution to American democracy. The Jewish school in America is conceived as a supplementary school to the public school. It is maintained as a voluntary school by a group of parents, by a congregation or by the larger Jewish community. It can be an afternoon school, or an all-day school, or a Sunday school, depending on the interests of the parents. It is this voluntary character which has been its asset in Jewish group life. "Because education of children has always been in the hands of parents and of the teachers who represented them," Dr. Kaplan reminds us, "the Jewish people survived in a hostile world." By the same token parents, with the support of an organic Jewish community, may hope to maintain a voluntary system of Jewish schools in which the emphasis will be on the cultivation of ethical and spiritual personality and on the progressive development of Judaism as a civilization, both of which can and will help to enrich American democracy and to build a better world. Its measure of success as a school will depend upon its purposes, its curriculum, its schedule, the qualifications of its teachers, the interest of its parents and the measure of its support by the community as a whole.

Conclusion

The philosophy of Jewish education in America as propounded by Mordecai M. Kaplan calls for a critical view of historic Judaism. Its purpose, however, is to preserve its traditions in such form as will release its spiritual, creative energies for the benefit of the Jewish and all other peoples. Its motivation is to claim the loyalty of the Jewish individual to his social heritage. To be sure, Dr. Kaplan has recommended changes. But "the criterion for determining such changes is the extent to which they will help to retain the continuity, the individuality and the organic character of Judaism."[25] He does not offer his theory of Judaism as an evolving religious civilization as just another form of truth about Judaism, but rather as a very necessary form of life. He seeks a maximum measure of Jewish living. He cannot conceive that that measure can be obtained without organized Jewish community life which is concerned with the observance and advancement of Judaism. For that reason he considers Jewish education for all age groups and by all agencies as the primary function of the Jewish community. His main concern in Judaism, however, is its religious purpose and character. In creative Judaism he finds a substitute for other-worldly salvation and offers it as "a motivation for eliciting the best in the individual Jew, for enlarging his mental horizon, deepening his sympathies, imbuing him with hope and enabling him to leave the world better for having lived in it, and for finding 'The Holy One, Blessed be He' ... The Jews who are likely to assume the task of thus conditioning Judaism are they who cannot do without it, and yet cannot do with it as it is."

NOTES

[1] Macmillan, New York, 1934.   [2] *Ibid.*, p. 508.   [3] *Ibid.*, Ch. XXXI.
[4] Macmillan, New York, 1930, pp. 40–41.
[5] Charles Scribner's Sons, New York, 1934, pp. 30–32.
[6] Columbia University Press, New York, 1940, p. 52.
[7] The following is based mainly on *Judaism As A Civilization*, Ch. XXXI; *The Future of the American Jew*, Macmillan, New York, 1948, Ch. XXII; and *Judaism In Transition*, Behrman, New York, 1941, Ch. IV.
[8] The following is based on *Judaism in Transition*, Ch. IV, and *The Future of the American Jew*, Ch. XVIII.
[9] Compare below, Eugene Kohn, "Mordecai M. Kaplan as Exegete," pp. 137–154.
[10] *Judaism As A Civilization*, Ch. XXI; *The Future of the American Jew*, Ch. VI. Also, compare above, Samuel Dinin, "Mordecai M. Kaplan's Concept of Organic Jewish Community" pp. 45–64.
[11] Compare above, Jack J. Cohen, "Mordecai M. Kaplan's Concept of Peoplehood," pp. 27–44.
[12] *The Future of the American Jew*, Ch. XXII.
[13] *Judaism As A Civilization*, Ch. XXVII.
[14] *The Future of the American Jew*, Ch. XXIII.
[15] *Judaism As a Civilization*, Ch. XXVII.   [16] *Ibid.*, Ch. XXIX.
[17] Compare below, Louis Kraft, "Mordecai M. Kaplan's Contribution to the Jewish Center Movement," pp. 119–135.
[18] *The Future of the American Jew*, Ch. XXIV.
[19] *Judaism As A Civilization*, Ch. XXX.
[20] Jewish Reconstructionist Foundation, New York, 1947.
[21] *Judaism As A Civilization*, Ch. XXXI.   [22] *Ibid.*
[23] *Education and Organized Interests in America*, G. P. Putnam's Sons, New York, 1936, pp. 3–5.
[24] *The Future of the American Jew*, Ch. XXV.
[25] *Judaism As a Civilization*, Ch. XXXII.

MORDECAI M. KAPLAN'S CONTRIBUTION TO THE JEWISH CENTER MOVEMENT

By Louis Kraft

On June 2, 1951 Dr. Mordecai Kaplan received one of the three annual Frank L. Weil awards, established for the first time in 1951, for his "lofty and creative contribution to the development of an indigenous American Jewish culture." The citation further states, that by his "creative interpretation of Jewish values, he has infused American Jewish life with new meaning and vitality." In acknowledgement of the debt which the Jewish Community Center movement owes to Dr. Kaplan, the citation stated, "From the earliest days of the Jewish Community Center movement and of the National Jewish Welfare Board, he has helped to give direction and purpose to the program, philosophy and development of the movement."

Young Disciples at YMHA

The formal recognition of Dr. Kaplan's significant role in the development of the objectives and program of the Jewish Welfare Board was unique in that Dr. Kaplan at no time had an official role as a member of any of the governing bodies of the Board. It was purely a tribute to an all-pervading influence through the written and the spoken word, and through direct counsel and teaching, that helped shape the basic philosophy of the Jewish Community Center. It is difficult to identify many direct references to the purpose of the Jewish Center in the writings and addresses of Dr. Kaplan. For his message was directed at all times to the larger, non-institutional Jewish community. He provided a frame of reference, a sense of direction for those individual Jews and Jewish organizations seriously concerned with the continuity of Jewish life and the development of a "Jewish civilization" in America. The Jewish Center movement, still in embryonic form as a national development after World War I, had articulated the basic concepts of its program in 1920, as a Center of Jewish life, a community home open to all Jews. It aimed for a program based upon the conservation of Jewish values. The evolution of the philosophy of the Jewish Center was the resultant of a number of factors, some of them identified in Benjamin Rabinowitz's *The Young Men's Hebrew Association 1854–1913*.[1] There is no doubt, however, that Dr. Kaplan's influence had played an important role in the thinking of some of the people who were responsible for launching the new program of the Jewish Welfare Board, and in the articulation of the philosophy of the Jewish Community Center movement. A social movement is an undertaking of individuals who are motivated by a social purpose and who have the ability to secure a following dedicated to the fulfillment of that purpose. Among those early pioneers in the establishment of the new program were disciples of Dr. Kaplan, who gravitated to him when he directed the religious activities of the YMHA at 92nd Street in New York City in the first decade of the twentieth century. He was teacher and philosopher, devoting hours, week after week, in discussion and elucidation of his conceptions of the meaning of Judaism in the light of the needs of modern living in America. His own experience in the YMHA, through direct contact with serious-minded Jewish young men, doubtless strengthened his faith in the dynamics of Jewish living. In the young people themselves with whom he met week after week, he helped to crystallize a positive outlook on the Jewish future in America; he provided an insight into the potentialities of the YMHA, broadened into the Jewish Community Center, as one of the instrumentalities for Jewish group survival.

Defining the Jewish Center

That conviction was further strengthened when Dr. Kaplan enunciated the philosophy of the Synagogue Center, called by him the "Jewish Center." For in this historic statement, sanction was given to the validity of informal educational, recreational and cultural activities, as essential complementary pursuits to the basic religious activities of the synagogue. "We state frankly," he said, "that we are establishing the Jewish Center for the purpose of deriving from it for ourselves pleasures of a social, intellectual, and spiritual character. We are not building a settlement, nor a communal center, nor a Young Men's or Young Women's Hebrew Association; nor do we expect the Jewish Center to be an institution for the doing of so-called uplift work. This time we feel that we are as much in need of being uplifted as they for the benefit of whom the city is dotted with communal institutions.... The Jewish Center will be dominated by a purpose of far-reaching significance, if we, who are about to establish it, will do so with the deliberate and conscious aim of conducting it as an experiment to help us solve the problem of Jewish life and religion....

"The elements which are indispensable to health in human life are four in number: atmosphere, light, food and exercise. Provide Jewish life with these constituents, and you will solve the problem of Judaism....

"Give it atmosphere, create surroundings that breathe the Jewish spirit. Let those surroundings be so inviting that we should look forward to them with delight; let every nook and corner convey a Jewish sentiment; let the furnishings be made expressive through Jewish symbolic art; let the books and pictures be such as deal with Jewish themes: and above all, let the entire atmosphere be pervaded by a spirit of piety and reverence....

"The second requisite to Jewish health is light, and by light I mean joy.... It is only by frequently resorting to entertainment and joy-giving recreations that our nervous systems are preserved from breakdown. If we want our religion to count as a factor in our lives, we shall have to imbibe it not merely during the few odd moments that we can spare from our work and our pastimes, but in the very course of these pursuits.... Great educators of the world have begun to realize that pastime and recreation are needed not only to build up the body, but also to build up the soul.... It is true that until the present time the Jewish environment provided by the synagogue did not have to contain game rooms, swimming pools, gymnasiums. But we forget that in the past the bulk of our people accepted the fact of their being Jewish as the most self-evident of all moral axioms....

"The third requisite to the health of Jewish life is the proper soul nourishment, that is, the food of knowledge.... Our sons and daughters, who learn something of the great world cultures and national literatures, but nothing of the culture and literature of our people, can at best be but starving Jews....

"Finally, the fundamental law to which we should give heed in order to secure a sound Jewish life is that, to keep any thought or ideal alive, we must be doing something with it. It is not enough to be talking about it. It must find expression through action.... By being in the van of all movements that make for justice, we can contribute more than our share to the establishment of the Kingdom of God on earth....

"Above all there is need for that form of practical action whereby the spiritual solidarity of Israel shall be made to operate as a real and active force in our lives. We should not content ourselves with merely securing justice for the Jew in the lands of oppression. We should make the upbuilding of Palestine as a spiritual Center of the world the foremost and distinctive contribution of Jewish life to the life of the nations....

"These, in brief, are the main elements essential to that normality and equilibrium of Jewish life, to that health which will efface forever from our lives the question, Why remain a Jew?...."[2]

The Synagogue and the Center

While Dr. Kaplan was urging an all inclusive function for the Synagogue as an institution, the practical and enduring contribution in the statement that stimulated the Jewish Community Center movement was the role assigned to the activities of an informal character, the responsibility of Jews towards Israel and towards social problems — all of these activities comprising Jewish duties and constituting "constituents of Jewish life." This conception gave Jewish purpose and Jewish meaning to the activities of the Jewish Community Center. It was not pertinent that the Jewish Community Center was not engaged in the normal activities of the Synagogue. From the standpoint of the way in which specialized institutions had developed and were continuing to develop in the larger and medium sized communities in America, the synagogue and the Jewish Community Center, while striving to serve the same broad purposes of Jewish life, could function as separate and cooperating institutions. And in the smaller communities, where communal life was simpler and the Jewish population more homogeneous, the Jewish Welfare Board willingly aided in the establishment of the Synagogue Center as defined by Dr. Kaplan.

In the decade 1921 to 1930, the Jewish Community Center movement expanded rapidly. New buildings were erected, a new profession was trained. At the same time the dynamism of the Conservative Synagogue manifested itself in similar rapid expansion. In some communities the simultaneous efforts of both organizations produced the appearance of competition. As early as 1926 the Jewish Welfare Board, at its annual meeting, adopted a resolution recommending consultation between the synagogue bodies and JWB, with a view to resolving any difficulties that had developed in the relationships of the Synagogue and Jewish Community Center. Dr. Kaplan took the lead in convening representatives of the groups, but with little success at the time. His interest in a solution of the problem continued and he wrote and spoke often on the subject. He participated, as a member of the JWB Survey Commission, in the formulation of recommendations designed to lead to acceptable working relationships between the Synagogue and Center, locally and nationally. Efforts are now being made to work out a program of cooperation between the Synagogue Council and the National Jewish Welfare Board.

A recurrent and constantly vexing aspect of the problem has its roots in what might be called ideological differences, or to put it differently, the labeling of Jewish Center activities as secular and, by inference, therefore destructive of Jewish values. There is confusion in definitions of terms: Why are Jewish activities of the Jewish Center "secular" (nonreligious)? Is the Synagogue an institution, or is it identical with Jewish religion or Judaism? Is it accurate in any event to speak of *the* Synagogue or Jewish religion, when there are at least three expressions of the Synagogue and of Jewish religious philosophy in many communities? Where does local community responsibility and authority fit into the plans of Synagogue and Center, or are both entirely private and completely autonomous organizations?

It would be unfair to quote Dr. Kaplan's views in support of either the Center or the Synagogue in this connection. His attitude on the centrality of religion in Jewish life is unequivocal. Nevertheless, the Jewish Community Center has sought validity through constant evaluation of its contributions to Jewish cultural life, as fulfillment of its function in the community. In the process, particularly in the dynamic development of its philosophy, thoughtful leaders of the Jewish Center movement have found encouragement and inspiration in the writings of Dr. Kaplan.

In a memorable address at the annual convention of the Jewish Welfare Board in April 1935,[3] Dr. Kaplan said "The Jewish Community Center is the resultant of two distinct factors. One factor is the Jewish will to live, or the will to live as Jews. And the other factor is the inadequacy of the Synagogue group to satisfy that desire or will to live as Jews."

But, lest there be misunderstanding that the speaker suggested that the Jewish Center could become a substitute for the Synagogue, he cautioned "It (the Center) should not . . . call itself a congregation or rival of the Synagogue group. But it should nurture the communal will into an awakening of itself, into an awareness of itself, give the communal will direction and help to implement it." He observed that the Jewish Center was at the time "in search of a philosophy," and emphasized that its purpose be sought in its communal character, which meant that in the Center there were "stirrings of a communal will, representative of all classes of Jews who wish to be united by an articulate desire to foster Jewish life." The times then were trying and spirits were low. With the country in the throes of an economic depression, with the Nazi influence casting a gloomy foreboding on the future of European Jewry, the call of Dr. Kaplan to the Jewish Center movement was an inspiring challenge. "This communal will, which has brought the Center into being, is a yearning, a deep seated irrepressible yearning. It is a yearning to belong to a fellowship, but not the ordinary kind of fellowship that only provides friendship and entertainment. It is a yearning for a fellowship that confers upon one status, a place in the world, a place in human life, the fulness of human dignity." The Jewish Center at the time had developed rapidly in physical facilities, in the range of its activities, in numbers of members and in the use of professional personnel. The outward signs of growth were evident, and even the economic crisis facing the country resulted in no serious impairment of the program. But Dr. Kaplan sensed, almost in the mood of the ancient prophets, that these evidences of seeming stability were illusory unless they reflected the existence of a solid and enduring purpose. "The only way the Jewish Community Center will acquire a philosophy is by adopting some inspiring ideal that would integrate its activities and redeem them from their present directionless character. What more inspiring ideal could the Center set before itself than that of helping the Jew to find what to live for as a Jew?"

Growing Emphasis on Jewish Culture

There were many among the lay leadership and the professional workers in whom Dr. Kaplan's message found fruitful soil. They had been motivated by the feeling that the Jewish purposes of the Jewish Center constituted its chief rationale. Dr. Kaplan's articulation of the need for a clear philosophy was a source of encouragement, and it became manifest in the growing emphasis on Jewish cultural elements in the program. Progress was slow, and difficulties were encountered in attempts to clarify and gain acceptance for the Jewish purposes of the Jewish Center. On the one hand, the criticism from some Synagogue leadership that the Center was a secularizing influence did not die. On the other hand, there were many who saw in the "Jewish" emphasis the danger of creating a social and cultural ghetto. The strong undercurrent of Palestine and Zionist influence, in the Jewish cultural aspects of the program, led others to raise the question whether the Jewish Center was not weakening loyalties to America. The validity of Jews' organizing separately for what appeared to be an American program of recreation was constantly challenged. The penetration of social theories of economic determinism and the influence of psychoanalytic approaches in the academic preparation of social workers, to some extent, also weakened the moorings of Jewish tradition in communal service. The Jewish Center, in common with other social services, was, for a time, affected by this emphasis. The preoccupation of the most able lay leadership with huge fund-raising endeavors for Jewry in other lands, and the trend towards building community organization around fund raising machinery, detracted from the support which was needed to help the Jewish Center to develop its potentialities as a center of Jewish life and living.

Few were the voices raised during this period, and stilled were the pens of those who could have employed the power of the word to give guidance and direction to basic efforts for the perpetuation of Jewish values. The urgent, immediate objective, the myopic view, supplanted the ultimate, telescopic vision. And confusion multiplied as the Jewish position oscillated between the impact of the tragedy of destruction of Eastern and Central European Jewry and the astounding victory of Israel.

During this time, many found anchorage in the thoughtful, challenging writings of Dr. Kaplan. He expounded his views on the vexing problems confronting American Jewry, especially as they might be dealt with through organized communal effort. Dr. Kaplan wrote for no special group — certainly not for the Jewish Center official family. His observations were directed to the general Jewish community; his was the large arena of contemporary, universal problems influencing Jewish life in America. Yet, so closely related were the issues with which he dealt to those confronting the Jewish Center in the aspects of its purpose and program, that there could at all times be found guidance and clarification in his writings. One need only to re-read *The Future of the American Jew*, published as recently as 1948, to find enlightenment on many of the questions that disturbed Jewish Centers then. It was just at that time that the Survey of the JWB, a monumental task directed by Dr. Oscar Janowsky, was undertaken. Dr. Kaplan, a member of the Survey Commission, was doubtless entirely at home with the problems, especially those relating to a redefinition of the purposes of the Jewish Center, for they reflected the issues facing Jewish life generally. He gave generous support to the recommendations, so brilliantly elucidated by Dr. Janowsky, because they represented the very goals which in 1935 he had urged and which he continued to elaborate and refine as guides to Jewish communal policy generally.

For example, on the question of basic purpose of the Jewish Center in America, the difficulty facing the Jewish Center movement, arising out of the varied purposes for which Jewish Centers were founded, could not be better expressed than in the following:

"It is not surprising to find both affirmative and marginal Jews supporting the same Jewish institutions, and cooperating in the same Jewish activities. On the face of it, a fact of this kind should be greeted with approval. What could be better than to have Jews of two diametrically opposed tendencies actually cooperating in socially important undertakings? Jews who otherwise would suffer want or illness are certainly better off, by virtue of the fact that those who are in a position to help them are willing to ignore their own differences.

"Yet, it is questionable whether, in the long run, more good than harm will result from this artificial coalition of tendencies as irreconcilable as the ebb and the flow tides. That some should expect to advance Jewish life through like activities that others use as a means of weaning Jews away from Judaism cannot but lead to unwholesome inner conflict. Marginal Jews combat anti-Semitism because it does not let them become one hundred percent Gentile! Affirmative Jews combat it because it does not let them live as Jews! Thus anti-Semitism in itself exerts an ambiguous role in Jewish life, routing some Jews out of Judaism and driving others back into it, thereby robbing Jewish life of focus and persistence."[4]

Integration and Survival

How could Jewish purpose be reconciled with the need for integration of the Jews as individuals and as a group into American life? Could Jews develop an indigenous Jewish culture, or for that matter work for the continuity of Jewish cultural life, and at the same time perform their full duty towards the development of American culture? Is there validity to cultural pluralism as the effective American way? Can Jews, or should they, resist the process of acculturation which has so effectively eliminated cultural patterns among other immigrant groups?

The fears implied in these questions are dealt with in clear logic by Dr. Kaplan. Recognizing that nationalism in its normal and legitimate form (e. g. democratic American nationalism) "calls upon all citizens to subordinate to the common good all differences that divide them — to weld all citizens into a homogeneous unity," he warns that "actual experience has proved that national homogeneity, unless qualified by cultural and religious heterogeneity, degenerates into total enslavement of the individual."[5] In this country, "all citizens share as individuals in the cultural, economic and political life of the nation."[6] Their rights as individuals are safeguarded by the basic law of the land. "Nevertheless, the very recognition of personal rights has resulted in the development of voluntary communal and religio-cultural institutions. This makes religio-cultural pluralism compatible with political monism."[7] Each cultural group, while sharing in the common American culture, "is free to develop additional cultural interests based on family tradition, religious affiliation, ethnic origin, race or any other natural factor."[8] "Being loyal to two civilizations is as ethical as being loyal to father and mother."[9]

The real difficulty confronting the Jewish Center is the lack, among many Jews, of a strong conviction about Jewish group survival in the Diaspora. It is a feeling shared by non-observant as well as some devout Jews, by non-Zionists as well as Zionists and by all who consciously attempt to escape from their Jewish origin. The Jewish Center has genuine purpose only for those who wish to live as Jews and have what Dr. Kaplan calls the "we feeling" toward other Jews. The Jewish Center has validity in the Jewish community only if it aids, as an institution and as a movement, in the process of Jewish survival. It is not sufficient that it be a "meeting place." It must have a conscious objective and a purposeful program based on its power to aid in the continuity of Jewish culture or civilization (Dr. Kaplan's meaningful term) in America.

Since the establishment of the State of Israel, this purpose has been questioned by many Zionists who see no future for Jews in the Diaspora, and by religious elements who see a future for Jews in America only as a religious denomination.

Many in the Jewish Center movement, devoted Zionists and many others who are loyal to the Synagogue, feel as does Dr. Kaplan. "Whatever the inherent merit of the Zionist solution for those who will or can go to Eretz Yisrael, it is no solution for the five million Jews in the United States, the only strong surviving remnant of our people; and without a satisfactory solution of the problem presented by modern nationalism, the status of American Jewry remains ambiguous. Such ambiguity is bound to undermine our children's happiness and peace of mind. In fact, every day that is allowed to pass without effort on our part to come to terms with so urgent and vital a problem as their Jewish status vis-à-vis the majority population adds to their inner tension and anxiety. The cliché that Jews constitute a religious community, allegedly united by some common beliefs concerning God and salvation, is flagrantly untrue. We contribute to our children's self-hate and self-contempt by failing to find the appropriate name for that which identifies them as Jews no less than by failing to render Jewish life intrinsically deserving of their loyalty."[10]

This does not contradict Dr. Kaplan's well known belief in the essentiality of a free and autonomous Jewish state. "Ever since that turning point in our career as a people which has fated us to integrate our lot with that of other nations, a Jewish land has become the *sine qua non* of the continuance of Jewish life."[11]

The Jewish Center has for many years drawn the Jewish content of the cultural program from two main sources — Jewish historic and religious tradition and Palestinian Jewish life — its music, dance and practical arts. It is not difficult for the Center to see the possibility of a continued connection with the new State, at least insofar as cultural interchange is concerned. Dr. Kaplan expresses the same conviction with regard to Diaspora Jewry generally. "With Eretz Yisrael, Judaism becomes a great historic movement with a present and a future as well as a past."[12]

"Moreover, by serving as the focal point of Jewish interests, Eretz Yisrael imbues the scattered remnants of the Jewish people with a sense of unity and creates an international Jewish public for the gifted Jewish writer, artists or musician. Such encouragement of esthetic expression is far more potent than that provided by the local Jewish community of Eretz Yisrael. In this respect the Diaspora becomes an impetus for fostering cultural life in Eretz Yisrael, no less than Eretz Yisrael is for fostering Jewish cultural milieu in the Diaspora."[13]

"Jews in the Diaspora will continue to owe exclusive political allegiance to the countries in which they reside. The tie that binds Diaspora Jewry to Eretz Yisrael is a cultural and religious one."[14]

The aims of the Jewish Center to provide opportunities for Jewish cultural expression and the stimulus given to the effort by the National Jewish Welfare Board cannot be affected by the current confusions regarding "dual loyalty", apparently induced in some minds by the establishment of the Jewish State. Although Dr. Kaplan's book antedates the establishment of the State, on this special problem of relations of Israel and the Diaspora, Dr. Kaplan's analysis applies today. "We Jews who have come to this country bore the gifts of a great historic tradition. To tell us that Judaism can have no future here is to tell us that these gifts are worthless and that, as a group, we can only be cultural parasites. Whatever the future holds in store for us is a matter of speculation, but that there are today five million Jews in the United States is not speculation but a fact that carries with it inescapable responsibilities. We Jews have the same need as have all other Americans of belonging to a community where we are wanted and welcomed, and where we can derive the moral and spiritual values that give meaning and dignity to human life. We naturally look to the Jewish community to give us a faith to live by and to live for. Whatever deprives us of faith in the possibility of Jewish life in America not only dejudaizes millions of our people; it demoralizes and degrades us . . .

"Until Jews realize that the Jewish problem in the Diaspora and the Jewish problem in Eretz Yisrael are one, they are running away from reality and defeating their own purpose.

Only as we assume the responsibility for having Judaism live wherever Jews are allowed to live are we likely to succeed in any of our Jewish undertakings . . .

"We are far from the land where the Jewish spirit is being reborn. But given the will, the intelligence and the devotion, it is feasible so to relive and to re-embody, within the frame of a democratic American civilization, the vital and thrilling experience of our people in Eretz Yisrael that, in the long run, we might achieve in our way as great and lasting a contribution to human values as they are achieving in theirs."[15]

So-called "Secular" Interests

The bogey of "secularization of Jewish life" still haunts the efforts of Jewish Centers to carry out Jewish cultural programs, and impedes general acceptance. The Jewish Center does not claim to be an institution comprising all Jews in the community, nor does its program assume to be inclusive of all Jewish interests. Many organizations, institutions and movements function to meet specific needs. The Jewish Center has gradually developed a distinctive function and a characteristic program that rules out the possibility of monopoly of the exclusive loyalty of individuals. At the same time the clarification of its function permits co-operation with other groups interested in positive Jewish living. The Jewish Center finds validity for its so-called secular Jewish activities within the framework of Dr. Kaplan's concepts of "peoplehood" and "Judaism as a civilization." Within the pattern of organized Jewish communal activities that includes the great variety of synagogues, schools, Zionist groups, social service organizations, fraternal bodies and many others, all part of the complex of Jewish life in America, i. e., "Jewish civilization," the Jewish Center finds a natural place in every community. It need not be, and in fact is not, a threat to any organization, nor does it weaken any legitimate program.

Dr. Kaplan has repeatedly urged the broad definition of constructive Jewish life or Judaism, that sanctions the purpose and work of the Jewish Center. In listing the objectives that need to be pursued for the reconstruction of Jewish life and thought, two come within the scope of the work of the Jewish Center (though not exclusively), namely, "the stimulation of Jewish cultural creativity in literature and the arts" and "the participation of Jewry in social movements that seek ample freedom, stricter justice and better co-operation among men and nations," the basis of the social action program of Jewish Centers.

At another point, this statement appears: "Emphasis on religion should not be interpreted as minimizing the importance of the so-called secular aspects of Jewish culture. Whatever enriches Jewish life can only help to re-enforce Jewish religion. Among the activities that enrich Jewish life, the arts must occupy an important place. Even in the ghetto, art was never completely lacking, although the scope of artistic expression was limited; the arts did not receive the attention that a modern civilization would accord them. In the reconstruction of Jewish life, we should make up this defect. We cannot afford to have the individual Jew find all his esthetic experiences outside the sphere of Jewish civilization. It was precisely the frustration of their esthetic interests by the limitation of their Jewish environment that led Heinrich Heine and many of his generation to abandon Judaism altogether. That situation must not be repeated.

"It need not be. As long as Jews react emotionally to the conditions of their life as Jews, there exist the potentialities of a Jewish art, since art arises from the effort to make emotional experience permanently significant. This is true whether the medium be literature, music, drama, the dance, or any of the graphic or plastic arts. Jewish art can express the experiences of Jewish life in a way that lifts that life above the commonplace, the sordid and the drab. The magic of the arts can renew the radiance of Jewish life.

"What consciousness is to an individual, culture is to a people. A people's culture finds expression in history, literature and art. The only way in which a member of a people can share its collective consciousness is by learning its history, reading its literature and fostering its art. The Jewish people has possessed all these means ever since it became aware of itself as a people ...

"As for the arts, we are only at the very beginning in the process of creating a modern Jewish art. We have highly talented Jews in all the fields of art, in music, drama, dance, painting, sculpture and architecture, but most of our people still lack the understanding that, unless all these arts begin to function in Jewish life, there can be no Jewish life in the Diaspora. If Jews are to continue living as Jews despite anti-Semitism, it is imperative to have Judaism spell deep joy for the harassed millions of our people in Western lands. That joy can be derived from nothing so much as from the flowering of the creative arts. These are the means of conveying the wide range of emotions that seethe in the hearts of Jews ...

"A conscious effort should be made to encourage appreciation of Jewish art in Jewish schools, community centers, youth organizations and cultural groups of all kinds."[16]

The Jewish Center movement has for years encouraged artistic self-expression, especially to give meaning to Jewish living. Under the leadership of the National Jewish Welfare Board, stimulus has been given to creativity, particularly in Jewish literature and music. The destruction of many historic sources of Jewish life and culture in Europe accentuated the tempo of this and other efforts to fill the vacuum in Jewish cultural development. Dr. Kaplan warned, "We are still living on the capital of habits and attitudes which represent the accumulation of centuries, during which our ancestors were socially self-governing and culturally a self-sustaining people".[17] "For the abundant and continuous supply of creative talent that could produce a vast variety of Jewish esthetic expression, we must have a responsible community ... a community that is organized for and around the purpose of transforming Judaism for each and every Jew from a burden to a privilege."[18]

Conclusion

Dr. Kaplan has written for Jews in all walks of life and not even solely for American Jews. The extent of his influence, while not measurable at this time, is clearly discernible in the development of the objectives of the Jewish Center, where the contribution of his thinking and the warmth of his understanding have been pervasive and will be enduring. A Jewish Center philosophy, appropriate to its function in American Jewish life, has been long in crystallizing. It is not yet certain that the current formulation, in Dr. Janowsky's survey, represents ultimate concepts. For, as Dr. Kaplan has pointed out, we are dealing with the factors of dynamism and change, in our efforts to develop a solid basis for Jewish living. There is perhaps no significant institution or movement on the American scene that more clearly reflects flexibility of method and program than the Jewish Center, as it attempts to meet the changing needs of American Jews. But withal, there is a basic framework, a large goal and a system of fundamental policies and practices, within which Jewish Centers serve Jewish needs. It is in this essential phase of the Jewish Center movement that the responsible leadership has absorbed understanding and purposefulness from the creative thinking and profound teaching of Dr. Kaplan.

NOTES

[1] Jewish Publication Society, Philadelphia, 1948.
[2] *American Hebrew*, March 22, 1918.
[3] *Jewish Center*, XIII, No. 2.
[4] M. M. Kaplan, *The Future of the American Jew*, Macmillan, New York, 1948, p. 5.
[5] Ibid., p. 18.
[6] Ibid., p. 70.
[7] Ibid., p. 70.
[8] Ibid., p. 70.
[9] Ibid., p. 104.
[10] Ibid., p. 24–25.
[11] Ibid., p. 9.
[12] Ibid., p. 125.
[13] Ibid., pp. 125–126.
[14] Ibid., p. 128.
[15] Ibid., pp. 129–130.
[16] Ibid., pp. 50–52.
[17] Ibid., p. 60.
[18] Ibid., p. 118.

MORDECAI M. KAPLAN AS EXEGETE
By Eugene Kohn

Of the many contributions of Mordecai M. Kaplan to Jewish life and thought, none is perhaps more important than his development of a method for reinterpreting Jewish tradition. The conviction prevails among modern scholars that the Bible and the Rabbinical literature stemming from it are not the record of a supernatural revelation, but are ancient human documents. This has resulted in a tendency on the part of many modern Jews to regard them as mere archaic relics irrelevant to the life of our day. Even if venerated as classics, they are apt to be treated, like most classics, as books to be kept on the shelf, but not to be read and studied. They are hardly expected, except in a few "purple passages," to have anything of interest to say to living men and women.

Convention has prescribed that they be used as a source of texts and quotations with which to embellish sermons and confer on preachers the prestige of erudition. But that convention no longer possesses its original significance. It was based on the assumption that the text of the Torah was the actual word of God, supernaturally revealed to Israel at Sinai. As long as all Jews believed that, preaching from a Biblical text had a function. It was a means by which Jews could learn what was expected of them by God and by the "holy congregation" of his worshipers. With the shift from supernaturalism to naturalism as the prevailing outlook on life, the sermon lost its significance and functional value. And not only the sermon, but the Bible and Torah literature as well. Yet none of our "spiritual leaders" saw, or admitted that he saw, the growing irrelevance of the Biblical and Rabbinic literature to Jewish life as it is lived today, until Dr. Kaplan had the courage to point it out. He was the first to grapple seriously with the problem of restoring the tradition to relevancy by a system of reinterpretation.

Genesis of Dr. Kaplan's New Approach to the Interpretation of the Bible

It was my good fortune to be a student at the Jewish Theological Seminary when, in the year 1911, Mordecai Kaplan, then a young man of 30, began to instruct as Professor of Homiletics. With a forthrightness that came as a great shock to the student body, he immediately started to revolutionize the teaching of homiletics. Until his time, it had been treated merely as a branch of public speaking. It was distinguished from other branches only by the convention that called for the use of a Biblical text and Rabbinic illustrative material. But he at once proceeded to an examination of the central problems which had hitherto been studiously evaded: (1) Why preach on a traditional text at all if one no longer believes it to be literally the word of God? and, (2) If one uses such a text, how should it be used?

Here is Dr. Kaplan's answer to the former question in his own words:

"It may be asked: but why start out with traditional concepts, and then subject yourself to the arduous task of revaluation? Why not begin with utterly new standards and values? The answer is that the tendency to reinterpret derives from the basic human need of feeling that there is some objective truth to the course which human history has taken. If all that man achieved of culture and religion should turn out to be illusory, what meaning can human life have as a whole? On the other hand, if we can discover some element of continuity between that which we find to be helpful to human life and development and that which was cherished by the ancients, we are fortified in our hopes and aspirations. The advantage of using traditional concepts is that they carry with them the accumulated momentum and emotional drive of man's previous efforts to gain greater spiritual power!"[1]

The Bible, he taught, was important to the Jew in every age as the original source of the basic concepts which functioned as sanctifying influences on Jewish life. Those concepts have changed in the course of time, but in all their changes a common core of meaning is discernible, provided we consider them functionally as they have expressed themselves in the life of the people. At one of his very first lectures to his class in homiletics at the Seminary, Dr. Kaplan left his students somewhat perplexed and bewildered by telling them that the Bible is, to the Jews, not a book, nor even a collection of books, but "an institution." The meaning of that somewhat cryptic utterance was made clear as he continued to explain that what the words of the Bible meant to successive generations of Jews was determined not exclusively by the significance of the words for their authors, and the people to whom they were originally addressed, but by the way they were subsequently interpreted and embodied in the laws, customs, mores and culture of the people. The Bible was thus, at one and the same time, the product of Jewish life and a determining factor in producing Jewish life. Being the record of Jewish experience in the formative years of Jewish civilization, it reflects precisely those vital reactions which have laid the foundation of the character of the Jewish people, just as the earliest experiences of an infant determine his manner of reacting to all the later circumstances that affect his life.

To attain Jewish self-knowledge, to understand how Jews have become what they are, to identify the values that the Jewish people has striven to embody in its life, the study of the Bible is as important for us as it ever was. Jews feel themselves challenged, by the various peoples among whom they live, either to justify their separate group existence or to merge completely with the majority and go out of existence. That challenge Jews cannot meet without the kind of Jewish self-knowledge which comes from the recognition of the spiritual identity of the Jewish group personality, through all the changes that have befallen it. To make that clear is the true function of the preaching and teaching of the sacred writings of our literature. That must be today the justification for drawing on Biblical and rabbinical texts for sermon material.

So much for the *why* of using the Bible and Rabbinic literature functionally in the sermon and classroom instruction. It is, however, Dr. Kaplan's answer to the second question, how to interpret tradition, which calls for a fuller exposition.

Perhaps, after all, the continued use of a Biblical text as the theme of the sermon, long after neither the preacher nor the congregation believed in its supernatural origin and authority, was not wholly a matter of convention; perhaps it was based, in part, on an intuitive perception of the value of that custom in helping to maintain spiritual continuity with the past. But obviously, its value cannot be realized by a form of preaching which merely reads contemporary ideas *into* a text and does not derive any ideas *from* the text. That had been the tendency before Dr. Kaplan expounded his method of reinterpretation. It is still the tendency of much preaching in our day. Texts are torn from their context and given a meaning entirely unrelated to their original intention. A license of interpretation is allowed in the pulpit which no modern commentator would seriously permit himself in a commentary that had to pass the scrutiny of scholars with a grounding in philology, archaeology, history, comparative religion and other branches of organized knowledge. Since it has long been obvious that the *peshat*, or literal meaning of the Biblical text, is often inacceptable to the modern mind or the modern conscience, many preachers assume that any Biblical statement may be treated as a figure of speech. Accordingly, *any figurative meaning* which the preacher may make his audience see in it is acceptable for preaching purposes. But it is obvious that a text which can mean anything means nothing. It is precisely the loose method of allegorical interpretation that enables the Devil to quote Scripture for his purpose.

If the Bible came to mean, to successive generations of Jews, something different from the literal significance of the text, it is because they seized upon certain of its implications that were relevant to their own experience of life and accepted them as its original meaning. But with our more informed present understanding of historic processes, we cannot so readily persuade ourselves that the implications of the text which expressed its meaning to later generations were necessarily those intended by its authors. Therefore, if we are to find implications in the ancient text which are relevant to contemporary life, we are in need of a method of perceiving in the text meanings that are derived from their authors' original intention, but are not necessarily identical with it. Those meanings would represent what the author would maintain if he were alive today and aware of the changes in the thought and behavior patterns of men that have occurred since his time.

The Meaning of Reinterpretation

To discover such implications of the text involves a Bible exegesis which thinks not in terms of *interpretation* but of *reinterpretation*. Even for people who lived in the same cultural world as the Biblical authors, many of their words might still have needed interpretation. There is, for example, in our own day, a whole body of literary criticism which is largely taken up with an interpretation of our contemporary literature. But such interpretation, in terms that have the same meaning for the original author, the interpreter and the public addressed, is a very different and much simpler task than what we mean by *reinterpretation*. Reinterpretation is necessary wherever the attempt is made to explain a work that belongs to one social and cultural milieu in terms that belong to another and very different social and cultural milieu.

The difference between the processes of interpretation and reinterpretation can perhaps best be grasped by the aid of an illustration. An American architect, if he were gifted with a simple, lucid style of exposition, could give an account of how a skyscraper is built, which would be informative to the American layman. That would involve an interpretation of certain physical and mechanical principles with which the lay reader is unfamiliar; but the task would not be too difficult, because skyscrapers and the processes of their building are part of the visible environment of the public addressed. But suppose the architect were to find himself somehow in the heart of the African jungle, and suppose that he were to try to explain to the people who live there what a skyscraper is like. Though their own homes are one-story huts, it might not be too difficult to give them the idea of a structure of more than one story; but when he told them of the number of stories in the Empire State Building they would certainly not believe him. They would point out that not only would such a building be sure to topple over, but that, even if it stood, it would be useless. How, they would ask, could anybody climb to the top of such a building? So he would have to explain the elevator. Then they would want to know how many persons were required to pull the elevator to the top? That would make it necessary for him to explain electric power. Then they would want to know the magic formula by which he could conjure the lightning to do his work. It is hardly necessary to labor the point further. It is plain that one cannot explain a skyscraper to one who has no familiarity with the culture that produces skyscrapers.

The reverse process would be almost as difficult. Were the primitive Africans to try to communicate to our supposed architect what their various taboos, tribal rituals, and ethnic customs mean to them, they would probably leave him perplexed and bewildered. The various interpretations that different anthropologists use to explain the same phenomena are evidence of the difficulty which our architect would encounter. Only long and patient study, plus a great deal of imaginative insight, make possible for us an understanding of the culture of people whose whole mental content is different from ours, who live in a different universe of discourse. But, once that understanding is achieved, it should be possible to restate the significance of the concepts of the one civilization in terms of the other, making allowance for the different thought symbols that must be employed. Such an explanation would be not merely an interpretation, but a reinterpretation.

The reinterpretation of an ancient text is thus the process of transposing its thought from the ancient universe of discourse into that of our modern age. By universe of discourse we mean the mental content of percepts, concepts and ideas common to a people who live in a particular cultural environment, as determined by time and place. To reinterpret the Biblical text is to restate some of its implications in the idiom of our modern universe of discourse.

Some Principles Underlying the Method of Reinterpretation

But how is that possible, in view of the difficulties indicated by the example we gave of our hypothetical architect's embarrassment in trying to explain a skyscraper to natives of the African jungle, and of their similar difficulty in explaining to him the characteristic features of their culture? That possibility is based on an acceptance of the truth of three fundamental propositions:

1. The authors of the Bible did not differ fundamentally, in respect to their physical and mental endowments, from the men of our day.

2. Their fundamental needs, based on that physical and mental endowment, and the interests developed in the effort to satisfy those needs, were also essentially the same as those of modern men.

3. Though human nature changes, if at all, only by unconscious and imperceptible steps, human knowledge is cumulative and human culture changes radically from age to age.

Let us examine these propositions a little more closely. There is no question that the bodily organs and tissues of men in ancient times were the same as those of men in our day. Since long before the dawn of history there have been no significant changes in the human anatomy. Presumably, then, the senses and sensations of our forefathers in Bible times were similar to ours. Since they had the same kind of nervous and glandular system, we must assume that their emotional responses to stimuli also resembled ours. A reading of the Biblical text confirms that assumption. Men showed anger by fighting or quarreling, grief by weeping, mirth by laughter, and all the other typical emotional responses, exactly as we do. Moreover, when they argued, they used the same kind of logic — sometimes the same kind of logical fallacies — as we do today. All of which confirms the first of the three propositions we have enumerated.

If the Biblical authors ascribed a supernatural, rather than a natural, origin to some of their ideas, or to decisive events in their lives or the life of their nation, that does not mean that they possessed spiritual powers not available to men of our generation. It merely means that, in the light of the knowledge of their day, they interpreted experiences in a manner different from the way we, with our present knowledge, would interpret them. In all ancient cultures, ignorance of the data on which the natural sciences have since been built made it necessary for people to rely more on imagination, and less on authenticated observation, than we would today. Hence, the prevalence in all ancient cultures of myth and magic, miracle and oracle. We cannot make sense of the Bible text either by assuming that its authors were endowed with occult powers lacking in ordinary human beings, or by assuming that, because its authors knew less about the world than we do, they responded to life with less of mature wisdom than we. The former of these assumptions leads to the abandonment of any effort to understand the Bible on the ground that it is too "deep" for ordinary human beings, who have experienced no esoteric mystical enlightenment. The latter leads to the sophomoric conclusion that, because our culture contains more knowledge than that of the ancients, they can have nothing of importance to tell us.

Our second proposition grows out of the first. Since the powers and faculties of ancient men were not different from our own, and since those powers and faculties express and serve functional human needs, it must be assumed that those needs and the interests based on them were also similar to our own. Then, as now, men needed food, shelter, clothing, security, love and fellowship, and were interested in satisfying their intellectual curiosity, in giving artistic expression to their response to the beautiful, and religious expression to their sense of the holy. In our reading of the ancient texts we must always seek the psychological response of the author to the specific life-situation to which he is reacting. If we can understand his psychological reaction, we can infer from it how the author would react to similar situations in the modern world. It is that which makes the Biblical text meaningful for our day. By the discovery of these "psychological equivalents," a term Dr. Kaplan frequently used in his teaching, the preacher is able to find meanings in the text of which the author himself may not have been aware, since he could not have anticipated the modern situation to which they apply. But these meanings, for one who knows that situation, are legitimate derivations from the author's thought.

In order, however, to discover those psychological equivalents and make a valid analogy with meanings relevant to our present situation, it is necessary to reckon with our third proposition: though human nature changes little, if at all, human culture changes radically as a result of changing circumstances and the constant accretion of new knowledge. To infer from the Biblical text the psychological attitude of its author to the life situation to which he is responding, we must, above all, know what that situation was. We must know Jewish history — the actual facts about the evolution of Jewish life and not merely the legend tradition has built up — in order that, by retracing our steps, we can put ourselves imaginatively into the situation the Biblical author had in mind when he uttered his words. Whatever a Biblical author said, even though it makes no sense for the modern reader on a merely casual reading, must have made sense for its author, and the people to whom it was addressed. That sense has merely been obscured for us because we live in a different universe of discourse from theirs. In view of the tremendous amount of knowledge that has accumulated since Biblical times, we need to make a deliberate effort to imagine how the world would look to us if we lacked that knowledge. Only so can we understand the premises of the thinking and the motivations of the actions of our forefathers in Biblical times. Only such understanding can make the text yield an intelligible meaning capable of being related to the thoughts and motivations of contemporary life.

The Outlines of a Methodology for Reinterpreting the Bible

From all of the foregoing, the outlines of a methodology for reinterpreting any passage in the Bible begin to take shape. It is obvious, for example, that we cannot treat any text as though it were an isolated literary unit. The text must be set in a context. That context must be not merely a literary one, relating the passage to others — a principle already recognized in the hermeneutics of the Rabbis — but also a social and historical context. The text must be oriented in time and space, in history and geography.

That gives us the significance of the so-called higher criticism for an understanding of the Bible. As a new approach to the study of the Bible, the higher criticism, particularly in its earlier days, when its techniques had not yet been perfected and it had not yet accumulated enough factual data, often arrived at fantastically erroneous conclusions. These have since been largely corrected by historical and archaeological research, and great progress has been made in reconstructing the historical background of the Biblical text, and thus providing for it the necessary context. The layman who is unfamiliar with this literature can hardly imagine the painstaking labors, the mental ingenuity and the fascinating problems which this effort to reconstruct the social and cultural world of the Bible involves. A great variety of sciences are drawn upon for that task: philology, archaeology, history, comparative religion, anthropology, ethnology and kindred disciplines.

But the higher criticism alone cannot make the Bible relevant to life today. Its pursuit is so fascinating to those who engage in it, and is so exacting in its demands, that it tends to become for them an end in itself. The ordinary layman, not having the time and energy left in his leisure hours to follow the intricacies of the higher criticism, nor the educational equipment to test its conclusions, finds the critical Bible commentaries as irrelevant to his religious and cultural needs as the unelucidated text of the Bible itself. A new type of Bible exegesis is therefore called for in our day, one that neither explains away difficulties by recourse to allegorical or metaphorical interpretation in the traditional manner, nor contents itself with merely freeing the text from scribal errors and later interpolations, and orienting it by the aid of the higher criticism.

The modern commentator who is concerned with making the text of the Bible yield meanings relevant to present spiritual needs must, to be sure, utilize the better established conclusions of the higher criticism as aids in reconstructing the life-situation which called forth the words of the Biblical author. With that assistance, he must then seek to enter imaginatively into the author's response to that situation and to discover not only what were his thoughts, but why he thought them.

Having thus arrived at a psychological insight into what the author himself meant by what he said, the modern commentator can then ask himself whether that meaning had any validity. He may come to the conclusion that the Biblical author was quite wrong; but he will then at least understand why he held that wrong view.

The text will then be significant for him in the same way as a discovered mistake in one's personal thinking is significant. We learn religious truth like all other truth by the method of trial and error. Once we accept the three assumptions that we have shown to underlie any rational method of reinterpretation, we need not be shocked to learn, for example, that, according to the Bible, the extermination of the Canaanites was commanded by God. We would certainly not then be tempted to use such passages as justification of genocide. We would see in them rationalizations of the behavior of the Israelites, which testify to a subconscious guilt-feeling in connection with the treatment of the Canaanites by the original conquerors of the land. And that subconscious sense of guilt at the conquest would thus carry with it the relevant implication that all wars of conquest are evil. Were we to assume that the Bible is a supernatural revelation, and that God actually did demand the extermination of the Canaanites, we would end up in a morass of untenable apologetics.

Nor need we fear that our discovery that

> "The things that you're li'ble
> To read in the Bible,
> They ain't necessarily so"

will deprive the Bible of its value as a source of inspiration and wisdom. The Bible could never have attained that influence which it has manifestly exerted over the minds and institutions of men, if it did not abound in valid insights into the problems of human life. But only through the imaginative reconstruction of the Biblical universe of discourse, and through the psychological interpretation of the authors' meaning are we enabled to uncover those insights and express them in terms of our own universe of discourse. Only thus can the gems of ancient wisdom be dug out of the debris of the ages, polished to their original lustre, and made to sparkle in the light of our modern day.

An Example of How Dr. Kaplan Applies his Method

To illustrate how Dr. Kaplan himself, in his sermons and writings, applied his method to the elucidation of obscure Biblical texts would be of great interest. Considerations of space, however, do not permit us to offer more than a single illustration of his own use of the method of reinterpretation as applied to the Bible. In 1927, Dr. Kaplan began a series of articles (unfortunately never completed) in the *S. A. J. Review*,[2] the modest predecessor of *The Reconstructionist*, on the subject, "The History of Judaism as Reflected in Its Literature." We shall take our illustration from that source. We can only give a few brief excerpts, which show how Dr. Kaplan finds relevance in those provisions of the Holiness Code of the Bible which deal with what, to the casual reader, are meaningless taboos. It should be noted that the articles are not formally exegetical, but historical. Nevertheless, they illustrate how the historical and social context, plus psychological insight, give meaning and relevance to otherwise arid passages of the Torah.

Dr. Kaplan accepts the view of those Bible critics who place the final adoption of the Holiness Code, as it appears in the Bible, in the age of Ezra, although recognizing that many of its specific provisions are centuries older. One reason for this assumption is the discrepancy between some of the laws as stated in the Torah and their equivalents as stated in the Book of Ezekiel. That discrepancy can best be accounted for on the assumption that those rules were still in a state of flux in the 6th century, B. C. E., when Ezekiel lived.

We now quote from the issue of January 20, 1928:

"We must not forget that we are dealing with a mental attitude that is radically different from our own. The ancients were as fearful of committing a *faux pas* in religious etiquette as we are in our social etiquette. Any supernatural being that was known as a god was necessarily holy. When entering into relationship with such a being one had to be free of anything contaminating. To approach a god with anything that might be repellent or offensive to him was a heinous sin. And how were they, the Jews, to live in continual vicinity of the one and only supernatural Being who was the true God, who was the sum and essence of all that was holy? . . .

". . . The laws of holiness are as old as religion itself. Even the crudest and most primitive religions abounded in taboos and prohibitions intended to emphasize the difference between a human being and a god. Likewise among the Israelites of old there existed such taboos and prohibitions since time beyond memory. But the spirit in which the Jews as a people became interested in the laws of holiness was altogether different from the spirit in which those laws were observed among other nations. The routine anthropological studies . . . . fail . . . . to take notice of the tremendous seriousness of purpose which marked the Jews when they applied themselves . . . . to the cultivation of holiness . . . .

"The most important expression of that element of seriousness was the *democratization* of the laws of holiness. Such democratization is far more characteristic of the code in the Torah than of that in the book of Ezekiel. In the code embodied in the Torah the cultivation of holiness is no longer limited to the priesthood. Every Jew is made responsible for the maintenance of the sacred proprieties. Even the laws pertaining to the priesthood were no longer to remain the esoteric knowledge of the priests themselves. By making those laws public, the priests were less likely to become negligent in their observance . . . .

"The distinction between clean and unclean animals, which had undoubtedly been observed by the more religious minded among the ancient Israelites, whether they worshiped their national God only or other gods besides, now acquired new importance.

" 'I am the Lord your God, who have separated you from other races, and therefore you must separate clean animals from unclean,

clean birds from unclean; .... You must be sacred for me, for I the Lord am sacred and I have separated you from other races to make you mine' (Leviticus 20:25-36, translation by Dr. James Moffatt).

It is no longer merely the priest, as in the holiness code of Ezekiel (44:31) but the entire people that is commanded to abstain from eating carcass (Leviticus 11:39-45)...

"Although the new rationale of holiness, which the priestly legislators began to apply to all manner of ritual, social and ethical ordinances, had the effect of intensifying the religious spirit of Jewish life, it had one serious drawback. It tended to destroy differences in spiritual and ethical evaluation. All laws came to possess an equal degree of importance. The commandment not to wear mixtures of linen and wool is seemingly put on an equal footing with the commandment not to bear a grudge against one's neighbor, and the law which forbids eating of the sacrifice on the third day is in close proximity to the greatest ethical principle which commands the Jew to love his neighbor as himself. From the legislators' standpoint, this effacement of differences in value was not intended to lessen in any way the importance of the ethical or social laws, but rather to augment the significance of ceremonial practices.

"But it is futile to argue away the fact that from the popular standpoint the only effect which the effacement of differences in valuation had was to undo the main contribution of the great prophets to the spiritual life of mankind. It negated the tireless strivings of those prophets to get the people to recognize that only the moral law had the right to be regarded as God's law."

Explaining the Method Further

A few notes may help to show how the above passage illustrates the method of reinterpretation we have outlined. By fixing the authorship of the final version of the Holiness Code as occurring in Judea in the early years of the Second Temple, Dr. Kaplan at once clarifies its motivation. Before the great prophets had taught the people to accept the concept of Israel's God as the Creator and sole Lord of the universe, the various ritual taboos, as well as the ethical laws of the code, would not have assumed that spiritual importance which they are given in the Bible. They would have been regarded more as practical precautions to be taken in approaching certain consecrated places and persons than as laws determining the people's relation to an all-powerful and all-knowing God of the world. Above all, in any period before the return from the Babylonian exile and the completion of the Temple as the chosen abode of the one and only God, these laws would not have been felt to be the necessary conditions on which the continued possession of the land depended. That they were so considered in the Holiness Code, Dr. Kaplan shows in a passage we have omitted, which quotes Leviticus 18:24-30.

Note how Kaplan's imaginative insight enables him to interpret the significance of the political, social and cultural situation to which the formulation of the Holiness Code was a response. Although his own scientific outlook on life recognizes the truth that the specific provisions of the laws concerning diet, ritual purity and the like have no more rational basis or intrinsic value than similar taboos among other peoples, he is able to put himself imaginatively into the frame of mind of a religious leader of those days. He realizes that, had he lived in those times, he too would have probably conformed to the prevailing taboos. Having no better explanation of their origin, since no better explanation was available before the developments of modern anthropology and social psychology, he would have ascribed to them a divine origin. Accepting the divine origin of these laws as a premise, he would then have reacted as the author of the Holiness Code reacted to the historical event of the completion of the Temple after the return from the Babylonian exile. This process thus enables him to discover and to explain the radical innovation, the significant *hiddush* or *novum*, in the Holiness Code, which was the specific contribution of its compilers to the religious development of the Jewish people — the "democratization" of the holiness laws that aimed at making of the entire people a "kingdom of priests."

Since, as already pointed out, our selection is taken from a historical essay rather than a sermon or commentary on a Biblical text, the final step in the reinterpretation of the significance of the Holiness Code may not be obvious. That step is, as has been stated, the translation of the principal values and ideas from the Biblical authors' universe of discourse to our own. Nevertheless, the relevant implications are evident if we but note some of the statements in our quotation. Dr. Kaplan recognizes, in the scrupulousness with which the Holiness Code guards against any form of ritual or moral behavior that might offend God, a religious value of supreme importance. The scrupulous observance of the "commandments" of that code enabled men to make the God idea operative in their lives. Ritual and ethical rules of conduct in modern times have a similar religious effect. The recognition of this psychological equivalence makes the Holiness Code of the Bible relevant to modern life.

At the same time, the psychological attitude of the Biblical authors was based on a premise which the modern man cannot accept, however natural it was in their day. We refer to the premise that the traditional taboos were self-revelations of the will of God. Kaplan therefore calls attention to the truth that the attempt of the compilers to raise the importance of ritual regulations, by conferring on them the same degree of authority as moral commandments, inevitably tended to undo the prophetic teachings, that only the moral law can be considered a revelation of God. This leads to the necessary conclusion that, however important ritual may be to religion, it must justify itself ultimately in its effect on human relations. Hence, in our day, the necessity of revaluating Jewish ritual practice from that viewpoint.

The Value of Dr. Kaplan's Method

To appreciate fully the value of Dr. Kaplan's method of reinterpretation of the Biblical text, we must understand its place in the Reconstructionist movement of which Dr. Kaplan is the founder. To reconstruct Judaism, in a way that shall maintain the unity and integrity of the Jewish people and, at the same time, permit an adjustment to the conditions of modern life that endanger Jewish survival, calls for a faith in the dynamic possibilities of Jewish tradition. Unless Judaism can change with the times, and yet manifest an identifiable spiritual continuity, it is lost. That is the situation which sent Dr. Kaplan in quest of a key to an understanding of Jewish tradition, consonant with the best in modern thought, and useful in the solution of modern problems. The method of reinterpretation which we have here described is that key. His philosophic intelligence, motivated by his passionate love of the Jewish people and Judaism discovered that key, and taught two generations of disciples how to use it. He has himself applied it to the redefinition of all the main concepts of Judaism: God, humanity, Israel and Torah. And still we are only at the beginning of that reinterpretive and reconstructive task which must be completed if the Judaism of our modern era shall be worthy of preceding ages of Jewish religious and cultural development. We have not yet, for example, produced a single Bible commentary that is based on the reinterpretive approach. That is a project which we should like to see inaugurated with the guidance, and under the direction, of Dr. Kaplan.

Notes

[1] M. M. Kaplan, *Judaism As A Civilization*, Macmillan, New York, 1934, p. 386.
[2] Society for Advancement of Judaism, New York.

MORDECAI M. KAPLAN'S THEORY OF RELIGION[1]

By Harold C. Weisberg

The proposition, that any important inquiry must be cognizant of the full dimensions of the problem-context to which it is directed, is well illustrated in the religious thought of Mordecai M. Kaplan. While others were going through the motions of theological adaptation, he took his age seriously and effected a major religious revolution in Judaism. Alone among his contemporaries, he did not merely make grudging concessions to the scientific enterprise; in fact, he welcomed its application to the field of Jewish religion. To be sure, there are those who feel that Dr. Kaplan's thought is not sufficiently naturalist. However, it is undeniable that his major categories reflect basic naturalist assumptions and the willingness to follow the path of unfettered rational and empirical inquiry. It may well be that future generations will honor Dr. Kaplan more for the general approach of his position than for any specific theory expounded in it. Surely, he has radically transformed the entire universe of discourse in Jewish religious thought and laid the foundations for any future naturalist reading of Jewish religion.

Theory As An Instrument of Reconstruction

To understand the nature of the revolution initiated by Dr. Kaplan, as well as the specific theories of religion he offers, it is necessary to view them in the context of the culture in which he lives and of the religious problems which dominated his maturing and mature years. Only then can we appreciate the value of his general theory of religion and comprehend the revolutionary character of his thought.

This is true not only because of the obvious fact that all inquiry begins with "problem irritation," but more significantly, in this case, because Dr. Kaplan himself has viewed his life work as an effort to respond creatively to the various intellectual and institutional challenges confronting the Judaism of his day. It is noteworthy that Dr. Kaplan refuses to be pushed into any of the conventional pigeon holes of academic classification, preferring instead to be known as an ideologian or ideologist.[2] That is, all of his work has been pervaded by a deep concern with ideology and is of a decidedly programmatic character. Dr. Kaplan is not an academic thinker who seeks to clarify problems in a given field through the making of fine distinctions or the formulation of novel theories. His ideas are truly instruments, seeking to reconstruct the civilization of the Jewish people. As such, the background of his thought clarifies his various positions and affords a broad perspective for judgment and evaluation.

Nowhere, perhaps, is this fundamental function more obvious than in the field of religion, which, of course, is a major concern of Dr. Kaplan's. It will be seen that he directs his attention to problems which others were either too insensitive to recognize or too timid to approach openly. His very vocabulary, the semantics of his religious discourse, indicates his deep awareness of the fundamental problems of his time. Dr. Kaplan is very much a contemporary. He not only sees and senses the problems of his age but, what is of greater importance, he correctly evaluates the nature of the challenge to religion in his age and offers directives for transforming it. His religious philosophy begins with analysis and culminates in programmatic reconstruction.

The Context and the Climate

Dr. Kaplan's primary categories in the general field of religion seem to be greatly influenced by two major intellectual forces: the growth in his day of anthropological and sociological studies of religion and the corresponding development of non-supernaturalist versions of religion. That there were other shaping forces will not be denied, but in the construction of his particular theories of religion these two trends contribute most. In responding to these forces, Dr. Kaplan becomes cognizant of a host of religious problems and possible solutions, in the areas of worship, ritual, the role of tradition, the function of religion and the like. From these disciplines he also takes much of his vocabulary of religion and his first principles of religious analysis.

In addition Dr. Kaplan has always sought to relate his thinking to the social problems confronting religion in a highly industrialized society. He reckons with the rapid adoption of religious functions by more efficacious secular institutions, and the assumption by the religious institutions of new social functions which were quite unlike any they had ever undertaken before.

Of course, the specific problems of Jewish religion, particularly those resulting from its being the religion of a minority in America, are sharply pointed up in Dr. Kaplan's thought. Certainly, too, the rise of Zionism, with its emphasis on peoplehood, on the one hand, and of Reform Judaism, with its insistence on the urgency of change, on the other, are also seminal influences.

Our analysis of these influences is not presented in the order of their occurrence in Dr. Kaplan's thought perspective. The exact sequence which Dr. Kaplan followed in developing his position and the order of problem awareness are not our concern. Looking back over the corpus of his opinion, the areas mentioned above seem to exercise most influence and form "cornerstone categories" in his thinking. Let us then examine more closely the twin threats of intellectual critique and replacement of function, which affected both Judaism and Christianity in the last half century or so, and the complex of problems exclusive to the Jewish religion of the corresponding period.

The Challenge of the New Sciences and New Social Conditions

The formative period of Dr. Kaplan's "religious and theological awareness" can be described as the "golden age" of anthropological and sociological studies of primitive and other non-Western cultures. Earlier challenges to the Western religions had come in the form of astronomical discoveries, critiques of medieval arguments for the existence of God, or geological and biological findings concerning the age and evolution of man and the universe. In the first decades of this century the challenges were expressed in studies of comparative religion, which cast grave doubts upon the claims of the Western religions to exclusive supernatural origin or ethical and religious superiority. Certainly the earlier challenges were still an issue which had not been met, nor was the original Darwinist controversy at an end; but the freshest and boldest attack, and the one which seems to have impressed Dr. Kaplan most, took shape when the implications of the anthropological study of religion were fully realized.

A brief look at the period 1885-1920 will suffice to indicate the strength of that challenge. The climate of anthropological and sociological discourse at the turn of the nineteenth century was still heavy with "social Darwinist" influence.[3] Studies of primitive and other cultures had been undertaken to demonstrate that the evolution of human societies and of biological species followed a similar course. John Fiske, the great interpreter of Darwin, still enjoyed much popularity, and even the "hurdy gurdy monotony" of Mr. Spencer echoed on until the beginnings of the First World War. Tylor, Morgan, Westermarck, and others had completed, or were in process of producing important primary studies in the fields of religion and culture. But other approaches to these fields were undertaken. Durkheim, Maret, Lowie and others were embarking on major investigations which went beyond "social Darwinist" analysis. The rediscovery of the primitive not only became source material for the earlier "social Darwinist" approach to cultural evolution, but involved unavoidable comparisons of Western and non-Western religious forms, and revealed interesting correlations and continuities between the "primitive" and the "civilized" religions. A growing suspicion was at hand that the religions of the West had no valid claim to divine preference, and might well be just another manifestation of a rather universal trait of human cultures.

This will explain Dr. Kaplan's overstatement that

"The chief opposition to the traditional conception of God .... arises not from the scientific approach to the study of nature in general, or even man in general."[4]

So great is the influence of the anthropological and historical critique that Dr. Kaplan's concern with other intellectual challenges is minimal. He is not much concerned with the implications of Newtonian or later physics; nor is he much interested in positivist and pragmatic theories of meaning which indicate that the problem of a spatio-temporal deity is logically meaningless. That he is not unaware of them is evidenced by his complete renunciation of a spatio-temporal deity, but his primary concerns are sociological and generally "biological" in the broad sense. The overwhelming problems for Dr. Kaplan are those created by the undeniable implications of the newer social sciences which dealt with the relations of religions to their cultural matrices. Thus he writes,

"The traditional conception of God is challenged by history, anthropology, and psychology; these prove that beliefs similar to those found in the Bible about God arise among all peoples at a certain stage of mental and social development, and pass through a process of evolution which is entirely conditioned by the developments of other elements in their civilization."[5]

How great a role sociological and anthropological themes play in Dr. Kaplan's theory of religion will be apparent when, in a later section, we analyze his specific propositions. For the present it suffices to show that they are the dominant instruments of his religious enterprise and that they offered a sharp challenge to traditional religion. We can also see how much of a twentieth century man Dr. Kaplan really is when we note his almost complete identification with the dominant philosophical direction of his age, although, at times, he unfortunately tends to a teleological vitalism.

Closely allied to the force of the anthropological studies is the influence of scientific Bible study on the age and thought of Mordecai M. Kaplan. I class this discipline with the others for, in addition to its own archaeological and philological tools, it learned much from comparative religion and cultural anthropology. Dr. Kaplan was directly influenced by personal contact with the critic Arnold Ehrlich; but, in addition, the themes of Bible criticism were generally very much in the air.[6] Cautious as well as extravagant hypotheses contributed to the reduction of the already diminished area of "religious truths"; and of the "debunking" of the Bible there was no end in popular circles. Dr. Kaplan's religious thought is, obviously, greatly influenced by his attitude toward the Bible, which not only forms the source material of his cultural analysis of Jewish religion, but (as is discussed elsewhere in this volume) serves as the basis for a fruitful theory of reinterpretation taken in conjunction with his broad civilizational approach.

The intellectual challenges to religion are matched by the institutional, and Dr. Kaplan's awareness of the latter is no less acute than of the former. He clearly recognizes that what he has termed "the modern economic order" generates as much trouble for religion as do the new intellectual ideas. He notes the effects of a scarcity economy, the rise of the labor movement, and increased leisure time on the usual forms of institutional religious expression. He is also alive to the Marxist challenge to the fundamental premises of traditional religion. In sum, he has been quick to see that competing schemes of salvation are available to modern man, and that these important alternatives to the conventional religious modes of salvation merit serious consideration.[7]

The Naturalist Response

The other side of the religious "condition" of Dr. Kaplan's age lies in the field of creative religious reconstruction, which was taking place in two areas; the modernist revision of Christianity, and the non-supernaturalist constructions of undenominational religions. It is not at all surprising that the successive blows of rationalist criticism, biological discovery and anthropological leveling would give sensitive thinkers cause for serious reexamination of the particular traditions with which they were associated, or for new directions in religious theory and function. The former role was assumed by the modernists, and the latter by a number of significant non-denominational thinkers. It is not important for us to outline the directions which these movements took except to point out that, on the whole, they attempted to make peace with the new intellectual ideas and institutions that threatened traditional religion, and that they went much further than the mild evolutionary efforts of a McCosh or an Abbot. What is of paramount importance is that Dr. Kaplan is the only *Jewish* religious thinker to attempt for Jewish religion what others have sought to do for Christianity. In fact, he surpasses these thinkers in his uncompromising stand on the side of the science of the century, and in his acceptance of its unavoidable implications.

As the only naturalist oriented thinker in Jewish religion, Dr. Kaplan has gained much from the efforts of his non-Jewish contemporaries. Not that this or that individual reconstruction has influenced him, but the very effort itself to create meaningful religion outside the framework of traditional categories has been a major stimulus. The extent and limits of Dr. Kaplan's naturalism will emerge as the discussion proceeds, but his fundamental participation on the side of the naturalists is undeniable, and can readily be seen from his forthright stand on the relations between philosophy of religion and theology. "Religious philosophy," he says, "approaches the idea of God independently of any tradition, and seeks to determine the objective truth, as far as it is possible to achieve it, with regard to God and His relation to man and the world. It does not recognize any authority other than that of the thinking, experiencing human mind." Further "religious philosophy itself must be based on the results of a descriptive study of religion," and must "harmonize with the rest of human experience both historical and scientific." Theology, which concerns itself with the interpretation or reinterpretation of a particular religious tradition, must function "in the light of the objective truth ascertained in religious philosophy."[8] Missing here, happily, is the attempt, so often encountered, to employ reason in a circumscribed context, denying it access to those regions where crucial doctrine awaits critical examination. Dr. Kaplan is open and specific. He goes where the inquiry bids him follow. We may disagree at times with his interpretation of the directions which reason offers, or with his equation of aspects of some human cultures with universal human traits; but he is willing, nay eager, to pursue a course of reasoned inquiry. This is his finest contribution to Jewish religion and it wears especially well in an age of religious absolutism and theological obscurantism.

The Crisis in Jewish Religious Life

The difficulties of traditional religion, to which we have already alluded, can in the main be said to apply to Christianity as well as to Judaism. Both suffered from the demands of an all-encompassing scientific search for reliable knowledge and from the changing social order which secularized so many functions formerly performed by religious institutions. There were, however, other problems confined exclusively to Judaism which posed major difficulties for the traditional religious way of life. Jewish religion, as part of general Jewish identification, was, in the United States, weakened to a considerable extent by the powerful trends of indifference and assimilation. The gap between the Judaism of immigrant parents and the social patterns of their children who were growing up in an American environment was not really being closed by any prevailing theology, institutionalized religion, or secular agency. Even Reform theology, which was supposed to be the best formulation of Jewish religion, was unable to stem the tide of assimilation and the general breakdown of Jewish religious concern and observance. With the exception of a few notable institutional achievements during a good part of the past fifty years, such as the founding of large theological seminaries and synagogues, Jewish religion in the United States was in a state of general decline.

The widespread indifference to Jewish religion is not, of course, unrelated to the general disrepute of the theological theories associated with the traditional religions. Even Reform Jewry, more progressive theologically than the other Jewish religious denominations, failed to respond significantly to the intellectual demands of the age. Its theology was set largely in the older framework of German Reform theology and, with the exception of Kohler's major work,[9] it consisted for the most part of the same kind of incipient neo-Hegelianism that was characteristic of most run-of-the-mill Protestant theology. The appalling state of Jewish theology in America is best understood if we note that, with the exception of Kohler's work and the theological essays of Schechter,[10] no significant theological formulations were made until the publication of Mordecai M. Kaplan's *Judaism as a Civilization* (1935).

What was occupying the interest of the better Jewish minds in America was, at one and the same time, a blessing and a curse. The more creative Jewish efforts were in the field of scholarship. The rediscovery of the Jewish past undeniably provided indispensable tools of great value for any approach to Judaism. Dr. Kaplan, in fact, realizes fully the importance of such an enterprise, and notes its intrinsic value as well as its usefulness for Jewish theology. Yet this great scholarly effort in America, which produced the works of Schechter, Ginzberg, Lauterbach, Kohut, Kohler, Morgenstern and many others, and generated the publication of such scholarly journals as the *Jewish Quarterly Review* and the *Hebrew Union College Annual*, was also a self-deluding enterprise. For, as close examination will reveal, there was little if any effort expended in translating the discoveries and creative hypotheses of these scholarly undertakings into theological attitudes. In fact, there developed a great compartmentalization in Jewish scholarship by which discoveries about the Jewish past were kept from association with problems concerning the Jewish present or future. The rich and varied historical enterprise was in reality, for all its drama and potential life-giving energy, but another strictly academic discipline unrelated to the realities and spiritual needs of Jewish living.

Needless to remark, Dr. Kaplan is the only one who, seriously and systematically, has applied the findings of modern scholarship in Judaism to the theological problems of our time. A good part of his life as teacher, homiletic interpreter and theologian has been devoted to the application of Jewish scholarship to the host of theological difficulties facing Jewish religion.

There are two other problem areas in Jewish religious life which have confronted a sensitive thinker like Dr. Kaplan. One is the condition of the synagogue, the other, that of Jewish ritual observance. In the former case, the synagogues have lost many of the religious functions and have been seeking opportunistically, in patchwork fashion, to replace those functions with auxiliary social services. Lacking a point of view on general service to the community, they have proceeded to harbor a strange mélange of activities under the synagogue roof, justified only on the premise that a synagogue is worthwhile so long as people use it for any kind of function.

In respect to synagogue worship the situation is no better. The service has become too often either a theatrical spectacle performed by rabbi, choir and organ for the entertainment of the congregation, or an incomprehensible hubbub of chant and song, confusing and meaningless to the second generation American Jew who has not been educated in the Orthodox tradition. Even the middle-of-the-road Conservatives, who have sought to modify Jewish service to some extent, have tampered only with the form; even they have not avoided the spectatorship which public worship in large synagogues almost unavoidably creates. Even when the services are esthetically enjoyable, the content of the prayers is often irritating to the minds of reasonably intelligent and educated people. Prayers for the reinstitution of the sacrificial cult, texts implying inequality of men and women, and affirmations of belief in physical resurrection are among the elements of the services that are jarring to the intelligent. God, who is addressed as an object of worship, is conceived in such anthropomorphic, or else in such platitudinous terms that most prayers of petition or praise of attributes offend the sensibilities of not a few worshipers. As for the preaching, that too is not afire with a meaningful message. Too often it is concerned with the commonplace laudation of virtue, too rarely does it address itself to the urgent theological and religious problems of the hour.

Jewish ritual observance has waned and attempts to rekindle interest have failed. Even rationalized appeals for a return to ritual, based on a "liberalized" reading of *halakhah*, do not bear fruit. Reform for a long time has been as intransigently opposed to traditional ritual usage as Orthodoxy is to innovation and change.

Only recently have some elements in Reform begun to reconsider their older positions on ritual, and this to a certain extent is the result of the influence of Dr. Kaplan's thought.[11] Ritual has long remained the weakest link in the chain of tradition; it has wavered between a sterile traditionalism or halakhic formalism, on the one hand, and a planless, and irresponsible latitudinarianism, on the other. For at least a good part of the half century just concluded, no significant proposals have been forthcoming which would indicate a methodological and intellectual tool for the satisfactory redevelopment of a healthy attitude towards ritual in terms of sensitive participation and group continuity.

The Effect of Reform and Jewish Nationalism on Dr. Kaplan's Thought

In all these problem areas Dr. Kaplan has leaned heavily on the instruments which the particular philosophy of religion to which he subscribes have offered him, but precisely in the field of Jewish religion he has been stimulated by two forces in addition to the anthropological, psychological and social disciplines mentioned previously. One was the license for revolt which Reform gave to Dr. Kaplan, or to any other independent thinker for that matter. Quarrel as he does with Reform theology and religion, Dr. Kaplan repeatedly praises its forthright stand and clear exposition of its position. From Reform he gains his right to demur, and perhaps too the very basic critical attitude to much of Jewish religion. He agrees with the Reformists in many areas, but, as we shall presently observe, differs on the decisive issues of the nature of religion and its relation to the Jewish people.[12]

The other great force is the emergence of Jewish nationalism and, more precisely, the thought of some of its leading exponents, both religious and secular. In the religious group the historical school, with its great effort to recapture the Jewish past, has excited Dr. Kaplan's imagination. From what was to be misnamed Conservative Judaism he takes the stress on *Kelal Yisrael*, He is much in debt to the Conservative insistence that the context of the people and the instrument of the people cannot be ignored in any discussion of Jewish religion. The happy marriage of this proposition with a group theory of religion gleaned from his philosophy of religion forms the major part of Dr. Kaplan's theory of Jewish religion.

Of equal influence is the nationalist thinking of the Zionist movement which, during the first half of this century, rose to its greatest heights. Particularly influential was the thought of Ahad Ha-am whose concern for the spiritual renaissance of the Jewish people made a permanent mark on Dr. Kaplan's consciousness. The concept of Jewish peoplehood was later to loom very large in Dr. Kaplan's thought.[13] This concept together with his Conservative concern for *Kelal Yisrael* and his group theory of religion, form the chief components of his structure of a reconstructed Jewish religious ideology.

Dr. Kaplan's Critique of Reform and Conservatism

Viewed against the background of an age which repudiated the intellectual structure of traditional religion and undermined its social function, Dr. Kaplan's religious philosophy emerges as a grand plan for total religious reconstruction. He was faced with the overwhelming problem of reconstructing Jewish religion without sacrificing canons of reason and intelligibility, rendering the religious significant in the framework of an industrial society, and preserving in it more than a faint resemblance to dominant themes in traditional Jewish religion. The difficulties of such an approach are illumined by the criticism of his opponents. On the one hand, he is opposed because, it is argued, he fails to reckon, in his naturalist approach, with features of the religious life which supposedly only a supernaturalist approach illumines. On the other, he is able so satisfactorily to translate Jewish religious values into the naturalist idiom that his critics declare the successful reconstruction to be outside the ken of genuine Jewish religion. To maintain intellectual honesty, ethical awareness and esthetic sensitivity, and still be true to the spirit and dynamic force of the tradition are the marks of Dr. Kaplan's religious philosophy and theology.

Dr. Kaplan's first efforts lie, logically, in the evaluation of the existing status of Jewish religion. He directs his critique not only against Jewish traditionalism, but as well against the later post-emancipation attempts at reworking the tradition. There is no point in our examining Dr. Kaplan's opposition to Jewish traditionalism, or even to the neo-Orthodox version of Judaism. Suffice it to say that, for the most part, he shares much of the Reform criticism of the Orthodox position and, in addition, offers the kind of critique which he also levels against the other two major groupings. In sum, he opposes the neo-Orthodox for resting Jewish religion on the fact of Sinaitic revelation, and he is critical of it for its unfortunate equation, though on a different level from Reform, of Judaism and Jewish religion.[14]

Of particular interest to us is the Kaplanian critique of Reform and Conservatism. Orthodoxy and neo-Orthodoxy, in the final analysis, are theoretically and practically re-wordings and restatements of a tradition they assume to be unalterable. Obviously, every challenge must be resolved in favor of tradition. Conservatism and, to a greater degree, Reform, however, claim to go beyond mere restatement and indicate some desire for genuine adaptation and transformation of the tradition. Since these are increasingly powerful institutions and movements in American-Jewish religion, Dr. Kaplan properly inquires into their value to the American Jewish community.

Dr. Kaplan levels many telling criticisms at both movements, but for our purposes we must limit our discussion to his critique of their implicit or at times explicit theories of Jewish religion.

He is apparently less critical of the Reform than of the Conservative position. He classes many Conservative theologians with those who tend "to blur the sharp outlines of the traditional ideology by surrounding it with a fog of words."[15] Reform on the other hand, while its theology is inadequate, nonetheless is clear and consistent.[16] Each position has some important features which are extremely valuable; yet as whole systems they are found wanting, since some factors negate the value of others. Reform thought fails for a number of reasons. The first is that it assumes the Jews to have been ahead of any other people in relation to the God-idea.

"The fundamental fallacy into which Reformism is forced by its habit of playing up the God-idea as the essence of Judaism is that of crediting the Jewish people as a whole with conscious self-dedication to a conception of God, which only its foremost thinkers were capable of achieving."[17]

Not only is Reform theology, as expressed, say, in Kaufmann Kohler's *Jewish Theology*, in error in ascribing such a high level of God-consciousness to the Jewish people as a whole, but, in addition, it fails to realize that Jewish religion, like all other religions, does not consist of a series of intellectual assents to universal propositions about the nature of God. Kohler, for example, so overemphasizes the centrality of the God-idea as the essence of Judaism (which incidentally he virtually equates with Jewish religion) that

"every aspect of Jewish life must justify itself by its relation to the God-idea, and God comes to be a hypostatized abstraction moving in a vacuum."[18]

The "vacuum" deity and the general Reform view which holds the intellectual affirmation of such a deity to be the essence of Jewish religion are indicative of yet another, perhaps the most painful shortcoming. This is Reform's inability to see Jewish religion as a part of Jewish civilization, which for Dr. Kaplan is a cardinal sin. Jewish religion, as conceived by Reform theology, "comes to be a series of general or universal teachings about God and man, apart from the specific social realities of the Jewish people."[19] Further, says Dr. Kaplan,

"The entire program of Reform is based on a misconception of the very nature of a religion like that of the Jewish people. Such a religion never existed apart from the people that evolved it and cannot be treated as a system of ideas and practices which might be fostered by a religio-philosophical group."[20]

For Dr. Kaplan, the essential failure of Reform religion lies in its inability to view Judaism as a whole, and Jewish religion as one manifestation of an entire civilization. To make a concept of God *the* differentia of Jewish identification is to conceive of Jewish religion as a soul without a body.[21]

It should be noted that Dr. Kaplan's dissatisfaction with the Reform notion of God-centricity is not to be construed as constituting a general criticism of all positions which make a concept of God central to a given religion. The brunt of his attack (outside of his specific opposition to the nature of the God concept offered by Reform, which, in the case of Kohler is "merely a rehash, not even warmed over, of medieval verbalism . . .")[22] comes in his disapproval of the intellectual abstractionism which, for Reform, constitutes the manner in which God awareness seems to emerge, and of the consequent divorce of this kind of religion from the rest of the group life. As we shall see, Dr. Kaplan's fundamental religious dictum is the inseparableness of religion and culture.

So much for Reform. Conservatism fares no better, although for other reasons. Dr. Kaplan neatly sums up the Conservative situation in this way; "The main weakness of Conservatism is that, in a situation in which there is no way of telling what the extremes are, it makes a principle of moderateness."[23] It is also possessed of a vaccillation which is accentuated by a "vague sentimentalism which hankers after a residue of Jewish life without knowing exactly why."[24] Viewed either as the "left wing of neo-Orthodoxy" or as "right wing" of Reform, Conservatism's greatest failing lies in its all-pervading confusion and unprincipled compromise. Dr. Kaplan holds up a number of thinkers in this school to considerable ridicule, viewing their work as "hybrid theology which would not be recognized by the ancient authorities as true, nor by cultivated men and women of the present as answering their needs."[25] He does not criticize Conservatism for failure to recognize the social context of religion; rather he opposes it because, failing adequately to understand the tradition which it inherits, it offers apologetics in place of solutions to genuine problems. Whatever kernel of religious theory lies hidden in the rhetoric of Conservative theology, it cannot do justice to the implications of its assumptions. It has no reliable criteria with which to evaluate the residue of earlier civilizational developments nor does it possess the imagination and ingenuity necessary to create new forms in the framework of a changed society.

The Rejection of Supernaturalism

Whatever his particular dissatisfactions with existing Jewish religious forms, Dr. Kaplan directs his major criticism against the basis of all of them, namely, the varieties of supernaturalism and consequent spatio-temporal God conceptions. Even though his primary dissatisfactions with Reform and Conservative religious thought are not expressed in terms of his anti-supernaturalism, and despite his praise of some Reform attempts at revising the conception of God, implicit throughout is an anti-supernaturalist critique, which emerges explicitly in later discussions. Dr. Kaplan's uniqueness is well evidenced in his open and clear-cut break with supernaturalism, and in his creative efforts to follow through the implications of such a break for possible future versions of Jewish religion. "Supernatural religion," writes Dr. Kaplan, "is the astrology and alchemy stage of religion,"[26] The only way in which Jewish religion can satisfactorily adjust to the modern world is by abandoning supernaturalism. Thus,

"To survive the present crisis, the Jewish religion will have to transform itself from an other-worldly religion offering to conduct the individual to life eternal through the agency of the traditional Torah, which is regarded as supernaturally revealed, into a religion which can help Jews attain this-worldly salvation."[27]

Courageously and openly he repeats the theme that Jewish religion, cast in the supernaturalist mold, cannot creatively survive.

Dr. Kaplan's rejection of supernaturalism is complete and extends as well to the supernatural God-idea. Not a few religionists deny the specific supernaturalist claims of a given historical religion, but they often affirm either that all religions are searching for a God who actually exists as a spatio-temporal Being, or maintain an argument for such a God on other grounds. It is true that Dr. Kaplan can be accused of hedging in his naturalism with categories of the "trans-natural" or "extra-experiential," which, when carried to their logical conclusions, commit him to some process or force inexplicable in naturalist terms and operating over and above nature.[28] Yet his deep anti-supernaturalism is everywhere evident. Perhaps it would be better to term him an anti-supernaturalist than a strict naturalist, for his vitalism is so pervasive and "extra" teleological categories are often introduced.[29] Yet with a few *tikunei soferim* (editorial changes) he may be converted to a stricter naturalist position.

It is also important to realize that Dr. Kaplan's opposition to theories of divine origin stems as much from their inability to do justice to the facts of religious life as from their logical and empirical disqualifications. True religion cannot ignore the findings of modern ethnology. A supernaturalist reading of religion fails to take into account all that the social sciences can tell us about religions and their cultural contexts, and misses completely the human factor in religious development. To assert that the interactions of a particular people with a particular environment are not the source of its religious institutions and ideas, and to postulate some extra-natural cause for the existence of religion, is for Dr. Kaplan the essence of *avodah zarah*— idolatry. It is to naturalist religion what idol worship was to Israelite and Jewish monotheism, a regression, a throwback, a product inferior to the more enlightened form.

The Basis of Religious Reconstruction

Granting, then, a complete rejection of supernaturalism, upon what basis can one found Jewish religion? Dr. Kaplan, in a sense, converts the facts of his religious doubts into values. That is, he rebuilds Jewish religion with the very instruments that bring destruction to its more traditional forms.[30] "The initial and hardest step in the process of religious adjustment at the present time," says Dr. Kaplan, "is to grow accustomed to the idea that it is possible to have religion without subscribing to the supernatural character of its origin."[31] Or again, "*Only religious fundamentalists and unimaginative pedants would insist upon limiting the name and conception of God to the God of supernatural revelation.*"[32] There is, according to Dr. Kaplan, a vast area as yet unrecognized by most Jewish religious thinkers, which offers tremendous possibilities for the reconstruction of Jewish religion on an entirely new base. It lies not in metaphysical schemes nor even in ethical reorganization. It is to be found in the study of man as a socio-cultural animal. The future of Jewish religion lies in an understanding of the nature of the adjustments men seek to their natural and cultural environments. Religion will then become part of the very nature of existence, as universal and undeniable as the "will to live" itself.

Dr. Kaplan's specific theory of religion begins with the assumption that religion is a manifestation of the general will to live. "In other words, for human beings the will to live becomes the will to salvation, to the achievement of the good life."[33] "*Religion is thus man's conscious quest for salvation or the achievement of his human destiny.*"[34] All men seek to find patterns of meaning and roads to salvation in the various environments they inhabit. Religion is part of man's adaptation to the world, of his adjustment to life. "Man seeks the good" can also be translated, "man seeks self-fulfilment," or religion.

Religion as the manifestation of the will to self-fulfillment and salvation is a universal phenomenon of man's existence. It is as much a part of the acculturation process as self-awareness. In fact, just as *"man becomes aware of himself as a person engaged in a struggle against dangers and difficulties, he also becomes cognizant of the help of a Power or powers to conquer obstacles."*[35]

The awareness of one's own personality is almost co-extensive with a similar awareness of forces which help shape the direction and future of that personality. Man's quest for salvation inevitably leads to a recognition of forces which sustain him and powers that help him. First conceived dimly, perhaps enmeshed in a network of magic and superstition, clearer lines emerge, and in a variety of outstandingly diverse ways men conceive of the powers that aid them as deities or divinities of some sort. "In time," says Dr. Kaplan, "man's capacity to generalize, which is itself a manifestation of the will to live, led him to conceive of God as a universal God. This is the correlative of man's will to live in its most generalized form, in the same way as the individual deities or divine beings are the correlatives of his specific hungers or wants."[36]

It can be seen from the foregoing not only that religion is a manifestation of the will to live but also that it involves, in one way or another, a conception of God. Dr. Kaplan, however, is not advocating a general theory of cultural evolution in which vague awareness of powers becomes in a later stage polytheism, and inexorably moves on to monotheism. He is only asserting the generic traits of religions and he finds, from his reading of human cultures, that such religions, though assuming many forms, have some kind of God conception. The conceptions of God which are associated with the so-called higher religions are only refinements of a general process, aided by the particular colorations of the culture in which they emerge. This leads to two fundamental assumptions:

(a) The will to salvation is always expressed in some cultural idiom, and thus religion is inseparable from a given culture context;

(b) Religions do not begin as intellectual exercises concerned with propounding universal propositions; they stem from the culture context and are expressions of the dominant life values of the culture.

This latter point clarifies Dr. Kaplan's strong opposition to Reform and points up the particular aspects of his cultural theory of religion to which we now turn. "Gods," he writes, "must be believed in before they can be beheld, imagined, or proved to exist."[37] Intellectualization of religion is a late, very late step. Tradition and even its many critics have confused the issue. One must not fail to distinguish the *belief* in God from a particular *conception* of God. Belief in God is the "basic substance of religion and is a constant factor in it," while, on the other hand, the conception of God "is a cultural formulation of that belief."[38] Religion cannot be thought up, or manufactured, without reference to a cultural matrix to which it applies and from which it in fact stems.

Religion is then, for Dr. Kaplan, unthinkable without a cultural origin and referent. True, indeed, that the quest for salvation is a general manifestation of all human life, but there is no unstructured quest. One's culture, one's people color and shape that quest, and give it the identifiable features which make it unique to a particular society or civilization. All men seek salvation, but no man seeks it outside a cultural frame.

Dr. Kaplan is particularly clear on this point and wants no ambiguities to appear.

"That is why, though the quest for salvation is common to all mankind, the particular values that constitute one's salvation and the particular method by which one seeks it, is determined by the civilization of the people to which one belongs. This accounts for the existence of the various religions of mankind. *Every religion is an aspect of a particular civilization. It is that aspect of a civilization which aims to render it worthwhile, both for the group as a whole and for each individual in it.*"[39]

This, in capsule form, is the essence of Dr. Kaplan's philosophy of religion. Its rich meanings can readily be seen to apply to Jewish religion.

Some Questions About Religious Reconstruction

This view of the origins of religions quite obviously breaks with prevailing opinion in Jewish theology. No act of supernatural revelation is needed to account for religious phenomena, nor is religion to be compounded of metaphysical first principles or ethical absolutes which require creedal assent. Religion, in Dr. Kaplan's sense, is natural to man and is part of the very life adjustment process. By so viewing religion, he clearly meets the criticisms which are usually leveled against the supernaturalist position. That position represents to him a past stage in the religious outlook. He now proposes to build religion on an entirely new foundation which, to his way of thinking, is apparent from the nature of human existence itself.

However, it is clear that the promulgation of a theory of cultural origins is by itself insufficient to account for the role of religions in cultures, nor does it necessarily provide the materials for a theory of the functions of religion for our own time. In addition, a naturalistic approach has problems of its own which, while certainly not of the kind hurled at traditionalist points of view, are such that they require, nonetheless, serious attention and clarification. Dr. Kaplan must go beyond the formulation of the general proposition that religions are man-made, and be prepared to answer questions like the following:

(a) What is the nature of the "religious"? That is, what are the generic traits of those institutions and behavior patterns which we classify as "religions" or the "religious"; and what distinguishes them from other cultural institutions?

(b) What is the relationship of a religion to the broader cultural matrix which it inhabits? What role does a religion play in a culture?

(c) Granting that the above questions can be answered in terms of a specific theory, then (1) What is the function of religion (particularly Jewish religion) in our own time? (2) What relationship does this function bear to the older functions? (3) What does the contemporary function of religion have in common with preceeding ones to enable it to maintain some kind of historical continuity and to merit the same adjectival labeling?

It is true that these questions apply, at least in part, to more traditional viewpoints, but they are particularly significant in Dr. Kaplan's case. Any theory which breaks with tradition must be able to show on what grounds it proposes to continue forms of religious expression that in some way resemble older forms. Dr. Kaplan must be able to indicate the continuities as well as the discontinuities with tradition and provide a rationale for both. Secondly, we cannot overlook Dr. Kaplan's ideological interests. We have mentioned repeatedly that his primary interests are not academic. He is more concerned with changing the course of Jewish group life than with proposing a theory of religion *per se*. A theory of religion, for him, must perform an important function in the effort of the Jewish people to live a creative life. As such, we shall soon see the great programmatic role which Dr. Kaplan provides for Jewish religion in the renaissance of the Jewish people.

Unfortunately, his great commitment to the end of cultural reconstruction often blurs distinctions between religious and other cultural forms. Despite his vehement opposition to the equation of Jewish religion and Judaism, he not infrequently sins on the other side by making Jewish culture into Jewish religion. In addition, his implied assertion, that the drive for self-fulfillment is more or less the social analogue of physical drives which motivate behavior, runs the risk of equating all cultural life with religion in that, in a very definite sense, all cultural forms are manifestations of a quest for human self-realization. There are times when clear distinctions between religious and other cultural institutions are made, but there are others when religion and culture are almost synonymous. Finally, the last set of questions must be faced by any position which seeks a new base for religion. We should know what religion is supposed to do for human life in our own time.

Dr. Kaplan is quite cognizant of these problems, and the greater part of his positive religious theorizing is devoted to answering questions like those we have just raised. Unfortunately, he does not always stress exactly the same roles for religion. Nonetheless, his position is quite clear, and consistent enough so that definite lines of thought can easily be noted. Most probably the occasional lack of consistency is more the result of a shift of emphasis than a logical lapse. For it is demonstrable that, in different works, Dr. Kaplan has stressed — at times — one feature of his religious theory over another. Not that the varied religious functions are contradictory, but that they play different roles.

The Three Roles of Religion

Roughly we may classify these roles and functions into three closely interrelated groupings:

(a) Religion makes one aware of the essential worthwhileness of his cultural life pattern, its history and climacteric experience. It manifests the values inherent in a given culture and attempts to embody them in a human conduct. (We shall refer to this theory as the "sancta theory.")

(b) Religion "fortifies the collective consciousness" and represents the "most intimate phase of the group consciousness."[40] It is a mode of adaptation to the group and makes one deeply aware of his membership in and involvement with his particular people. It sensitizes one to the realization that his personal destiny is bound up with the destiny of his group. (We shall refer to this theory as the "group theory.")

(c) Religion seeks to satisfy our most distinctively human needs. It endeavors to supply the spiritual necessities which every human being demands. Religion provides "morale" and courage in meeting the problems of existence. (We shall refer to this theory as the "needs theory.")

This classification is not arbitrary. Certainly, the three functions are interrelated, and surely the last mentioned function is always culturally determined; but it is demonstrable that, despite their interrelatedness, they do have varied and specific functions to perform. Dr. Kaplan no doubt would argue that you cannot have one function without the others so that *sancta* make us aware of our involvement in the group and the group-culture provides the materials of "courage" or morale.[41] But it is apparent that at certain times he felt that certain functions of religion were more important than others. Thus, for example, in his early *Judaism as a Civilization*, a "sancta" theory and a "group" theory are offered, but one senses that the most important function of religion is that which makes Jews conscious of their folk and group. In *The Future of the American Jew*, published a dozen or so years later, "group" theory is hardly mentioned, "sancta" theory has an important role and a whole new approach — the "needs" theory — is treated at considerable length.

Turning to the first function, we noted that it was the assertion that religion manifests the highest values of the society and aims at bringing an awareness of these values to the individuals who make up the group. Whatever the group deems valuable is the focus of religious interest. "The religious element in a people's civilization is objectified in those institutions, places, historic events, popular heroes, and all other objects of popular reverence to which superlative importance or sanctity is ascribed. *These sancta, the attitude towards life they imply, and the specific observances that they inspire, together constitute the religion of a people.*"[42] These highly valuable ways and forms in group living are viewed "as in some measure a manifestation of God in human life."[43] Each civilization is differentiated by the nature of its particular *sancta*, and these in turn are an indication of the particular God conception advanced.[44]

Now, it would appear from the foregoing that we have a specific theory of the role of religion in culture. The business of religion according to this function is values, and it is that instrumentality which makes man aware of the values in his culture which help him to "achieve his destiny as a human being." However, a few questions arise: Does religion in this usage generate values or is it merely a sensitizing agency? For Dr. Kaplan, religion goes far beyond its worship and ritual functions alone; but he never makes it quite clear whether religion seizes hold of the values of the culture and makes one aware of these general values which inhere in the entire cultural framework, or whether in addition it also generates values peculiar to religion out of the life process itself. When Dr. Kaplan speaks of "basic values of Jewish religion" he implies that there are values which are the exclusive province of a cultural entity known as religion. Religion performs a function — morale building — in its own terms. However, when he discusses "the relation of Jewish religion to Judaism," for example, he says, referring to Jewish religion: "The sum of these teachings and ritual practices is not a random conglomerate. It is animated and unified by the one dominant function of helping the Jew to achieve his destiny as a human being."[45] Now in this sense, even though it is made in the context of a passage explaining religion as relating to a belief and faith in God, religion is virtually coextensive with whatever in the culture helps man achieve his destiny. Yet who can deny that the *whole* of culture and society sustains man? Values are generated by a complex of institutions and forms. Viewed in this sense, culture and religion are equated. Dr. Kaplan himself says, "The purpose of *society* (my italics) should be to enable each individual to achieve salvation."[46]

Dr. Kaplan realizes the difficulties and reiterates time and again that religion has a special province — relating to belief in God. He carefully shows that the belief in God is determined by what in the culture is looked upon as of supreme worth. Yet one cannot escape the fact that certain passages unavoidably and perhaps unintentionally make the total values of the civilization coextensive with religious values without too clearly indicating what it is that makes something religious as distinct from valuable alone, or what traits differentiate religion from other institutions such as law, or government.

We have digressed for a moment only to point up some questions implied in the "sancta" approach. What is important for us to remember is that religion for Dr. Kaplan is unthinkable outside a cultural matrix. Inside that matrix, religion has the function of sensitizing us to the values or *sancta* of that culture, and of stimulating us to live out our lives in accord with them.

The Group Theory Applied

Group theory, as we mentioned above, emphasizes the role of religion in making one aware of his group membership. Religion serves as a group binding agency. Religion makes one feel a part of his group. Thus, says Dr. Kaplan, "In reflecting the most important group interests by means of rites and symbols derived from the activities by which these interests are furthered, a religion fortifies the collective consciousness."[47] Therefore, in addition to the awareness of the group values, religion makes one conscious of the power and force of the collective entity itself, and brings one to the realization of his ultimate dependence on the group. Not only the sancta but the god concepts serve to emphasize the group consciousness. The gods "symbolize and represent to the individual what he would otherwise have been unable to grasp — the clan, tribe or nation as organic entity."[48] The gods, thus conceived, are not only generalizations of what the group deems valuable; they also operate as instruments of group awareness. "It was through the medium of the gods that the individual grew aware of his people not only as a group existing in the present, but as one whose life extended far into the past and was expected to endure eternally."[49]

It can readily be seen that this is another aspect or function of religion. While directly involved in the first function, it emerges as a second pattern. Dr. Kaplan here clearly follows Durkheim when he makes of religion the agency which brings about consciousness of group. Yet there are other factors beside the intellectual attractiveness of a particular theory which lead Dr. Kaplan to its acceptance. In this case surely his ideological interests dominate. The great stress which he puts on the group-identifying features of religion clearly apply most decisively to Jewish religion. The existence of the group, the creative future of the folk, are served by the religion of the folk. Past cultures were, at times, able to survive primarily through the individual's awareness of his place in the group. In fact, people at times subsumed their personal interests to the group. Dr. Kaplan proposes a similar revitalizing role for Jewish religion.

The Jews suffer from a lack of identification with their folk. They are not sensitively aware of their dependence on the group. There is no pervasive group consciousness. This is why Dr. Kaplan stressed at one time the group-identifying features of Jewish religion. For this reason, too, he played down the role of "personal religion," leaving that either to great personalities of the past or to some future religion of mankind, or as a supplement to folk religion.[50] The need of the hour, particularly in the period 1910–35 when awareness of group was so low and assimilation so powerful, was for the Jew to become aware of his people, to feel with them, to be a part of them. This religious function seems to dominate *Judaism as a Civilization*. One's folk must not be ignored and Jewish religion is the great instrument to bring about that group consciousness. Values, goods, all of life's beneficial sources are found in group existence. *"This implies that one's people will always constitute one's chief source of salvation, and therefore one's chief medium of religion."*[51] *The function of group religion is to help a civilization reach "the point of self-consciousness essential to its perpetuation."*[52]

The Role of Personal Religion

At this point it may be objected that Dr. Kaplan's religious thought seems to be concerned only with finding some role for Jewish religion in the framework of Jewish culture. What place is there for what may be termed "personal," individual religion? It has often been charged that Dr. Kaplan has no role for such personal or individual religion. It is said that his group concern precludes the religious functions which may conceivably lie outside the ken of group values. Finally, it is charged that he opposes that religion which makes individuals seek values outside their own culture. This is usually presented in the form of a contrast between Dr. Kaplan's religion theory and Whitehead's. Dr. Kaplan it is maintained, could never subscribe to the dictum that "religion is what man does with his solitariness."

That support for such arguments can easily be found in Dr. Kaplan's writings will not be disputed. But it is also true that he does give an important role to individual religion. This will be readily apparent as we consider his third area of religious function.

The charge seems justified when we recall Dr. Kaplan's strong opposition to "personal religion" in *Judaism as a Civilization*. There he contends that personal religion comes about when the group life begins to breakdown. It arises when one *"emphasizes the authority of one's own personality in contrast with, and sometimes in opposition to, the authority of the group."*[53] As such only great men of religious or philosophical genius can have personal religion. Group religion is the norm, personal religion an aberration. It seems that Dr. Kaplan opposes personal religion for the masses because the great need of the day is for reorientation to Jewish religion as a folk religion. A more personalistic religion would be detrimental to this attempt.

Now Dr. Kaplan does not deny outright the value of such religion but he feels it is beyond the grasp of all but the gifted few. The question obviously arises: Should we not all have the authority of our own personality as the measuring rod of our religious affirmations? Is it not what we as persons want to do that should shape our religious interests? Does Dr. Kaplan propose that we subsume our very selves to the group? No, he does not. He is chiefly interested in showing that the cultural matrix cannot be ignored, that historically all religions have made their great appeal inside a given cultural framework. And that we have responsibilities to the group which at times transcend our limited personal interests and values.[54]

Nor does Dr. Kaplan deny the central position of individual personality. He wishes to bring the interests of the group and the individual into harmony. He has embarked on his program of reconstruction precisely because he wishes to eliminate the sources of personal religious discomfort which exist today in Jewish religion. His rebellion is highly personalistic, in the sense that it wants to make Jewish religion and Judaism more meaningful for individual Jews. However, he reiterates that he is unable to spin religion out of the fibres of the imagination. He must refer to his cultural existence. He lives as a Jew. He is a member of a Jewish group. His fundamental life perspectives have come about under Jewish auspices. To make religion more meaningful to him personally, he must make *Jewish* religion more meaningful. And, recalling his general reconstructionist theory, this cannot be done without the revival of all of Jewish civilization.

But Dr. Kaplan's affirmation of personal religion goes much deeper. After all, he is a personal rebel. He has followed his own conscience and gone contrary to dominant values in the group. Yet he does so both as a personal and a group venture, personal in that it makes his religion more meaningful to him, collective in that it transforms the group matrix, which he cannot disavow, into an instrument of religious self-fulfillment. Thus the personal and the collective are harmonized.

Finally, Dr. Kaplan's religion is intensely "personal" where personal means attempting to make religion valuable to the needs and wants of a given individual. As we mentioned previously, it might well be true that the third "needs theory" of religion is part and parcel of the "sancta theory." However, Dr. Kaplan is not only advancing a claim that religion dedicates us to the valuable in the group life; he also emphasizes a general human spiritual need which all religion reckons with. Man as creature has certain spiritual needs. Religion seeks to provide for them. Of course, each culture handles these needs differently; yet each caters to a not dissimilar set of needs. All involve some notion of a god, of the worthwhileness of life, courage, hope, absolution from the sense of guilt, and so on. It is here, by the way, that Dr. Kaplan's vitalism comes in, for he believes that religion makes us aware of forces "higher" than those of "natural selection." Religion, conceived in this sense, is that instrumentality which makes life inherently worthwhile.

Dr. Kaplan postulates a very clear function for religion in this theory. Religion here is not the conglomeration of all of the values of a culture; it is a specific set of values which are the peculiar concern of religion. Roughly, they might be termed "morale." Religion gives the essential morale for existence. It seeks to make us unafraid, to drive us to do the good, to have faith in the essential goodness of life. Each religion takes its sources of morale from the particular cultural setting in which it operates, and it strives to give to the members of that culture the courage and the will to continue to live in face of all of life's manifold difficulties.[55]

This kind of religion is personal in that it endeavors to provide a personal rationalization for each man, so that he may live without fear and in hope. It is personal also because it enables him to master the hardships of existence with morale and courage. In addition, this kind of religion is personal because its values must be attuned to the needs of the individual in yet another sense. Not only does religion offer morale and courage in response to seemingly universal needs, but, most significant of all, it changes the emphasis and form of the "morale" when new conditions render older forms obsolete. This takes place on an institutional and intellectual level. Thus, what may have served to build morale in one age may be bankrupt in another. New sources of morale must be found and new values promulgated which give to religion that kind of contemporaneity which makes it relevant to the major problems of our own times. The brunt of Dr. Kaplan's reconstructionist mission is to redevelop Jewish religious values in just that fashion, towards just such ends.

A substantial portion of his work — especially his later *The Future of the American Jew* — seeks to retranslate the basic religious values of Judaism for our own time.

Reconstruction Applied to Jewish Religion

The great gap between traditional religious theories and the Kaplanian variety can now be measured. Religion for Dr. Kaplan is neither ethics nor metaphysics, although such conceptions at times do enter into a particular religious point of view. Fundamentally, religion stems from man's quest for meaning and purpose in the difficult business of existence. As a manifestation of the will to salvation, it is a universal feature of the life of the species. However, the search for meaning and the quest for the good can only come in a specific cultural medium. The content of one's salvational search is socially determined and reflects the ways and habits of one's people and civilization. Thus, man's awareness of powers which aid his drive for meaning becomes the unique apprehension of powers in the peculiar mode of a given culture. The functions of religions in cultures are threefold. (1) They make one aware of the basic worthwhileness of the life pattern of the group and sanctify that which the group deems of utmost worth. (2) Through the *sancta* and commonly held values the cohesiveness of the group is maintained and the consciousness of group is served. (3) Religion provides morale for the immense effort expended in the difficult processes of human existence.

Gods, in such a conception, are not the creators of religion. Man, in his cultural setting, "creates" the gods. He generalizes from his own cultural experience, and arrives at some god concept unique to his group.

Following this general approach to religion, it would seem that Jewish religion would be affected in this way:

1. Dr. Kaplan believes that a civilizational concept would enhance the value of Jewish religion. Not only is the non-supernatural character of that religion more in line with present-day knowledge, which is in itself of primary importance, but people would be more willing to subscribe to a religion which is viewed as part of a dynamic civilization than to a fixed set of creedal assumptions.

2. The civilizational aspect of Jewish religion means also that it is a dynamic religion. It discards old functions and creates new ones. *Sancta* can become meaningless and cease to be "genuine" *sancta*. A civilizational concept views the past as source material for new growth and dynamically develops newer forms and expressions.

3. Jewish religion, with its stress on the *sancta* of Jewish civilization, contributes heavily to the continued growth of the Jewish people. But this is a reciprocal activity. Without the awareness of our Jewish values we lose sight of the meaning of our group existence, yet there can be no Jewish religion without the Jewish people. Jewish religion centers attention on those values and creates the dynamism of cultural survival.

4. Jewish religion can no longer claim a superiority based on exclusive rights to divine revelation. It is unique only to the degree that its own cultural patterns are unique—and this only in the sense of "different," not "better" or "superior."

5. Religious diversity is a fact of Jewish religious life. It is by now painfully clear that there can be no uniformity of Jewish religious outlooks and observances.

6. The reconstruction of the Jewish religion, once the cultural referent is granted, can proceed with full regard for the intellectual and cultural challenges of the age. New revisions

of older materials can be made and new religious goods introduced. Since religion is not a corpus of opinion to which one gives intellectual assent, but a culturally conditioned life process, one can adjust former schemes of salvation to new conditions, always maintaining the "folk" element, without which change is meaningless.

7. The Jewish religion of the future will adjust its concept of salvation to the world view of modern man. Its *sancta* will reflect the bi-cultural status of its Diaspora existence. It will shift from otherworldly to thisworldly orientations. Its God concepts can also change to reflect a more reasonable formulation of those powers or that Power in nature which seems to sustain human life. Conceived by our ancestors in one way, as anthropomorphic deity, we today may abandon their particular *conception* of God for our own peculiar formulation of the common *belief* in God.

8. The motive for Jewish ritual observance can be discovered in realizing the civilizational context of the ritual prescriptions. If the "halakhic method," on the one hand, is seen to reflect an earlier, no longer functional viewpoint, and the Reform license, on the other, loses sight altogether of the cultural context, a fresher view will see Jewish ritual as in part conditioned by the culture complex it traditionally inherits, and the wider base of civilizational referents which it can call upon to aid in ritual modification.

9. Prayer too assumes new roles. Petitionary prayer can no longer be expected to actually change the physical nature of things. Rather it is the soteric-psychological function of prayer as an aid in human self-adjustment to life's great crises which is involved in a reconstructed form of petition. Certainly, the nature of the very God invoked or addressed in traditional prayer no longer needs be accepted.

10. Most important of all, hope for the future of Jewish religion lies ahead, not behind. The great process of religious reconstruction opens doors to a fertile source of newer and

richer religious meanings. Drawing on the "givens" of the past, we reach out to new sources of energy, nurtured by our collective will to live as a people and the specific cultural values which we hold. We ever remake our religions with all available cultural goods. In our own day, respect for human reason and the spirit of open inquiry must pervade all our reconstructive efforts. Only when the Jewish religion is brought into line with the best in the patterns and intellectual perspectives in which we live at present, can it become the glorious instrument for our own age that it was for earlier ages and different cultural settings.

While we may disagree on a number of points, it is undeniable that we have in Dr. Kaplan's thought one of the most fruitful approaches to Jewish living generally, and to Jewish religion in particular. In a world ravaged by fears of every sort, willing to sacrifice its intelligence on the altar of absolutism, Dr. Kaplan's thought restores us to our senses, and illustrates that human reason can explore the greatest depths of the "mysteries" of existence.

Notes

[1] Dewey's distinction between "religion", "religions" and "the religious" are accepted by the writer; "religion" is employed here only in deference to popular, though inexact, usage.

[2] Compare below, M. M. Kaplan, "The Way I Have Come," pp. 283–321; also "The Influences That Have Shaped My Life," *The Reconstructionist*, VIII, no. 10, and "A Heart of Wisdom," *The Reconstructionist*, XVII, no. 6.

[3] See the excellent study by Richard Hoffstader, *Social Darwinism in American Thought*, University of Pennsylvania Press, Philadelphia, 1944.

[4] *Judaism as a Civilization*, Macmillan, N. Y., 1934, p. 39.

[5] *Ibid.*

[6] See "A Heart of Wisdom."

[7] *Judaism as a Civilization*, pp. 28–35.

[8] *The Future of the American Jew*, Macmillan, N. Y., 1948, pp. 167–168.

[9] Kaufmann Kohler, *Jewish Theology*, Macmillan, N. Y., 1918.

[10] Solomon Schechter, *Studies in Judaism*, Jewish Publication Society, Philadelphia, Reprinted 1945.

[11] Dr. Kaplan was called upon to help in the preparation of the "Columbus Platform" in 1937.

[12] Compare below, Roland B. Gittelsohn, "Mordecai M. Kaplan and Reform Judaism," pp. 233–242.
[13] Compare above, Jack J. Cohen, "Mordecai M. Kaplan's Concept of Jewish Peoplehood," pp. 27–44.
[14] *Judaism as a Civilization*, pp. 133–159.
[15] *The Meaning of God in Modern Jewish Religion*, Jewish Reconstructionist Foundation, Inc., New York, 1947, p. 10.
[16] *Judaism as a Civilization*, p. 126.
[17] *Ibid.*, p. 114.
[18] *The Meaning of God in Modern Jewish Religion*, p. 15.
[19] *Ibid.*, p. 14.
[20] *Judaism as a Civilization*, p. 124.
[21] *The Meaning of God in Modern Jewish Religion*, p. 14.
[22] *Ibid.*, p. 16.
[23] *Judaism as a Civilization*, p. 131.
[24] *Ibid.*
[25] *The Meaning of God in Modern Jewish Religion*, p. 10.
[26] *The Future of the American Jew*, p. 193.
[27] *The Meaning of God in Modern Jewish Religion*, viii (Preface).
[28] Compare below, Henry N. Wieman, "Mordecai M. Kaplan's Idea of God.", pp. 193–210.
[29] Compare *The Future of the American Jew*, p. 193 (where God is viewed as the "soul" of a "living" universe; or p. 183 in same text. On the other hand, compare *Meaning of God*, pp. 25–27.)
[30] Compare above, Ira Eisenstein, "Mordecai M. Kaplan and His Teachers," pp. 15–25.
[31] *Judaism as a Civilization*, p. 306.
[32] *The Future of the American Jew*, p. 192.
[33] *Ibid.*, p. 173.
[34] *Ibid.*, p. 172.
[35] *Ibid.*, p. 171.
[36] *Ibid.*, pp. 171–2.
[37] *Ibid.*
[38] *Ibid.*, p. 182.
[39] *Ibid.*, p. 173.
[40] *Judaism as a Civilization*, p. 333.
[41] See *The Future of the American Jew*, p. 174. Also *Judaism as a Civilization*, pp. 332–349, especially, 347–349.
[42] *The Future of the American Jew*, p. 46.
[43] *Ibid.*, 174.
[44] Though *The Meaning of God in Modern Jewish Religion* is mainly an attempt to reinterpret the God-idea, it is also an excellent analysis of the way in which *sancta* operate in a religion. In this book Dr. Kaplan illustrates the way in which traditional *sancta* can become valuable in our time and clarifies the meaning of the Sabbath and other festivals as reinterpreted *sancta*, from his own particular theological point of view.
[45] *The Future of the American Jew*, p. 162–63.

[46] *Ibid.*, pp. 206–207. Compare with definitions of religion in the same book, p. 109, and in *Judaism as a Civilization*, pp. 327–28 ff.

[47] *Judaism as a Civilization*, p. 333.

[48] *Ibid.*

[49] *Ibid.*, p. 334.

[50] *Ibid.*, pp. 337–338.

[51] *Ibid.*, p. 335.

[52] *Ibid.*, p. 342.

[53] *Ibid.*, p. 337. (On this point, it is true that Dr. Kaplan looked upon "personal religion as a check and corrective" to some aspects of folk religion. And certainly it is granted that in *Judaism as a Civilization* he has a definite function for it. However, this function is almost completely subsumed under the plea for a Jewish folk religion.)

[54] *Ibid.*, p. 334.

[55] *The Future of the American Jew*. See especially pp. 245–46. Also sections on "Faith," pp. 256–266, "Hope" pp. 266–274, "Inner Freedom" pp. 283–295.

MORDECAI M. KAPLAN'S IDEA OF GOD
By Henry N. Wieman

Dr. Mordecai Kaplan is moving out into regions of religious inquiry which could not have been entered with much confidence prior to our time. Only since the Renaissance, more especially since the eighteenth century, most of all since the beginning of the twentieth, the human mind has become equipped with sufficient understanding of the processes of the temporal world, and with sufficient confidence in them, to venture successfully into this field to seek answers to religious questions. Of course, nothing is entirely new. Some men in all ages have founded their religious faith on some kind of temporal process. But since the time of Plato, on the one hand, and since the time of the earliest Jewish supernaturalists, on the other, the religious leaders of Western culture have generally looked to a timeless reality to find what religious faith demands. But today human living is confronted with problems that cannot be surmounted unless we find the source of human good in those developments of history which determine the destiny of man. This means to commit ourselves in religious faith to a temporal process. The question is: What process?

Since the first World War, still more since the second, it has been obvious that Western culture is caught in a whirlpool which may engulf us. Whether we shall escape engulfment or not, no one can surely predict. But we cannot conduct the religious inquiry, imperatively needed, if we fail to see that the disaster threatening Western culture is only a whirlpool in the broad and mighty stream of temporal process which shapes the world. They who cannot see beyond the whirlpool have become despairing pessimists, able to keep up their hope only by looking beyond the temporal world to a timeless reality. But Dr. Kaplan and others like him are able to look beyond the whirlpool to the stream that swells from out of the remote past and moves on into the future. Destruction hangs over us, to be sure. Perhaps it hangs over the entire human race. But this is no new thing. Men have always lived under the threat of annihilation, whether they knew it or not. He whose religious faith does not enable him to live effectively and courageously under such a threat has not yet found the faith that "provides salvation," to use Dr. Kaplan's phrase.

We begin to understand a man when we are aware of the problem which he is trying to solve, and see how his proposed solution is related to other attempted solutions. Let us, then, first get an over-all picture of the state of religious thought today. In that picture we can locate the work of Dr. Kaplan and his interpretation of the meaning of God. This should enable us to apprehend the significance of his treatment of the problem which underlies all the other problems in human living.

Four Approaches to Religion

All the great world-religions have been splintered into four divisions by the impact of modern civilization. Judaism, Christianity, Mohammedanism, Hinduism, Buddhism, all display these four groups and these four directions of religious thought and action. I shall distinguish them as they appear in Christianity, because I am better acquainted with them there; but they are also found in Judaism. In Christianity the four may be characterized as follows:

(1) Traditional Christianity, intensified and hardened to resist the disintegrating impact of modern life.

(2) Neo-orthodoxy, which holds to most of the affirmations of traditional Christianity, but reinterprets them in such a way

as to lift them completely into the non-temporal realm, beyond the reach of human reason and empirical inquiry, thus delivering them from any attack or challenge that modern thought might make upon them. Traditional Christianity, like traditional Judaism, has always looked to non-temporal reality for the last support and final salvation; but it has also made claims about the temporal world which expanding knowledge renders untenable. Neo-orthodoxy remedies this weakness in the traditional formulation of the faith by reinterpreting these claims in such a way that nothing which the human mind can ever know will refute them. This escape, however, is costly. It is accomplished by lifting the most important claims of Christian faith beyond the reach of any knowledge attainable by way of rational inference and observation.

(3) The third group is so indefinite and diverse that naming it is a difficult task. It began with the philosophy of idealism and still continues in that form, but has since developed many offshoots that can no longer be classified with the philosophical idealists. It is sometimes called religious liberalism. But liberalism defines not a content of thought; it defines an attitude which may be found with almost any set of beliefs. It is sometimes called modernism. It strives to retain all that it can of traditional Christianity, but, when a traditional affirmation is challenged by modern thought, the traditional idea is relinquished and the modern substitute adopted.

All this is done, however, without any radical change in the basic presuppositions of the Christian faith. Consequently, the resulting set of beliefs becomes increasingly incoherent and indefinite. Individuals and groups tend to improvise their own set of religious beliefs with their limited resources, fabricating the best mixture they can of modern knowledge and traditional belief. This cannot go on indefinitely. It breaks down the unity of religious fellowship, the coherence of religious belief, the assurance of religious commitment, the co-operation of many men striving together in deep community of faith. The result of all this is to bring on the disintegration of our civilization. If I understand Dr. Kaplan aright, this third group represents what he calls transvaluation of the traditional faith, in contrast to his own procedure, which is revaluation.

(4) Religious naturalism is a revolutionary shift in the presuppositions on which religious living has been founded and religious inquiry conducted. The presupposition which it *rejects* is that of a timeless reality which is supposed to have originated the temporal world, to sustain the temporal world in being, and finally to bring it to an end. The presupposition which it *accepts* is that this temporal world, with its knowable possibilities and with the creativity which occurs in it, is the only reality we can ever know, hence the only reality wherein we can find the creative, sustaining and saving source of human good, and to which we must commit ourselves in religious faith if we are to be saved, sustained, guided and transformed toward the greater good.

I shall not attempt to name these four groups in the form in which they appear in Judaism. But from what I have read and from what I have heard, I am quite sure that they are present, even as they also appear in Mohammedanism, Hinduism and Buddhism. Doubtless they will be somewhat different in form in each of the great religions. My description of them in Christianity may not be an accurate description of them in these other faiths. But something akin to this fourfold division is, I believe, present in all.

The names I have used to distinguish the four groups in Christianity may not be acceptable in other religions. Indeed, these names are not acceptable to many representatives of the four groups in Christianity. If I had names more widely acceptable to all members of the four groups, I should gladly employ them. But since I do not know of any better words to use, I shall speak of the four groups, respectively, as traditional orthodoxy, neo-orthodoxy, religious idealism and religious naturalism. Naturalism, especially, has unsavory psychological associations for the religious man. But I have given this name to the group with which I am myself allied.

Let me summarize the picture I have drawn of religion today as it struggles with the problems of human living in the civilization of our time.

Modern civilization presents the human race with a problem which can only be solved by way of an adequate religious faith. Adequate religious faith here means personal and social commitment to whatever will bring forth the greatest possible good in human life when required conditions are met. There are four ways in which religious leaders are trying to solve this problem. One of these four ways is the right way, the others are wrong. If we surmount the present crisis in the history of man, and pass on through it to some greater good beyond, when other problems and dangers await us, it will be because this problem was solved more or less in the right way.

Will we find the sustaining, guiding and saving faith by building up more securely the defenses of traditional orthodoxy? This is the first of the four ways. Will we find the reality we need by extricating the important claims of the traditional faith from all involvement in this temporal world, when they are exposed to refutation by expanding knowledge? This is the second way. Will we find the reality that sustains, guides and saves when we commit ourselves to it in faith, by retaining the presuppositions of the traditional faith but modifying our beliefs in adaptation to modern thought? This is the third way. Will we find what we seek by rejecting the traditional presupposition that timeless reality sustains and shapes the temporal world, and adopting the presupposition that in this temporal world we must find what sustains, guides and saves when men commit themselves to it, to be transformed by it and to provide the conditions that it requires? This is the fourth way.

Dr. Kaplan the "Religious Naturalist"

Here we have the over-all picture of religious thought today, showing how the religious leaders in all the great faiths are struggling with the most important problem of civilization and the most important problem of human history; also showing the four different ways in which they are trying to solve this problem. I think it is not difficult to locate Dr. Kaplan in this picture. He belongs to the fourth group and is trying to solve the problem in the last of the four ways. The name "religious naturalism", I believe, best applies to him. The way is now open for me to undertake the task specifically assigned to me. That task is to examine Dr. Kaplan's treatment of the idea of God. Perhaps it is best to start with some quotations, so that we shall have his own words before us. In that way, both writer and reader can guard against attributing to him what he does not say. I think that I see a development in his idea of God, with his most mature statements in his latest book, *The Future of the American Jew*. So my quotations will be taken from it almost exclusively. In this book he writes as follows:

Does awareness of God depend upon our conceiving God as a personal being, or may God be conceived in other ways, and yet be the subject of our awareness, or the object of our worship? In strictly philosophical thought, the very notion of a personal being, especially when not associated with a physical body, is paradoxical. Nothing would, therefore, be lost if we substituted for that notion the one of "process," which, at least with the aid of science, most of us find quite understandable. Why, then, not conceive God as process? (p. 182-3)

.... we suggest that God be thought of as the cosmic process that makes for man's life abundant or salvation. As cosmic process, God is more than a physical, chemical, biological, psychological, or even social process. God includes them all, but what is distinctive about the God process is that it is superfactual and superexperiential. (p. 183)

God as the Power, transcending ourselves, that makes for salvation, also inheres in all the forces of our minds and wills. As such, God functions not only in our own bodies, but also in our relationships to one another and to the environment in which we live. (p. 184-5)

When we sustain a tragic loss, and for the moment are paralyzed by despair, what enables us to get back to life and resume our tasks, if not a Power beyond us that impels us to go on living? It is that same Power that impels us to make the best use of our lives as human beings. That is why human beings will continue to pray and worship, regardless of the mental image or concept, with the aid of which they think of that Power. (p. 184)

When a man prays that part of him which is the actualized element in him addresses itself to that part which is potential. It is then that one's entire personality is implicated. When one's personality is entire, it necessarily includes something of the divine which transcends it. (pp. 184–5)

There can hardly be a more real and more God-revealing experience in the inner life of a child than that of growth..... The experience of growth thus offers not merely an analogue to salvation, but can actually be made to constitute salvation to the child. It conveys in very realistic fashion the polarity of salvation: on the one hand, God, or the Power outside, making for growth and, on the other, one's self or the Power within, which does its part in meeting the necessary requirements to growth. (p. 186)

The Jews evolved a civilization of which they are actually aware as more capable than any other of helping them to achieve salvation. This means that they did not think of their way of life as an artificial device which may or may not prove successful, but as an instrument supplied by God to enable them to attain the ultimate good. They, therefore, called it the Torah of God. As Jews, we have to cultivate the knowledge and practice of that civilization. That is to say, we have to study and practice Torah.... Torah reveals the power that makes for salvation. (p. 187)

The following passages are taken from *The Meaning of God in Modern Jewish Religion:*

It is sufficient that God should mean to us the sum of the animating, organizing forces and relationships which are forever making a cosmos out of chaos. This is what we understand by God as the creative life of the universe. (p. 76)

.... that Power on which we rely for the regeneration of society and which operates through individual human beings and social institutions. Faith in the sovereignty of God comes then to mean faith that in mankind there is manifest a Power which, in full harmony with the nature of the physical universe, operates for the regeneration of human society ... (p. 110)

Whenever we recognize the inadequacy of our acquired personality to do justice to the demands of a new situation, and we try to overcome the obstacles that prevent our lives from manifesting the divine, we are practicing repentance, or the return to God. (p. 184)

According to Dr. Kaplan, a religious faith with its corresponding idea of God is intrinsic to a civilization. The religion apart from its civilization is futile and empty; the civilization apart from its unifying and directing faith is doomed to disintegration. The formulation of a faith with its idea of God will be different for each civilization, and should be so, for otherwise the religion would not meet the distinctive needs of the civilization to which it belongs. On the other hand, this faith with its idea of God must be so shaped as to enable the individual to serve that process which can transform man, through history, toward the greatest possible good ever to be attained. This requires that the individual, moulded as he must be by his own civilization, and in full community with it, serve a process which transforms both himself and his own civilization, and likewise transforms other civilizations in the direction of what is better, and away from what is worse. It can do this, however, only when required conditions are present. One of these conditions is that men commit themselves to it in religious faith.

Nothing can glorify a man's life more, nothing can sustain him more in time of disaster, give him more profound sense of community with all men, lift his vision more loftily, than to feel himself identified with such a process that works through all ages, and in the lives of all peoples, and will in the end bring forth the greatest good that life can ever attain. According to Dr. Kaplan, salvation is to have one's life thus glorified, sustained, and given the deepest community and highest vision.

The Meaning of "God" as Process

If I understand Dr. Kaplan aright, the word "God" is used by him to designate whatever is of such a nature as rightfully to command from man the ultimate commitment of faith, because it transforms man and society in the direction of the greatest possible good when men commit themselves to it, and do what they can to provide the other conditions that it requires. Anything having that character should be called God, no matter how much it may differ from any of the many diverse mental pictures men have had of this reality. When the word "God" has been used in the great religions by earnest religious people, it has been their name for what they *thought* had the character described in the first sentence of this paragraph. Therefore what they intended to designate by this word was what actually does operate in the way described, even though they may have been quite mistaken in the descriptions by which they tried to represent it.

I think that I agree quite completely with Dr. Kaplan in this undertaking. I think I have spent all my life trying to do the same thing. But I think he would agree with me in saying that he and I, and all others engaged in this undertaking, have to date only begun — perhaps not even begun — to get a correct and adequate idea of this kind of process which calls for the religious commitment of faith. Therefore, what he says about it, what I say about it, and what others say about it may, in many cases, be quite mistaken. Such being the case, perhaps the most illuminating thing I can do is to set down my idea of this process and place it alongside his idea. Agreements and disagreements will then emerge. This kind of cross reference between the two ideas seems to me to be the most clarifying thing I can do.

Dr. Kaplan calls this process of creativity a cosmic process. I interpret this *not* to mean that the process commanding the religious commitment of faith is the totality of everything going on in the universe, such as Hitler's killing of six millions of Jews and all the other horrors of history. He does not mean cosmic in any such pantheistic sense. I understand him rather to mean that the process in question is rooted in the nature of things. But the cosmos includes many other processes besides this one, and many of the other processes are opposed to the one which commands our commitment of faith. Therefore, the God-process must be clearly distinguished from these other processes, and to that end I use the word creativity. I find that term also used by Dr. Kaplan.

Dr. Kaplan points out that this process of creativity is distinguished from all others by being "super-factual and super-experiential." By these words he means to refer to ideal possibilities not yet actualized in existence. Creativity carries ideal possibilities, not only those which the human mind has envisioned and strives to actualize, but also others which the human mind cannot discern nor appreciate until it has been further developed by creativity. In this sense creativity as God does in truth include the super-factual and super-experiential.

Dr. Kaplan refers to this process as a Power, and so do I. I do not challenge him on this point, but since I myself have been challenged on it, I think it well to point out a source of confusion when this word "Power" is used in this context.

Is the Power something that causes the process called creativity? Or is the Power simply another word for the process itself? Is power identical with process, or is power the cause of the process? My own answer is unqualified. Power is process; process is power. Examine any instance of power, such as the explosion of an atomic bomb, or a leader inspiring many men to heroic struggle and utmost effort. What do you find? You always find a process of transformation and nothing else. The individual engaged in action, when such action is called an instance of power, can introspectively be aware of many felt qualities variously called the felt qualities of effort, hope, fear, determination, decision and the like. A streaming flood of felt qualities may pour through his consciousness. But a stream of felt qualities is a process.

In opposition to the view just stated as my own, many will insist that process and power are not identical; that whenever a process occurs, there is something else, called power, which causes it. I have no interest in arguing this point because this alleged distinction between power and process is one which no possible experience can reveal. In one sense of the word *metaphysics*, it is a metaphysical issue. Therefore, I am perfectly willing to go along with any one who wants to distinguish power and process, providing only he will recognize that process is what we experience; and process is what we must work with, even though every process has a power "back of it." I myself do not make that claim; but I see no point in arguing it.

Further Thoughts on "Process" and "Event"

I think the word *process* as used in present-day philosophy calls for further interpretation, and especially when God is identified with a process.

Process, as I understand it, is any set of events which have something in common by which they can be distinguished from other events. The process of getting downtown begins with the event of getting on the bus and ends with the event of getting off the bus. It includes all the intervening events which are a required part of the total undertaking. The living organism which is my body is made up of all those events which build up the living tissue, and all those events which burn up the living tissue, in the process of living. Everything that exists is process. The table before me is involved in a process. It began with the event of putting its parts together, and it continues in process of wearing out and being used. It will end when it breaks or otherwise disintegrates.

It remains to explain the meaning of "event". An event is any duration of time that is marked off by the occurrence of some difference at its beginning, and the occurrence of some other difference at its end. The difference occurring to start the event may be the beginning of some sound, or some change in the quality of sound that I am hearing. The difference occurring at the end may be the cessation of that sound, or some difference in the quality of sound. The difference that initiates the event may be the entry into my field of vision of some color; or it may be the beginning of a motion or change in some motion. The difference that initiates the event may be inferred but not directly observed, such as the events that occur in the atom.

So far we have used as our examples very small events. Let us now look at a very large event. Six hundred thousand to a million years ago there began to emerge on this planet a new kind of animal called human. The end of that event, called human life on this planet, has not yet occurred.

Every event seems to be made up of sub-events included in it, because every duration of time is not only marked off from past and future by the occurrence of differences at its beginning and ending; it is divided into segments by the occurrence of differences throughout the duration. Each of these segments can be called an event in its own right; but such events are sub-events included in the larger event.

Since time cannot be separated from space, every event is not only a stretch of time, but also an expanse of space. Events can have every sort of spatial and temporal configuration. The totality of all events is the totality of all that exists. The totality of all processes is also the totality of all that exists, and nothing exists that is not a process. The only difference between events and processes is that a process is some combination or class of events having a distinctive structure.

Events (processes) are concrete reality; and concrete reality is infinitely complex. It is infinitely rich with felt quality when the events are experienced. The event of my existence between nine o'clock in the morning and one half hour later can be called a single event with subdivisions making up a chain of events. This chain of events is a process. This process is rich with felt qualities. It includes the qualities I feel in my body, the qualities I feel when I remember the past, the qualities I feel when I anticipate the future, the qualities I feel when I observe what is going on around me, when I listen to others tell me what they think, feel, have experienced, hope, fear, and the like.

To say that God is a process, is simply to say that God exists, because process and existence are identical. But none of the examples used in the last few paragraphs to illustrate event and process can be identified with God. What then is God? God is that kind of process previously described as creativity. In human life it is the expansion of shared meanings in community.

A process is a combination of events having a structure which distinguishes it from other combinations of events. Creativity is a combination of events having a structure which distinguishes it from other combinations of events. Many structures are transitory, in the sense that some events display them and some do not. Every event seems to participate in many different structures, some of the structures being more transitory than others. The bus, for example, participated in that structure of events which I called going down town. But the bus has a structure of its own, which continues long after it has ceased to play any part in getting me down town. There may be one structure that is everlasting, in the sense that every event must have it in order to be an event at all, although every event may also participate at the same time in many other structures that are not everlasting.

An everlasting structure would mean an everlasting process. If there is an everlasting process it runs like a golden thread through all other processes having different and transitory structures. I think it might be demonstrated that creativity is an everlasting process of this sort. If creativity at the most elementary level is the formation of the most elementary structure, without which events could not be distinguished from one another as coming before and after, then creativity is everlasting because, without it, there could be no time, no order or structure of any kind, but only chaos.

God-Process as Creativity

Let me now state more precisely what I understand this God-process to be, which I call creativity. Of course any attempt to describe it, or anything else in existence, must necessarily fall far short of the total reality of it. To substitute the description for the reality is, therefore, an absurdity. Some people think it very funny in mockery to substitute an attempted description of God for the reverent words of worship, which do not attempt to describe but only symbolize. This is absurd, of course, and if any one likes to make merry by doing it, it is his privilege. But if he thinks that, in so doing, he is presenting any evidence whatsoever that the descriptive statements are false, he is quite mistaken. Any description is an abstraction that falls infinitely short of the total reality. To substitute an abstract and partial description for the reality under consideration, especially in cases of worship, is absurd. But the absurdity is not in the description; the absurdity is in the attempt to make this foolish substitution.

Creativity, as it works in the midst of human life, is progressive expansion in what the individual can know, control, suffer, enjoy in community with others. It is, therefore, expansion in the range of meaning which signs can have for associated individuals. How much of the past can I know, feel, suffer, enjoy? How much of the anticipated future? How much of what is happening to other people around me can I know, feel, suffer, enjoy? How much of what they hope and remember, suffer and enjoy, seek and avoid can I share, not only when I agree and approve, but also when I am convinced that they are mistaken in their ideas and evaluations?

Over against all such sharing, there is a privacy of the individual, which must not be violated. There is also the privacy of the small "in" group. There is even the privacy of an entire civilization, as over against other civilizations. But over and above this privacy are all those concerns which we must share if every individual is not to be frustrated, misunderstood, often persecuted, and deprived of every cooperation and sympathy. Indeed, the newborn infant cannot even reach the level of human living if he cannot acquire from his mother and other intimate associates some of the language and meanings of his culture. But this is precisely the expansion of shared meanings in community which I am describing. Psychiatry has revealed the disastrous consequences that occur in the development of a personality when this kind of sharing between the child and intimate associates is unduly obstructed. Disasters even greater occur when this expansion of shared meanings in community cannot be created between peoples, classes, groups and ages.

The Three Levels of Creativity

So far I have been describing this creativity at the top level, so to speak, where it works in human society and history. But its roots are much deeper. We can trace it up through three levels. By making further distinctions, one can multiply the levels which creativity builds as it works from the lowest to the highest.

(1) At the bio-chemical level, this creativity creates living tissue out of inanimate matter, when required conditions are present. This it does for the individual up to the point of death. This it does through the ages from the first emergence of life on this planet, progressively building up more complex and sensitive organisms, able to discriminate more finely.

(2) At the physio-phychological level, this creativity creates minds by developing the ability to respond to signs and to what signs can signify. This it does for the individual from infancy on, so long as conditions permit progressive expansion in what the signs can signify for the individual. This it does through the ages by progressively creating minds that can respond to signs that signify things more finely discriminated, more extensive in scope, richer with felt qualities, more widely and fully shared in community with others.

(3) At the social-historical level, this creativity produces minds able to respond to signs which signify progressively more of all that exists, more of all that has existed, more of all that is conceivable. At the level of human history, when required conditions are present, this expansion in the range of

what can be known, controlled, enjoyed and suffered has no known limit. This expansion of human concern in community through history is what we call the progressive creation of a civilization or culture.

I have tried to emphasize, by reiteration, that this creativity does not occur unless the required conditions are present. Inevitable progress is not claimed and is not a fact. But progress, in the sense of expanding and enriching meanings in community, does occur when the required conditions are present. The most important problem in human life is to discover what these conditions are, and to provide them so far as man is able. But creativity itself man cannot achieve. It is impossible for a man to imagine a meaning which is beyond the reach of his imagination. Creativity is precisely expansion in this reach of imagination.

The Two Dimensions of Meaning and Salvation

Man is distinguished from everything else in the known universe by the degree of his capacity to undergo progressive transformation by expanding the meanings which make up his mind, his personality and his community with others. The destiny of man is to undergo this transformation beyond any known limit, by committing himself most completely to creativity and serving it above all. In this way a community is created which includes not only human beings in association, but increasingly more of the universe, in the sense that this community can feel more of the qualities that the universe can yield in the form of qualitative meaning. Qualitative meaning calls for careful exposition and understanding, for it is the heart of the matter.

Qualitative meaning is one dimension of meaning and can best be understood by contrasting it with non-qualitative dimension of meaning. The purest example of the non-qualitative dimension of meaning is a mathematical formula enabling one to take account of a vast complexity of events and possibilities, without any feeling of the qualities pertaining to them. Example: actuarial tables showing the ratio of births and deaths in a population of millions.

The purest example of the qualitative dimension of meaning is in art and in the meanings conveyed by symbols in love and devotion. Example: *Death of a Salesman* by Arthur Miller. For an example in actual life, observe a daughter telling her mother about the infant born to the daughter. The glow on the faces of the women, their tones and laughter, make it obvious that they feel abundantly the qualities of the infant when they use signs to refer to him, his birth, the gurgle of his laughter, his little hands and kicking feet, his soft flesh, etc. etc. He is to them "the sweetest little thing that ever was." Births represented in the actuarial tables, brought to consciousness, have no such awareness of qualities.

The actuarial tables refer to deaths, but as one reads them he feels none of the tragedy in those deaths. *The Death of a Salesman* also refers to deaths. While one man plays the part of the salesman, the drama is presented to symbolize any death and all deaths of men who live in a certain way. So it is a sign referring to many deaths, even as the actuarial tables. But when observing the drama, one feels the qualities of such deaths. This is the qualitative dimension of meaning.

The expansion of non-qualitative meaning in the form of science and technology is the chief way in which man's power of control is extended over the world. There is reason to think that this dimension of meaning has been disproportionately developed in our culture, not because man can have too much power, but because power becomes destructive when magnified without proportionate increase in community of shared qualitative meaning. In such case, psychic ill and social conflict mushroom.

All enjoyment is of felt qualities. Signs, with the dimension of qualitative meaning, bring felt qualities to consciousness and hold them before the mind for contemplation. Thus all enjoyment depends upon the qualitative dimension of meaning.

All expansion and enrichment of enjoyment can occur only as this dimension of meaning is expanded and enriched.

Expanding the range of the cognitive dimension of meaning is to increase what the individual can know and understand. Expanding the range of the technological dimension is to increase what the individual can do. Expanding the range of the qualitative dimension of meaning is to increase what the individual can enjoy and suffer. Expanding the range of *shared* qualitative meaning is to increase the love and community which the individual can have with others. Trouble mounting to disaster begins when the cognitive and technological are not held subject and instrumental to the maximum creation of qualitative meaning in community. As this last increases in society and through history, men move toward the "Kingdom of God." This is the destiny of man. Complete commitment to the creativity that transforms man and his world in this direction is salvation.

I am quite sure that Dr. Kaplan is not a pantheist, but on the other hand, he may not accept my interpretation of the cosmic process that is God. Whatever the disagreement between us, and however wide of the mark my interpretation of his thought may be, I am sure that he is on the right track. Many others will follow after him and widen the blazed trail he has made. In time it will be a broad highway down which millions of men will travel. I am very confident that sooner or later the dominant form of religion by which men find salvation will be developed along the lines indicated by Dr. Kaplan.

I have tried to give my version of Dr. Kaplan's idea of God. Better stated, I have given my version of the idea of God which I think is basically in accord with Dr. Kaplan's. I have made this statement paralleling his, in the attempt to interpret him to myself and to others. Also I have made it in the endeavor to cooperate with him in the attempt to develop an idea of God to meet the needs of our time.

MORDECAI M. KAPLAN AND JEWISH LITURGY

By David Polish

The deepening penetration into Jewish life and thought of Mordecai Kaplan's views on Jewish liturgy was attested when the Reconstructionist Prayer Book was publicly burned in New York, in 1945. This incident represented more than a recrudescence of medieval fanaticism, doubly abhorrent because it was incited by Jews. It recorded a tremor within Jewish tradition, a tremor transcending approval or disapproval, that had shaken up and rearranged traditional Judaism's liturgical household which had long stood undisturbed, defying disarray. While the Reconstructionist Prayer Book was the palpable target of recrimination, the real adversary, which was beyond reach and beyond interdiction, was a body of belief, incorporated in all of Kaplan's writings, that compelled a radical reorientation, not only to liturgical forms but to the religious concepts embodied in those forms. Dr. Kaplan's opponents and adherents alike correctly assessed the new prayer book as the symbol of a revolution in theology.

In this light, the introduction to the Sabbath Prayer Book may be regarded as even more trenchant than the Prayer Book itself: "If prayer is to be genuine and not merely a recital of words, the worshiper must, of course, believe in God... He must be able to sense the reality of God vividly, as an intense personal experience. Our ancestors possessed such a sense of the reality of God. The modern Jew, however, is disturbed by the current conception of nature. Nature is generally viewed as blind, mechanical and unresponsive to man's prayers. This view of nature leaves in his mind no room for God or for worship. Therefore it is necessary for the modern Jew to strive to formulate his idea of God in terms which can serve to inspire him with faith and courage, and which at the same time conform to his knowledge of the world..... For purposes of common worship ... it is essential to arrive at an idea of God, broad enough to bridge the differences in individual outlook and capable of resolving the inner conflicts which paralyze the impulse to pray."[1]

Validity for this proposition, that our liturgical symbols be made to conform to our changing theological concepts, is to be found in some current psychological insights into the human soul. Writing of Carl Jung, Schaer says: "The twilight of antiquity was really a vast dying of God. Neither for the individual nor for the community is this moment easy to bear. For Nietzsche the statement that God is dead was bound up with a profound spiritual shock that can be noticed in his writings. And the extraordinary religious insatiability that appeared at the end of the classical era, an insatiability that sought peace and salvation everywhere and found it not, gives us some idea of the inner horror of the experience that God is dead.... One of the infallible signs that a God-image is dying is that people begin asking what is the meaning of the God-image or God-symbol. Whether a God-symbol dies or not depends, as in the case of all symbols, on whether it still corresponds to the state of a man's consciousness. If he has evolved so far that a symbol is no longer the best possible expression for some intuited fact that is of importance to him, then the symbol becomes lifeless.... There is, however, not only the 'God-death', the extinction of the God-symbol, but also a renewal of it. God may change with a modification of the God-image. The symbol may in the course of time be replaced by a new one. From the point of view of the psyche this is, indeed, an absolute necessity. In this practice Jung has observed people during the period when a new intuition of God was taking shape in them."[2]

The Functions of Public Worship

Throughout Dr. Kaplan's expositions of prayer, the major stress is placed on public worship. What are the effects of communal prayer?

A. Just as God is a prerequisite for prayer, God's presence is made more manifest through prayer, particularly group worship. In consonance with his conception of the folk aspect of the Jewish religion, he invokes psychology and sociology to demonstrate the primarily gregarious aspects of prayer. "Public worship is a means of giving a people that collective consciousness which unifies its life and integrates all of its individuals into an organized totality."[3] This awareness of God's Being in the midst of a Congregation is discussed in almost mystic terms by Dr. Kaplan, who invokes Rabbinic intuition as his starting point. "The reason that ten men are required as a quorum for public worship is stated to be that 'wherever ten men gather for prayer the *Shekinah* is with them.' "[4] To Dr. Kaplan, public worship is the principal avenue of encounter with God as a Living Presence. "To appreciate fully the meaning of the awareness of God as a Presence, one must actually experience the influence of public worship. Inasmuch as such experience takes possession of the whole personality, it partakes in each individual instance of the uniqueness of that personality, and hence is never wholly communicable. To analyze it can never do it full justice. Nevertheless, some of the communicable elements of this experience may be described, as an intimation of what one who has not experienced such communion with God may expect of it." "The feeling of togetherness is the raw material of religion, just as the undifferentiated sensations of the new-born infant are the raw material out of which he later fashions his world of sensory objects and their relations in thought. This feeling is early recognized as God-feeling. As social experience classifies the objectives of human behavior, and the conception of God is accordingly ethicized, this God-feeling becomes an ethical force. But on the higher level of spiritual thought and conduct, as on the lower level, the feeling of togetherness is indispensable to the realization of God, for without it we cannot experience God at all."[5]

Public worship makes not only for an encounter with God but for a spiritual encounter with our fellows. Collective worship makes for human cooperation. Our competitive society vitiates man's deep-rooted drives toward collaboration. If there is such a force as a competitive impulse, there is "also an impulse to cooperate," (a religious verity whose scientific implications men like Ashley Montague are now uncovering) and this impulse can be effectively motivated and unleashed through communal prayers. This mutuality not only results in social attainments, but actually induces a Divine response. To understand this we must comprehend Dr. Kaplan's stress upon God as implicit in human relations. "God functions not only in our own bodies but also in our relationships to one another and to the environment in which we live. By becoming aware of these forces and relationships, we induce them to function most efficiently."[6] Dr. Kaplan uses the example of two shipwrecked men in a row-boat, strengthening one another morally as well as physically in their common struggle against the sea. Each, by working with his fellow, possesses more than twice the strength and resources than he could muster if he were on his own. "Thus public worship not only enhances our strength by its suggestion of human cooperation, but by banishing morbid fear it gives us renewed confidence in nature itself, enabling us to see in it, as well as in humanity, the immanence of God. Thus public worship makes us feel not only that we have brothers on earth, but that we also have...a Father in Heaven, a Power in nature that responds to human need, if properly approached."[7]

B. Group worship, by identifying us with our fellows and their problems, has an edifying effect upon the individual. It seems to identify us with others who, like ourselves, suffer from all the privations of the human spirit. This sense of relatedness generates "for the time being" a spirit of love and understanding.[8] The group therapy technique, employed now with increasing efficacy, is predicated on insights such as these.

C. Public prayer affects yet another area of relationship — the relationship of the individual to his own being. The emotionally debilitating effect of brooding over our personal problems, disappointments and limitations is dissipated by merging our identities with "the multitudinous life of our people," by "sharing in a common life that transcends our personal organism." Through immersion in the group, the fear of death is mitigated, if not lost, and a conviction of our own worth and immortality takes hold. We leave the confining chrysalis of personal preoccupation, and enter into a greater life which is the God whom we experience. We pass from the restricted zone where we fear death and know *about* God, and enter the borderless terrain where we retrieve our immortality and *know* God.[9] "When one's personality is entire, it necessarily includes something of the divine which transcends it. Franz Rosenzweig put it well when he wrote that 'prayer is its own fulfillment; the soul prays for the power to pray.' "[10] "In the higher civilizations, when the pious sang praises to God, they gave utterance to the ineffable delight they derived from communion with Him. The modern equivalent of that experience is a glimpse into life's unity, creativity and worthwhileness. To articulate that experience in the midst of a worshiping throng is a spiritual necessity of the normal man. He needs it as a means of affirming the meaning of life and of renewing his spirit."[11]

The Problem of Prayer in our Time

If this metamorphosis of the human spirit can be achieved through group worship, why is it that masses of our people are stubbornly immune to its effects? This failure to respond is due to the tenuousness of their identification with the worshiping community. Ignorance of our past, indifference to our present, apathy to our problems keep them out of tune with the spirit of their people and disqualify them from enjoying the effects of communication with them. Since the traditional liturgy speaks primarily of a God who is revealed to the Jewish people through its history, the spiritual cravings of the peripheral Jew cannot be satisfied. In the past, the liturgy adequately served this function, but its ability to fulfill this function has been steadily weakened.

Just as group worship is indispensable for collective and personal salvation, personal worship alone, personal worship devoid of relationship with the community is mischievous and deleterious. The individual who considers himself spiritually self-sufficient is feeding upon his own self-consciousness and runs the risks attendant upon any recourse to personal isolation: morbidity, world-weariness, spiritual narcissism accompanied by rejection of forces beyond ourselves.

While assigning a subordinate role to personal religion, Dr. Kaplan interposes it as a rein against group religion's running wild, against "its apotheosis into a consecrated chauvinism."[12] He intimates that the more gifted souls in the community, the more metaphysically trained, the more mystically inclined require the more rarefied atmosphere of personal religion that folk worship alone cannot afford. They are not mutually exclusive. Folk worship is a deterrent to excessive introspection which often leads to spiritual aberrations. Personal religion exerts a modifying effect on collective religion. "Thus far no civilization has made any contribution to the problem of so balancing the functions of folk and of personal religion as to insure their reacting beneficially upon each other. Here is an opportunity for the Jewish civilization once again to become creative in a phase of human life which it enriched by its achievement in the past."[13]

The Need for Revising the Liturgy

In order to help bring the Jew into rapport with his God and his people, a radical revision of our liturgy is imperative. It is, indeed, inevitable. The change in our world view and the change of attitude toward the efficacy of prayer compel a new orientation to our ritual. To a great extent, it has manifested itself largely in rejection. The thaumaturgic concept of God responding to man-made formulae is being rejected. "Jewish religion should discountenance the use of ritual for the purpose of influencing the course of events in other ways than by its influence on the mind and heart of the worshiper." The authoritarian insistence upon uniformity and its intolerance of the heresy of deviation are likewise rejected. "Legalism and endless repetition of prescribed formulae have banished from Jewish worship all that freedom and spontaneity without which art cannot flourish . . . . We should frankly accept the conclusion to which all modern and enlightened people have come, that the realm of law . . . must not extend to matters of ritual."[14] Finally, uniformity for its own sake, uniformity that does not edify is renounced.[15]

The new approach to our liturgy must be accompanied by a new attitude toward prayer. "Worship will henceforth have but the one function of imbuing the human being with God-consciousness, or the consciousness of life's significance and momentousness. It will therefore express itself in words and gestures of *tehillah* rather than *tefillah*, of praise rather than prayer."[16] Prayer as petition must be replaced by prayer as striving toward self-and group-fulfillment, and as communion with God. Also, in addition to strengthening our Jewish consciousness, it should "interpret the divine aspect of life as manifest in social idealism . . . the potentialities of the individual soul . . . [and] the aspiration of Israel to serve the cause of humanity."[17] Thus relevance, social consciousness, Jewish mission, personal salvation are all motivating factors in Jewish liturgy.

To offset the inadequacies of the traditional liturgy, a new mode of worship must evolve and it should be in consonance with the conception of Judaism as a civilization.[18] The writing of new prayers, services, hymns and other devotional literature should be encouraged. The retention of traditional forms should be contingent on their value to the services.[19] The content of the prayers should concern not only the Jewish past but the realities and the challenges of contemporary Jewish life. Such subjects as the "renascence of the Jewish spirit and the reclamation of the ancient homeland" as well as peace, justice and freedom should predominate.[20]

All this presupposes a radically different attitude on our part to public worship. It posits the full utilization in the service of poetry, music, song, drama and the dance. As long as these forms (which incidentally had their origins in formal religious observance) are congruent with the purposes of public worship, they should be embodied in it. The creative genius of Hebrew poetry which reflects a distinctive sensitivity to spiritual themes, the emergent patterns of Jewish religious music, the religious potentialities of pageantry — all open new horizons for our liturgical and ritualistic self-expression.[21]

Some Attempts at Revision

The first attempt at applying these concepts was made by Dr. Kaplan in his *Supplementary Prayers and Readings for the High Holidays*, published in 1934 by the United Synagogue of America. With minor modifications (which are indicated by marginal notations in Dr. Kaplan's own copy, the only extant copy of the United Synagogue publication available) several of the prayers are incorporated in the *High Holiday Prayer Book*, published in 1948 by the Jewish Reconstructionist Foundation. The foreword to *Supplementary Prayers* reflects Dr. Kaplan's views on the need for contemporary relevance in prayer:

"In English-speaking congregations that use the traditional liturgy there are unmistakable signs of a growing demand for supplementary prayers and reading, which would translate the religious aspirations of our ancestors into terms of present-day experience. This condition is not without precedent in Jewish life. The large output of *piyyutim*, or sacred verses, during the Middle Ages came in answer to a similar need. To be true to the living spirit of the Jewish religion, we should not content ourselves with past formulations of its ideals, but always seek to reformulate those ideals in terms of current situations and thought patterns. Every age should have its own *piyyut*; and none should be more creative in that respect than ours. The infinite ramifications of modern life and knowledge reveal new and unsuspected implications in the religious insights of our prophets and teachers.

"Both the intrinsic nature of Jewish services and the atmosphere most congenial to them logically require that all prayers and readings in the synagogue be rendered in Hebrew. It is only as an interim concession to an immediate need that those contained in this booklet are given in English. It is hoped that before long the Jewish spirit of our synagogues will be sufficiently rehabilitated to make it feasible for these prayers and readings to be published and recited in Hebrew."

Dr. Kaplan's influence is apparent in the Reconstructionist *Haggadah*, the *Sabbath Prayer Book* and the *High Holiday Prayer Book*, although the actual editing of these books represented a collective effort, including the work and counsel of Dr. Kaplan. Their effort at casting our prayers into a pattern which utilizes historical materials to adumbrate contemporary situations is true to Dr. Kaplan's concept of the transvaluation of Jewish values.

The salient characteristics of the *Haggadah* are the inclusion of new readings and music; the incorporation of midrashic material concerning the Egyptian enslavement, and Moses; the addition of Biblical verses accentuating the ethical meaning of the Exodus; but above all the homiletical nature of the entire text, pointing recurrently to the meaning of freedom for our own time and in our own lives. The concept of the chosen people is omitted from the Kiddush, for the first time in Jewish liturgical history.

The stress upon relevance and new form and content is developed further in the *Sabbath Prayer Book*, which includes a supplement that is more extensive than the Sabbath services themselves. The supplement consists of readings, poems and prayers by contemporary, recent and medieval writers, on a wide range of subjects. These readings are intended to be incorporated into the services in such a manner that they constitute a central theme. Interpretive material, intended to give added meaning to traditional prayers, is embodied in the service. For example, a meditation on the "Unity of God and Our Love for Him" precedes the *Shema*. The preface indicates that such traditional doctrines as the chosen people, supernatural revelation, personal messiah, retribution and resurrection are absent from the prayer book. The *High Holiday Prayer Book* is similar in conception and structure.

Most recently, Dr. Kaplan has been advocating that Jewish worship be integrated with group study by basing the services upon specified Torah lessons. The Torah lessons would serve as central themes which would recur and be developed throughout the services. The use of the Torah would be predicated upon Dr. Kaplan's view that it can serve us only in the light of what it means to us today, not what it might have meant to our fathers or our ancestors. "We have to achieve a type of Midrash that fits into the contemporary world outlook, a kind of reinterpretation that will indicate its bearing on what profoundly concerns us. The Pentateuchal Torah should help us identify our people, not so much by its outward history as by the contents of the collective mind and spirit".[22]

Dr. Kaplan's outlook is strikingly in the spirit of a Talmudic comment which might well serve as a basic text for Reconstructionism. Ben Zoma discusses the verse: "Behold the days come . . . that they shall no more say, 'As the Lord liveth that brought up the children of Israel out of the land of Egypt', but 'as the Lord liveth, that brought up and that led the seed of the house of Israel out of the north country, and from all the countries whither I had driven them'; and they shall dwell in their own land". (Jeremiah 23:7-8)

The question is, does this verse imply the obsolescence of the concept of the Exodus? Not at all. But it does indicate that the Exodus will become secondary and the release from the servitude of the kingdoms (*shi'bud malkhuyot*) will become primary. This is analogous, we are told, to a man who, while walking by the way, is attacked by a wolf and rescued. He recites his encounter with the wolf, but later is set upon by a lion and is again rescued. This time he tells about his escape from the lion. Still later a snake attacks him and once more he escapes. "He forgets about the first two and tells about the snake. Even so with Israel. The most recent troubles make us forget the earlier ones."[23]

Notes

[1] *Sabbath Prayer Book*, Jewish Reconstructionist Foundation, New York, 1945, pp. xviii–xix.

[2] Hans Schaer, *Religion and the Cure of Souls in Jung's Psychology*, Bollingen Foundation, Inc., New York, 1950, pp. 143–145.

[3] *Judaism as a Civilization*, Macmillan, New York, 1934, p. 346.

[4] *The Meaning of God in Modern Jewish Religion*, Jewish Reconstructionist Foundation, New York, 1947, p. 245.

[5] *Ibid.*, pp. 246, 250–251.

[6] *The Future of the American Jew*, Macmillan, New York, 1948, p. 184.

[7] *The Meaning of God in Modern Jewish Religion*, pp. 247, 248.

[8] *Ibid.*, pp. 256, 257.

[9] *The Meaning of God in Modern Jewish Religion*, pp. 247–263; *The Future of the American Jew*, p. 184.

[10] *The Future of the American Jew*, p. 185.

[11] *Judaism as a Civilization*, p. 347.

[12] *Ibid.*, p. 348.

[13] *Ibid.*, p. 349.

[14] *Judaism as a Civilization*, pp. 346, 458; *The Future of the American Jew*, p. 49.

[15] *Judaism as a Civilization*, pp. 347, 429.

[16] *Ibid.*, p. 506.

[17] *Ibid.*, p. 347.

[18] *Ibid.*, p. 430.

[19] *The Future of the American Jew*, p. 49.

[20] *Judaism as a Civilization*, p. 348.

[21] *Ibid.*, p. 506.

[22] "The Torah as our Life and the Length of our Days", *The Reconstructionist*, XVI, no. 11.

[23] *Berakhot*, 12b–13a.

MORDECAI M. KAPLAN'S CONTRIBUTION TO CONSERVATIVE JUDAISM

By Alexander J. Burnstein

Wherever and however one enters upon Professor Mordecai M. Kaplan's writings, one is brought back, it seems to me, to the main fact, the most interesting and decisive fact about Dr. Kaplan, his genius as a religious thinker and a religious reformer of a very high order, who succeeded in developing new ways of thinking and many new and promising approaches to traditional thought and contemporary Jewish problems. Dr. Kaplan's wide-ranging critical study and sympathetic appraisal of Judaism, a task which no one among the moderns has as yet performed, places him squarely alongside those men who have made Jewish thought relevant to the needs of their own time. In the performance of this function he is to be ranked with the classical Jewish thinkers of the Middle Ages, with Saadia, with Maimonides, with Crescas, who dominated the minds of thinking Jews for centuries. The greatness of those men does not consist in their having originated new ideas; their greatness lies in having successfully harmonized widely circulated new ideas with their traditional religious beliefs.

Dr. Kaplan has performed analogous services, particularly for American Jewry. Even those who do not find themselves in agreement with some of his assumptions and conclusions will admit that he is the first to have given us a full-scale, objective and serious sociological study of the nature and structure of Judaism, and the first to have offered a creative, courageous exploration of the ultimate reason for the existing upheavel and break-down in Jewish life. He has taught, with tireless industry and rare patience, a whole generation of Jews to distinguish between the modes of sociological functioning which prevailed in the past, in an era which has come to an end, and the new forces which operate in the world today. He has endeavored to relate the basic Jewish values and ideals to the thought-movements of our time, and to every issue of human life. He has brought his comprehensive thinking to bear upon problem after problem confronting the modern Jew. While the solutions which he found may be questioned by some, he has shown himself to be an animator of thought and feeling. There is hardly a phase of Jewish life, whether it be the synagogue, the school, educational theory, the field of Jewish social work and organization, or Jewish theology, which does not exhibit the impress of his activity.

Surely no Jewish thinker of recent times perceived so clearly the inherent relations which ought to subsist between religion and social and ethical progress. No religious teacher of the present age has labored so fearlessly and selflessly to correct the widely diffused misconceptions of the true function of religion. He is among the very few who have made an honest attempt to grapple with the many theological questions raised by modern science. No man ever tried harder than Dr. Kaplan to initiate the necessary changes in thought and action which our contemporary experience has made compelling. He will, therefore, always stand out as a religious reformer who has infused our ancient faith with new motive, new direction, and a new relevance to the modern world. And by all who have come under his influence, his personality is cherished with gratitude and affection.

With this preamble, let us now look at some of the currents of influence which Dr. Kaplan set in motion within the Conservative movement.

Scientific Candor and Clear Thinking

Dr. Kaplan has affected those who studied under him in the Jewish Theological Seminary — and I am privileged to number myself among them — in so many ways, and at so many different levels, that it is difficult to know where to begin and what influences to regard as more important than others. But some features of his influence are especially pertinent to any discussion of Dr. Kaplan's major contribution to the Conservative movement. They provide a glimpse into the process by which Dr. Kaplan has come to make so profound an impression on that movement.

First and foremost, it is as a teacher that he has had so commanding a share in inspiring and shaping the ideas of the teachers, preachers, and exponents of Conservative Judaism. There are certain characteristics of his teaching one can never forget.[1]

Dr. Kaplan's teaching has, for instance, exhibited the spirit of scientific candor. He has always displayed a wonderful openness of mind, and a readiness to receive new truths. He has never been appalled by the novelty of an idea, and has approached every belief with respectful inquiry. As an ideal teacher, he seeks not so much to persuade or to indoctrinate his students, as to challenge and stimulate them to examine the foundations and superstructures of their assertions and beliefs, to subject these beliefs to the stern test of reason and experience. He treats every problem with utter honesty, and with an attitude of mind which is mainly the result of the habit of scientific research. In his teaching we discovered a new fearlessness and a new unhesitating directness of thought about many things, to which the smothering influence of ancient custom had made a direct approach difficult. We found that directness evident in his psychocultural interpretation of Judaism, in his passionate and commanding insistence upon the necessity of renewal, and the desperate need of a program, or, better, of guiding principles, through which such renewal and re-animation of Judaism can be achieved. In a very real sense candor has become a more widely diffused attitude in our day, within our own ranks, because of Dr. Kaplan's teaching. And in that sense, we may call it a gift of Dr. Kaplan to Conservative Judaism.

Then there has been Dr. Kaplan's emphasis upon the need of clear thinking. Theological discussions too often fall prey to the temptation to wander off into a misty land of abstraction where nothing stands out in clear definition. But there has never been any fog floating about in Dr. Kaplan's class room. Sermons, he stressed, must be presented in a clear-cut, logical, and orderly fashion. And woe to the student who has tried to substitute rhetoric, grandiloquence, wordy formulas for well-organized thought and ideas! But not even logical definition satisfies Dr. Kaplan's conception of the moral obligation and responsibility of the rabbi. In his view the preacher must not only know the meaning, and work out all the implications, of his own assertions, but he must learn that simplicity and clarity of speech which set forth thought in so sharp an outline that it cannot possibly be misunderstood.

And finally, it would be impossible to list these characteristics of Dr. Kaplan's teaching without mentioning its aliveness. He has presented to us not a worn-out system in whose channels men's minds move with difficulty and to whose deeper meaning our hearts do not respond. Rather has he given us a philosophy responsive to the yearnings and gropings of our modern thought-life. We always saw in him a man, who had an extraordinary sense for what was significant in other people's ideas, and who put his heart into the process of dialectic. And we saw the twinkle of friendly, sympathetic eyes as we watched this masterful teacher at work, always seeking to provide a principle of integration for the diverse facts, conflicting values and religious and moral ideas of the modern Jew.

This, then, is the sort of teaching which has brought not only distinction and commanding dignity to the Seminary for more than four decades, but has given us, graduates of the Seminary, and hundreds of other students and exponents of Jewish thought, a new belief in the future of the Jew, a new spirit, and a new mood about the creation and preservation of Jewish loyalties and ideals in the Diaspora.

Judaism As a Civilization

In assessing Dr. Kaplan's contribution to the Jewish Theological Seminary, the seat of Conservative Judaism, one is at the same time paying tribute to the school which, in turn, provided him with a rostrum, a stimulus, and the necessary academic freedom to enable him to spread his basic convictions and message with fearless independence and intellectual integrity.

Yet even this does not suggest the full measure of Dr. Kaplan's influence. It is still too early to summarize with any degree of historical objectivity, the impact of his teachings upon every section of the Conservative movement. But it is possible to state with certainty that some elements of his thought have already entered deeply into the making of the mind of Conservative Judaism insofar as that mind may be said to have clearly defined character. He has given us at least three ideas which are bound to have increasing influence within the Conservative movement.

First comes Dr. Kaplan's fresh and original conception of Judaism as a civilization. The concept has been so much used within our movement, and has had so much wear, that one might fear it would become threadbare. But there is so much truth in it, and there is so much that is suggestive in it that few have grasped as yet its far-reaching implications. Judaism, according to Dr. Kaplan, is not a creed or religion, nor does it consist of a set of divinely revealed teachings. It includes teachings, but is something very much bigger, very much more alive than any teachings or doctrines can be.

Dr. Kaplan's argument is that, if we get away from theological definitions and take the historical point of view, we shall see that this is so. Judaism has always functioned as a civilization. It is a great social, cultural, and spiritual movement in the life of our people. It is a great stream, taking its rise back in the second millenium before our era and flowing on down the centuries into our own times. It is not simple but complex, as all living things are. Consequently, it has not the form of unity and identity that an unchanging dogma or an unchanging "atom" (as originally conceived) may possess; it has the same sort of identity and unity that characterizes all living things, — the sort that we, as human beings, possess.

A man may be considered the same person he was 20 or 30 years ago, because his life today is continuous with his life of yesteryear, and also because, though he has changed in many ways, there are certain fundamental characteristics which were his then that are his still. So it is with Judaism. Its present has grown, by a continuous and unbroken process, out of its past; and in spite of all the changes which it, as a living thing, has naturally undergone, it has been characterized, throughout its long course, by certain fundamental traits which are constant and decisive. The basic elements or factors which make up the complex phenomenon of Judaism are: religion, the peoplehood of Israel, its tradition, culture and folkways. In short, Judaism is the evolving religious civilization of the Jewish people.

The Need for Adaptation

But there is a corollary of this conception which has guided Dr. Kaplan's thinking, and which some within our ranks have not apprehended as yet, namely, that, like all other living things, Judaism is constantly adapting itself to new situations. This involves change. Change is a condition of its life. With every new land in which Jews settle, with every new generation, new problems arise to which Judaism must respond by some fresh intellectual formulation. New situations demand of religious leaders that they discriminate between the details which have become irrelevant and the main principles which forward human and moral progress. Constant alertness, constant inventiveness is the condition of Jewish life.

Now, "Conservative Judaism," Dr. Kaplan contends, "does recognize change in the beliefs and practices of Judaism as an historical fact. Such change, having taken place at a stage of human development, when the authority of tradition was paramount, necessarily insinuated itself quite unconsciously. Only as we look back over the long past of Judaism do we discern in it the process of evolution. It is this kind of evolution which Conservatism has raised to a norm. Accordingly, it yields to change which has come to stay, but it does not initiate change."[2]

There is much in Dr. Kaplan's criticism that is true. Conservative Judaism has been to a great extent defensive rather than constructive; indefinite, apologetic and ineffective rather than positive and affirmative. Its deep commitment to the institutions and traditions of religion and Jewish Law has made for an emotional conservatism, difficult to overcome, which has kept many a Conservative rabbi from facing squarely the issues raised by historical needs and life. Yet who can fail to discern the shift in religious orientation within our ranks and the new trend of interest in the problem of adjusting some of our observances to contemporary life? Especially among the younger men in the Conservative movement, the growing influence of Dr. Kaplan's meaningful interpretation of Judaism has been marked, and has contributed not a little to the remarkable stirrings within the councils of the Committee on Jewish Law and Standards, and to the yearnings and demands for far-reaching revision of Jewish Law.

Dr. Kaplan has also taught the significant principle of the peoplehood of Israel, which has clearly defined our status as Jews, and has been largely appropriated by many of the adherents of Conservative Judaism. Here Dr. Kaplan has presented to us a concept that can be tested both as a rational ideal and as a psychological fact. As a psychological fact, the idea of peoplehood is objectively given, something structural to the organic nature of any living society, something rooted in history, and something that serves to satisfy the deepest needs of man, because, in the words of Dr. Kaplan, "as human beings, there are two states or conditions we cannot do without. We cannot do without being needed, and without something of which we are proud."[3]

As an ideal, Jewish peoplehood stands up as a phenomenon of life-giving vitality, widening the mental horizon of Jews and enlarging the scope of their interests. But, if that ideal is to serve as a unifying force in Jewish life, it needs constant correction, must be charged with new meaning and significance, and must be re-defined in terms "that would make our status creative of new social and spiritual values as well as compatible with unquestioned loyalty to the non-Jewish people with which our lot is cast."[4] At the same time, since the intellectual affirmations are of secondary importance, this dynamic concept is capable of including Jews whose social, philosophic and religious views vary greatly. There is much in it which can be applied empirically, and it is bound to gain in influence as against all static views and definitions of the Jewish group.

A New Approach to Religion

But perhaps the most significant contribution Dr. Kaplan has made to the Conservative movement is his stimulating and provocative interpretation of religion. To this he gives marvelous expression in all his writings, notably in his *Meaning of God in Modern Jewish Religion* and in *The Future of the American Jew*.

Space does not permit a detailed analysis of the basic elements of his religious philosophy. We can scarcely afford, however, to omit those characteristic expressions of his thought that have become part and parcel of the mental furniture of a substantial number of Conservative Jews.

First, there is Dr. Kaplan's non-dogmatic and non-theological definition of religion as "the organized quest of a people for salvation, for helping those who live by the civilization of that people to achieve their destiny as human beings."[5] In other words, religion is *not* independent of the remaining portions of a culture, but is ultimately integrated with them. Dr. Kaplan treats religion as a culture pattern, emphasizing the shareable social, ceremonial, and cultic features inherent in it. His attempts to relate the festivals and institutions of Jewish life to the ongoing process of reality and history, in a broad and organic sense, have given us a new spiritual altitude from which to view the religious practices and values of our faith.

Second, emphasizing the volitional and practical in religion, Dr. Kaplan has been fastening our attention on two antithetical truths; the one that true religion is the assimilation and imitation of what is best in the past, and the other that transience of conditions renders the primary postulates of the traditional religious view of man and the universe irrelevant to the present. The problem of modern Jewish religion is contained in this antithesis.

That problem is: how to understand our inheritance from the past in the most comprehensive sense of the word, and at the same time become fully aware of the change that has taken place in the outlook of contemporary man. It is fallacious and intellectually dishonest to try to conceal or to minimize the gulf that separates the past from the present. But it is also a mistake to suppose that religion can be rebuilt out of the blighted resources of the present alone, — a hopelessly impoverished and ruined present. We must restore our broken connection with the past, and the best way of finding our way back to it is through "revaluation," which, according to Dr. Kaplan, "consists in disengaging from the traditional content those elements in it which answer permanent postulates of human nature, and in integrating them into our own ideology."[6]

Certain basic insights and values in our heritage, according to Dr. Kaplan, are true, of course, but the Jewish theologian has been more concerned with *defending* tradition than with *discovering* truth. The consequence is that, in this modern world, he is left hugging words and dogmas to his heart when the strength of truth is no longer in them. We need to recover in religion the reverence for truth shown by the scientist, and his humility as he searches for it.

For religious ideas that are sound and true have everything to gain and nothing to lose under the light of examination. The details of ritual and some of our doctrines may have to be completely revised and transformed; the things believed about God may have to be expressed in different language. But we need not "tremble for the ark of God." Religion cannot retire into some sequestered corner of experience. Only religious ideas that have stood the test of careful scrutiny can face the world unafraid. Sincere, progressive and effective "religion must be based on faith in reason, and resort under all circumstances to the rational conclusions of empirical experience."[7]

Many of us, I hasten to add, are not in full agreement with some of Dr. Kaplan's theological views, especially his provisional definition of God in impersonal terms "as a cosmic process that makes for man's life abundant or salvation."[7] Needless to say, this does not in any way minimize or lessen our tremendous indebtedness to Dr. Kaplan for the new, daring philosophic pattern which he established in his studies of the whole subject of Judaism, and which none of us can afford to neglect or ignore. Dr. Kaplan's, thought because of its novelty, complexity and the uniqueness of its method, may for some time have to be mediated by others.

Whatever the difficulties of interpretation, his thought is bound to have increasing significance within the ranks of thinking Jews in the Conservative movement. For he is not only a theoretical thinker of great stature, but one whose thought is practical, pragmatic, and strikingly relevant to every major problem facing the modern Jew. The principle he employs may be abstract, but his thought is not. It deals in terms of vigorous realism with the very stuff of life. Many of us have already received from him much more than we can possibly acknowledge. The best homage which we can pay to this great master in Israel is to revaluate and rethink the problems which he has raised, and to emulate his courage in answering them. May he continue his vigorous and blessed activity for many years to come!

Notes

[1] Compare above, Mortimer J. Cohen, "Dr. Kaplan as Teacher," pp. 3–14.
[2] M. M. Kaplan, *The Future of the American Jew*, Macmillan, New York, 1948, p. 25.
[3] *Ibid.*, p. 82.   [4] *Ibid.*, p. 93.   [5] *Ibid.*, p. 172.
[6] M. M. Kaplan, *The Meaning of God in Modern Jewish Religion*, Jewish Reconstructionist Foundation, New York, 1947, p. 6. Compare above, Eugene Kohn, "Mordecai M. Kaplan as Exegete," pp. 137–154.
[7] *Ibid.*, pp. 355–356.

MORDECAI M. KAPLAN AND REFORM JUDAISM: A STUDY IN RECIPROCITY

By Roland B. Gittelsohn

One of the more common misconceptions of Reconstructionism is that it represents merely an off-shoot of Conservative Judaism. Perhaps it is only natural that this be so, since the founder and leading philosopher of the Reconstructionist movement is so distinguished a Conservative spokesman and teacher. The fact is, however, that there are nearly as many Reform as Conservative rabbis among Dr. Kaplan's disciples, and that many such men have found the climate of Reconstructionism thoroughly compatible with their orientation as teachers of Reform Judaism.

They have discovered that there are large areas of agreement between the thinking of Dr. Kaplan and that of Reform Judaism, and that there has been between them a reciprocal relationship of benefit to both. In tracing the broad outlines of that relationship, let us deal first with the threefold influence which Reform has had on the leader of Reconstructionism.

The Threefold Influence of Reform

To begin with, Reform Judaism blazed a pathway, or, at the very least, cleaned out much annoying brush along the pathway later followed by Dr. Kaplan toward an evolutionary view of Judaism and of Jewish life. It is relatively easy today for the spokesmen of Reconstructionism to speak of Judaism as an *evolving* religious civilization, to stress the importance of adjusting the eternal message of the Jewish spirit to "changes in conditions or in mental outlook."[1] It would have been infinitely more difficult to take such positions if the pioneers of Reform three to four generations ago had not anticipated and prepared them.

To be even more specific, Dr. Kaplan and his disciples have insisted quite properly that the adaptation of Jewish religion to the intellectual and philosophic climate of our day makes impossible a literal acceptance of Biblical miracles, that our ancestors' stories of miraculous events must now be reinterpreted as parables, the moral value of which is far more important than their literal truth. Reconstructionists are still subject to severe criticism in some quarters because of their approach to the matter of miracles. How much greater would be both the criticism, and the heartache of surmounting it, if Reform had not first served as a kind of mine-sweeper, clearing out at least the more obvious and explosive obstacles before the ship of Reconstructionism tried to enter the harbor! This was no small service; to ignore it, or even to take it for granted, would be an act of historic injustice.

This impact of Reform Judaism in helping to shape Dr. Kaplan's acceptance of Judaism as an *evolving* civilization is not limited either to the past or to principle. It seems to be a common trait of progressive religions to think faster than they act. Long after the philosophers of a given faith have reasoned out both the necessity and the rationale of change, its adherents are very apt to defer putting such change into living practice. Reform has been peculiarly and fortunately free of this limitation. There are some, to be sure, who would say, "altogether too free." But the fact remains that while Reform and Reconstructionism seem to stand abreast of each other today as far as the *principle* of evolutionary change is concerned, Reform is far ahead when it comes to *practice*.

It anticipated Reconstructionism, for example, by the better part of a generation in counting women in the *minyan* and extending to them the privilege of reading from the Torah. It has sloughed off the impedimenta of outworn custom and ceremony with far less restraint than have other Reconstructionists. The *Guide Toward Jewish Ritual Usage*,[2] worked out by Dr. Kaplan and his closest associates some few years back, could be accepted almost without amendment by most Reform rabbis today as a statement of their own criteria of change. But the very men who themselves worked out these altogether acceptable criteria are often timid about accepting them in their own personal religious life. This is not meant to be adverse criticism. I happen to be among those who believe that a certain amount of tension and strain is good between those who would experiment boldly and those who would accept reluctantly. And I think that Reform has served and continues to serve usefully in the capacity of challenging Dr. Kaplan's group to implement more eagerly their own principle of evolution in religion.

The Diaspora Not Galut

There is, then, a second kind of influence which must be credited to the early leaders of American Reform in anticipating an important part of Mordecai Kaplan's thinking. They were the first to insist that we Jews in the United States are not languishing in *galut*, yearning for a return to Zion. To be sure, here again the virtue sometimes became a vice. Too often the insistence that we are at home on the American scene became an uncomfortable concomitant of an almost hysterical anti-Zionism. But the core of truth was important none-the-less, that there is room in the cultural life of the United States for many groups, not the least of which is the Jewish group, whose members are here as permanent residents, not as tenants restless to move. Today this is the accepted belief of Reformists and Reconstructionists and of countless other Jews who belong to neither group. It was Reform's original emphasis.

In many areas the thinking of Dr. Kaplan has exercised a restraining influence on the exuberance of Reform. In at least one respect, however, this direction has been reversed. The third contribution of Reform to Reconstructionism has been its consistently alert emphasis on the priority of religion in

Judaism, an emphasis which provides a healthy counterbalance to what might otherwise have been a tendency of Reconstructionism to minimize the role of religion. It would be unfair as well as inaccurate to accuse Dr. Kaplan himself of any such tendency. Many times he has underscored both the historic importance and the present need for religion as the principal component of Jewish civilization. It was not a parenthesis in Mordecai Kaplan's thinking when he wrote: "Jewish religion is nothing less than the soul of Judaism."[3] "If the glory of a civilization consists in the uniqueness of its contribution to human culture, then religion was, and will remain, the glory of the Jewish civilization."[4]

Notwithstanding which, there is a very real danger that, in stressing the importance of community, in reacting against the absurd but popular notion that Judaism is merely a religion in the creedal sense, in opening the door quite properly to the Jewish secularist also, Dr. Kaplan's followers may tend to forget the primary role of the religionist and of religion. There are unfortunately some among us who would seize all too eagerly on this phase of Reconstructionism to justify their own indifference to religion.

The gap here between Dr. Kaplan and what Milton Steinberg, *alav ha-shalom*, called "new-type Reform" may be only one of emphasis, but it is vital withal. Perhaps it is only the difference between those who look upon religion as a means of keeping the Jewish people alive, and those who see the Jewish people as a vehicle for the preservation of our religious values. But even so apparently slight a difference as this can be fundamental. Though the emphasis of Reform on religion as such may not be necessary for Dr. Kaplan himself, there have been and no doubt will continue to be occasions on which his followers would do well to hearken to the warning of Reform: "Though we recognize, in the group-loyalty of Jews who have become estranged from our religious tradition, a bond which still unites them with us, we maintain that it is by its religion and for its religion that the Jewish people has lived."[5]

Such, then, are the several aspects of the contribution which the philosophy of Reform Judaism may be said to have made, directly or indirectly, to the thinking of Mordecai Kaplan and of those who surround him most closely.

The Emergence of the New Reform

Not less, by any means, have been his great contributions to the ideology of Reform. One might almost say that Dr. Kaplan has been one of the midwives responsible for the birth of the new Reform from the womb of the old. Few men from within the movement itself have exercised greater influence on this transition than has he from without. First has been his role in helping to enlarge the compass of Reform to embrace the concept of *k'lal Yisrael*. From the very beginning there has been danger that Reform Judaism might divorce itself from the mainstream of Jewish life, that, like the Karaitic movement, for example, it might prove to be but a temporary incident in time, — a little sect which would play out its role, exert perhaps a wholesome influence on the mainstream, then vanish. If that danger has by now been largely averted, Mordecai Kaplan is among those to whom credit is due. His part has been considerable in broadening the vision of Reform to include the whole people of Israel, and to see itself as an integral part of that people.

Similar to this is Dr. Kaplan's role in opening up for the leaders of Reform Judaism a wider view of what constitutes the totality of Jewish thinking. There still are some among the adherents of Reform — fortunately fewer by far with the passing of time — who look upon themselves as Americans of the Mosaic persuasion, and upon Judaism as nothing more than a doctrine or creed. For them, Judaism is a religion only. For Dr. Kaplan, it is a religion, plus. For them, being a Jew means assenting with the mind to a set of abstract principles. For him, it is an assent of heart and hand as well as of mind. His has been a liberating influence to the extent that it has opened up new and wider vistas which encompass the whole of Jewish living, rather than any narrow formulation of only a part.

As one reads through *A Program for Jewish Life Today* and the *Guiding Principles of Reform Judaism*, there is not a single trace of incompatibility, not one word in either document which cannot be thoroughly acceptable to those who adhere to the other. But it is immediately apparent that they are of altogether different dimension. Dr. Kaplan has provided a wider frame, so to speak, within which the more specific view either of Conservative or of Reform Judaism is immediately at home; not only at home, but enhanced, even as it is the function of any frame not merely to surround but to enhance the canvas within it.

When the *Guiding Principles* state quite simply that "Judaism is the historical religious experience of the Jewish people," the initials of Mordecai Kaplan are over every word of that statement. I suspect that even those among its formulators who may be most anxious to dispute the validity of his thought have been moved by it in ways of which they may not yet be consciously aware themselves. The "historical religious experience of the Jewish people" is a far, far cry from "Americans of Mosaic persuasion." So far, in fact, that the pitiful few within Reform who are afflicted with Zionophobia have found it necessary to cling with frantic compulsion to the rigid patterns of their past. But the movement as a whole has moved a great distance indeed toward its own way of saying that Judaism is the religious civilization of the Jew.

One aspect of this second Kaplanian influence is the great change of Reform toward Zionism. Surely there is no need at this late date to retrace the familiar course of that change. It may be that such change was historically inevitable, that it would have occurred in any event, even if Mordecai Kaplan had never lived or spoken. Perhaps so. By the same token and with equal validity it might be suggested that Dr. Kaplan himself would have progressed in his thinking without the influences of Reform which have already been noted. At the very least, however, it would seem reasonable to assume that each has had an effect on the other in hastening a process which would otherwise have taken much longer. It would be both inaccurate and ungracious for Reform Jews today to deny that the Kaplan school has had great effect on them, — generally in enlarging their ideological perspectives, — specifically in bringing them back to the love of Zion. Traces of Kaplan are to be found in more than one part of the *Guiding Principles.* Just how far is it — really? — from his doctrines to this: "We affirm the obligation of all Jewry to aid in (Palestine's) upbuilding as a Jewish homeland by endeavoring to make it not only a haven of refuge for the oppressed but also a center of Jewish culture and spiritual life."

Reformulation of Jewish Theology

I have purposely saved for third and last what to me personally has been Mordecai Kaplan's greatest contribution to Reform Judaism — or for that matter, to Judaism at large — his reformulation of Jewish theology. Here one begins to see quite clearly how inappropriate both "Conservative" and "Reform" can be as adjectives describing their respective interpretations of Jewish religion. Reform, which has advanced so eagerly on the front of ceremonial observance, often seems more hesitant than Conservatism in the realm of theology. The boldest and bravest recasting in our generation of Jewish thinking about God has been done by men like Solomon Goldman, Milton Steinberg, Eugene Kohn, and above all, by Mordecai Kaplan.

I often suspect that when everything else about Dr. Kaplan has been either forgotten or taken for granted, when the issues of organic Jewish community and the sancta of ceremony and the delicate balance of Israel and Diaspora have been settled by the stubborn facts of history, the name of Mordecai

Kaplan will live longest in the courageous company of those who have dared to rethink the eternal values of Jewish religion in the light of new circumstance and perspective. He belongs with Philo, and even more with the Rambam. Where they talked of God in the language of Plato or Aristotle, he has described Him in the climate of Darwin and Freud and the newer physics. To do so does not mean to be irreligious or to assign God a lesser place in the total scheme of things. Quite to the contrary, it means putting the concept of God into the only terms which will enable it to function in our lives with something of the intensity and validity it had for our fathers.

Some day there may be food not only for speculation, but for fascinating psychological research in the respective roles of Conservative and Reform Judaism vis-à-vis both ceremony and theology. Perhaps some of Dr. Kaplan's disciples have had to cling rigidly to the accustomed routines of ceremonial observance precisely for the security they have momentarily relinquished in departing from the old ways of conceiving God. And perhaps others of his followers, in the Reform wing, have held close to the old ways of describing the *ribono shel olam* exactly for the security they have surrendered in departing from so many of the old *mitzvot*.

But this is only speculation. What is fact is that Mordecai Kaplan, more than any other Jew of our generation, has translated the idea of God into a terminology acceptable to Jews of the twentieth and twenty-first centuries. He has understood that we stand on the threshold of a time when men will be able to think of the Creative Power responsible for the highest values they know, not necessarily as a personality, but as a quality of the universe and of life. For daring to touch the sacred concept of the Eternal Highest, he has been excoriated and excommunicated. One day he will be universally revered for precisely the same reason. One cannot help but apply to him Dr. Sachar's perceptive comment about an earlier sage: "The writings of Maimonides were constantly under fire because he applied reason not only to ethics and metaphysics, but to the very sanctities of religion."[6] Like the Rambam, it will be Mordecai Kaplan's inevitable fate to go through the cycle from heresy to respectability to orthodoxy. It may even be that the Reformers of a later day will rebel against the very ideas of his which seem so daring to some of us now. If they do, it will be with the benevolent blessing in advance of Dr. Kaplan himself, who, even in the midst of his highest creative zeal, is able to write: ". . . . the quest for an adequate concept of God should not be expected to yield the same results for all Jews. Jews will conceive of God in different ways."[7] It would be hard to find anywhere a statement which applies more eloquently to the specific realm of theology what has from the beginning been the essential spirit of Reform Judaism.

And Kaplan has done one thing more, without the mention of which even this inadequate word of evaluation cannot be concluded. He has helped to give us of the Reform rabbinate a common ground on which to stand with our colleagues of the Conservative wing. If there are growing numbers in each group who see areas of agreement, and more important, possibilities of common activity and effort, this is but another testament to the genius by which we have been privileged to be touched. He has helped all of us understand more deeply than ever the ancient admonition: *eleh v'eleh divre elohim hayyim*.[8]

The mutual effect of Dr. Kaplan and Reform is deeper by far than many of us have suspected. Those of us who are privileged to be at once among the disciples both of this man and of Isaac Mayer Wise perceive that clearly. We believe, with honest humility, that the priceless heritage of Isaac Wise has smoothed a way for Mordecai Kaplan's view of Judaism as an evolving civilization, even while it challenges his observance to keep pace with his thinking, and reminds the more zealous of his followers that religion is and must remain the essential heart and core of Jewish civilization. And we acknowledge, with inexpressibly heartfelt gratitude, that he for his part has enlarged our vision to include *kelal Yisrael*, our thinking to encompass the whole of Jewish existence, and our minds to see God as tomorrow will see and know Him.

NOTES

[1] *Program for Jewish Life Today*, Jewish Reconstructionist Foundation, Inc., New York, 1951, p. 10.

[2] *Toward a Guide for Jewish Ritual Usage*, Jewish Reconstructionist Foundation, Inc., New York, 1941.

[3] M. M. Kaplan, *The Reconstructionist*, V, no. 19.

[4] M. M. Kaplan, *Judaism As A Civilization*, Macmillan, New York, 1934, p. 306.

[5] *Guiding Principles of Reform Judaism*, Central Conference of American Rabbis, 1937.

[6] "The Writings of Maimonides", A. L. Sachar, *History of the Jews*, Alfred A. Knopf, Inc., New York, 1948 edition, p. 191.

[7] *Program for Jewish Life Today*, p. 10.

[8] "Both these and those are the words of the living God."

MORDECAI M. KAPLAN AS A PHILOSOPHER OF DEMOCRACY

By Joseph L. Blau

The record of the achievements of Mordecai M. Kaplan is a full and inspiring one. He has added new meaning to the older conception of the rabbi as teacher, during his years in the pulpit and in the classroom. His part in the creation of the Society for the Advancement of Judaism and the Jewish Reconstructionist Foundation, and his important services to the cause of Israel and to Jewish culture and education might well serve as a definition of the newer conception of the rabbi as leader. To these two, out of his own qualities of mind and heart and spirit, he has added a third conception of the rabbi as spokesman for the vital values of Jewish civilization in the American democratic environment. Equipped with a broad knowledge of the modern sciences of sociology and psychology, and a wide reading of recent philosophic literature, as well as with a comprehensive familiarity with the traditional literature of Judaism, he has produced a creative synthesis which has served as a Guide for many of the Perplexed of our times.

In this collective volume of tribute to Dr. Kaplan on his having reached three-score and ten, it is my small part to draw together his thoughts on the nature of democracy. It will not be possible here to go beyond this limit and to indicate the relation of this special aspect of Dr. Kaplan's work to the total pattern of his philosophy. The thoughtful reader of these essays should, however, find no difficulty in estimating the role played by Dr. Kaplan's theory of democracy in the larger symphony of the whole.

The Cultural Matrix of Democracy

To appreciate Mordecai M. Kaplan's philosophy of democracy it is necessary to consider it in its broadest context. This inclusive matrix is his theory of culture. For if "culture, in the concrete, exists only as cultures",[1] it will be the case that some of the particular cultures which exist are democratic cultures. The attempt to formulate a philosophy of democracy becomes, then, the attempt to define the ideal ends and functioning of such a democratic culture. Such a definition of the ideal of one type of culture demands formulation in terms of the nature of culture in general. Dr. Kaplan's general view of the nature of culture is akin to that of the secular sociologists and anthropologists, but goes beyond that secular notion by avoiding its narrow limits. The measure of the difference is the measure of Dr. Kaplan's originality as a religious thinker.

E. B. Tylor, one of the nineteenth century anthropologists who helped in the creation of the culture concept, described a culture as "that complex whole which includes knowledge, belief, art, morals, law, custom and any other capabilities acquired by man as a member of a society."[2] More recent anthropologists and sociologists who have used the concept, in keeping with the attempt of their disciplines to scientificize themselves, have emphasized the study of "culture traits" or the external and visible behavioral indications of the culture complex. They attempt to limit themselves to what is objective in order to get away from certain "metaphysical" views of culture. Thus Melville J. Herskovits and Malcolm M. Willey wrote "Culture . . . is the mode of life of a people. It must not be assumed, of course, that culture is a metaphysical entity which operates of itself. It is rather a generic term that covers an amazing number of types of behavior."[3] Dr. Kaplan does not dispute this definition; the study of the behavioral patterns of individuals in society has been a major aspect of his thought. What he does is to supplement this positivistic definition, and thus to retain its empirical values, while recognizing an ulterior element in culture. This ulterior element may be regarded as the psychological foundation of culture, underlying its behavioral expression.

The psychological component upon which Dr. Kaplan sagely places stress is the factor of awareness of kind. He does not say that awareness of kind is the *cause* of identical behavior patterns, nor does he say that identical behavior patterns *cause* awareness of kind. What he says is that a culture is internally grounded on awareness of kind and externally expressed in identical behavior patterns. They are the two faces of the same coin, and therefore inseparable. Internal awareness without identical behavior does not constitute belonging to a culture, nor does identical behavior without internal awareness. Not every person whose behavior pattern is like my own is recognized as a *Landsmann*. The combination of internal awareness and external behavior constitutes belonging to a culture and it is by means of culture that "human societies are enabled to operate as units and to perpetuate themselves as units."[4]

Awareness of kind, however, is not an altogether beneficent element in the human makeup. To have a sense of likeness towards some people implies having a sense of unlikeness towards others. Awareness of kind involves an awareness of difference, which is often expressed as xenophobia. "The culture that evokes awareness of kind in relation to members of the same society evokes the awareness of difference in relation to members of other societies."[5] Towards those a little less than kin we are apt to be a little less than kind. There may have been a stage in human history when cultural groups and political groups were coextensive. Today, however, we are more likely to find a culture which spreads over a number of nations and which does not completely include any one of these nations. Each cultural group may be multi-national; each national group may be multi-cultural. For many centuries of Western European history the integrating element in the culture pattern, the factor which induced a strong sense of kinship among members of different national groups, was the

Christian Church. True, the Church-dominated culture of Europe was unkind to outsiders.[6] But it had an historical mission: to produce a cultural fusion among the physically fused cultures of Western Europe. "The historical process whereby this fusion is effected usually gives rise to new sancta, new myths and new religious rites. From these emerge values, norms, and interpretations of events which become the context of the new awareness of kind."[7]

Under the impact of various fundamental changes in the outlook of part of Western European society, a disintegration of this synthesis took place. The Church-dominated culture proved insufficiently flexible to make the necessary adjustments, and modern national cultures arose to take over the job. This is not necessarily to be construed as a weakness or a flaw in the Church or in the synthesis created under its influence. The very strength which the Church developed to meet the challenge of anarchy after the downfall of the western branch of the Roman Empire may have been the factor which led to its inflexibility in the face of the new outlook. In any case, the fact is that the culture as then synthesized failed to adapt itself to new conditions, and what had been an integrating factor in Europe itself disintegrated, and modern nationalism replaced it. "Modern occidental nationalism, or awareness of kind growing out of common political and economic interests rather than out of a common acceptance of a revealed religion, played the chief role in overcoming feudalism and ecclesiasticism which would have stymied the three fundamental changes that spell modernism."[8]

For a time this form of cultural integration was able to maintain social control. But just as the Christian cultural synthesis had shown an inability to adjust to one form of change, modern nationalism showed a dangerous tendency under the impact of another type of change. Modern western nationalism becomes totalitarianism; it ceases to be merely political and economic and becomes religious. As Dr. Kaplan has pointed out on many occasions, the chief problem of democratic life in the world today is to resist totalitarianism in whatever local and temporary form it may manifest itself.[9] The growth of totalitarian political religions emphasizes the need for world peace based upon more than formal covenants among nations. There must be a genuine attempt to educate for international amity. "Human brotherhood can no longer be reserved for pious wishing in religious rituals which are never meant to guide national policies."[10]

The method of theological change which Dr. Kaplan has advocated and exemplified and to which he has reserved the name of "reconstructionism" involves the conscious acceptance of new ideas and their deliberate rooting by attaching them to older formulas and practices which are thereby given new significance. It is a cultural reconstructionism which Dr. Kaplan suggests as a means for the development of a program for world peace and against totalitarianism. Western man must find a new principle of integration whereby his national cultures may attach "a new significance to the awareness of difference which always accompanies the awareness of kind. Awareness of difference should not stress unlikeness, but otherness, i. e., the realization that peoples living in other climes and amid other circumstances have an inherent right to be what they are . . . . This points to the necessity of adopting some kind of cultural currency, or a kind of international stabilization fund of cultural values, . . . a kind of valuational Esperanto . . . . Without such a basis for mutual understanding there is no likelihood that men would ever acquire a feeling of common humanity. Without the feeling of a common humanity, all covenants and machineries for world peace lack the motive power to make them work."[11]

There is another use to which Dr. Kaplan believes this "valuational Esperanto" may be put in the struggle against totalitarianism. The aggressor nations have developed highly integrated value-systems in their emphasis on awareness of kind. Meantime each of the democratic nations has failed to weld its diverse elements together into a unity adequate to defense.

Where totalitarianism has arbitrarily simplified the composition of modern society, the problem in a democratic nation is to develop a frame of reference which does not reject complexity and yet provides for the integration of conflicting trends into a cultural whole. In describing his sense of this need, Dr. Kaplan indicates well what the conditions making for disunity are:

> How essential such integration is becomes evident when we realize the precarious condition of the unity of a democratic nation like ours. One has only to consider some of the factors that make for inner division and that are likely to be taken advantage of by an aggressor: the existence of various religious groups, and the almost equal number unaffiliated with any of those groups; the lack of mutual understanding between the different races, between the "grass roots" population and those whose foreign provenance is still recognizable, between agriculture and industry, between labor and capital, between skilled and unskilled industry. In addition, each specialized function in the various fields of human endeavor calls for so much concentrated attention in the way of knowledge and training that it isolates culturally those who master that function from the rest of society. The more complicated society grows, and the more dependent it becomes upon every individual's performing his part in it efficiently, the less each individual knows about the whole of society and the less he realizes his responsibility in maintaining its wholeness or health. With the competition for jobs becoming ever keener, and with the consequent tendency of vocational preparation to invade more and more the education of the country's youth, the less likely are people to acquire a common fund of ideas and values as a basis for mutual awareness of kind. They speak the same vernacular, but what they think about the things that matter may place their worlds so far apart as to render them completely out of touch with one another.[12]

Within Mordecai Kaplan's theory of culture, then, the democratic nations of the world must develop a democratic pattern of values both as a basis for the maintenance of international accord and as a method for overcoming internal divisive forces and disintegrative elements. This is democracy's task which must be carried forward without violating democracy's distinctive character.

Definition of Democracy

From this view of the task of a democracy we come naturally to inquire what Dr. Kaplan means by his use of the term "democracy." He has given a formal definition of the term, and it is with this that we must start our inquiry. " 'A democracy' is a form of nationhood dedicated to a way of life based upon certain empirical values, or values which represent forms of experience, among them being those which have served as a basis of the American way of life, viz., life, liberty, and the pursuit of happiness."[13] This definition, to be sure, does not describe any actually existing society; it attempts to define an as yet unrealized goal which was set forth in the past, has been translated into present-day terms, and must be held before ourselves as a future possibility.

The statement of the democratic ideal was basically the contribution of the so-called Age of Reason in the eighteenth century. Dr. Kaplan does not encourage the myth, which much recent scholarship has tried to foster, that Judaism or any of the other historic faiths "has always taught the gospel of democracy, as we understand it." Quite the contrary; his evolutionary view of Jewish civilization leads him to the assertion that "one must expect to find in its early stages" or in the early stages of any other of the traditional religious bodies, "much that has become unacceptable." The orthodox method is to teach a religion "as an eternally fixed system of truth [and that way of teaching it] is to prevent it from being a force for democracy."[14] In fact, in a recent aphorism, Dr. Kaplan has pointed out that "Communism, Catholicism and Jewish Orthodoxy demand of Democracy freedom in the name of *its* principles, and deny freedom to Democracy in the name of *their own* principles."[15] This is not to say that there is any opposition between any religion and democracy. In the first place, there is a sense, to be discussed later, in which Dr. Kaplan regards democracy as itself a religious faith. In the second place, he does not advocate any such static teaching of religion as that which he has described as unacceptable within a democratic frame of thought. Where religion is taught, as Dr. Kaplan has taught Judaism throughout his ministry, "as a dynamic life pattern, with a design whose beauty of meaning unfolds gradually to meet the growing needs of human life, then it can function as a potent factor for democracy."[16]

In its original statement, democracy was aimed at the destruction of the tyranny of the few. Its traditional function was to carry on the struggle against special privilege. Democracy's problem today is no longer the same. "The danger which threatens to overwhelm democracy nowadays . . . lurks in the tyranny of the many." To carry on the struggle against this totalitarian menace "as though it were merely an intensified form of the struggle against special privilege" would be a serious error.[17] It is in part because democracy did not adequately fulfil its goal of eliminating the tyranny of the few that we now have to combat the tyranny of the many. Dr. Kaplan has gone as far as to suggest, tentatively, that "had the liberal democratic movement been carried to its logical conclusion, or had any serious attempt been made to translate the ideal of 'liberty, equality and fraternity' into political and economic law, the long awaited millennium might actually have come about."[18] Thus, although there is an historical relation between the problems of today and those of yesterday, the democracy which attempts to solve today's problems with the weapons of the past is foredoomed not merely to fail, but also to create new and more difficult problems.

To say that democracy is a "form of nationhood," or, as Dr. Kaplan has expressed the same thought in other places, a "quality of nationhood," is to state the obvious as a necessary reminder. Although the idea of democracy may be an abstraction, any steps toward the realization of the ideal must be taken within the concrete framework of a social order. In the exemplary case, the social order with which we are concerned is a nation. We have already seen that Dr. Kaplan is keenly aware of the pluralism and diversification of the modern nation as well as of the element of solidarity which constitutes the nation a unity. Any form of nationhood presupposes some type of unity of diverse elements. The particular type of unity which is presupposed by a democratic form of national organization is based upon the idea that "the interests which unite human beings, if they are well aware of those interests, are strong enough to deprive differences of their divisive power."[19] Essentially, then, a democratic nation is one whose bonds of unity are moral rather than coercive. The purpose of democratic social organization is ethical. It is "to have justice and kindness instead of tyranny and cruelty prevail in all human relationships. That purpose is to bring under control the inherent tendency of human beings to seek power and to exercise it for its own sake regardless of the harm it does."[20]

To assert the moral quality of democratic social organization requires a conception of the democratic nation as a community. "Society is neither an organized mob that imposes its will by violence on other social groups or individuals nor a mechanism in which every man's life follows a predetermined pattern, wherein his own choices hardly count for anything. We have to be aware of society as functioning in the spirit of a community. *A community might be defined as that form of social organization in which the welfare of each is the concern of all, and the life of the whole is the concern of each.*"[21] It may be observed here, although the observation is not germane to our central inquiry, that one of the chief concerns of Dr. Kaplan's specific ministry has been the attempt to rebuild an American-Jewish community which foundered in the nineteenth century on the rocks of diversity. His proposals for reconstituting the Jewish community in America take full account of the diversity of Jewish group interests. His suggestions are for the creation of a *democratic* social structure for the Jewish community.[22]

To insist as Dr. Kaplan does upon democracy as a quality of community extended to the nation is to get away from the shallow and superficial individualism which has too often been identified with democracy. There is no basis, he claims, for regarding as the essence of democracy "the principle that the primary unit in all political and economic problems should be the individual and not the nation or the state."[23] To view the individual as thus implicated in the essence of democracy leads to a view of the democratic society as merely a mechanical aggregation of individual citizens, not a true social organism.

The Democratic Values

A *value*, in Dr. Kaplan's usage, means "anything whatsoever that is regarded as furthering the achievement of human destiny," while a *disvalue* means "whatever is regarded as hindering the achievement of human destiny."[24] The classic formulation of the values of democracy is that of the French Revolution, "liberty, equality, fraternity." Dr. Kaplan's thought on these values is devoted primarily to the discussion of freedom (he rarely uses the term "liberty") and equality and their reconciliation. Fraternity does not appear directly, but it is understood as the basis of community, equivalent to "free voluntary cooperation, the ultimate objective of democracy."[25]

Freedom is a vital value in Kaplan's social ethics. "The triumph of democracy is the triumph of social order based on freedom.... Democracy is freedom conceived as a condition of society, or as a quality of social relationships. It is freedom embodied in political forms or institutions."[26] This freedom is not anarchic. It is not license. Freedom is an aspect of self-realization. It "should be a means to growth and life abundant. It must, therefore, be offered not as an alternative to security but as an addition to security." The democratic nations have thus far failed to grasp this ethical interpretation of freedom; they have chosen, rather, to understand freedom as *laissez-faire*, "with cutthroat competition, whether it be on an individual or on a collective scale." Thus the democratic nations have failed to eliminate special privilege for the few who have won both freedom and security, while the bulk of the citizenry have lost both. The democracies have allowed "the struggle for freedom [to degenerate] into the freedom to struggle," and, as a consequence, faith in freedom reached its nadir in the totalitarian wave of recent years. To restore faith in freedom, there must be a guarantee, universal in its applicability, of both security and true freedom.[27]

"This freedom which occupies so central a place in man's higher life is not the freedom of one or more dominant impulses, desires or passions, but of our whole being.... When the whole of us acts through every part of us, we are initiators of action, creators and not merely passive and helpless automatons."[28] Creative living is the social development of true individuality; both the right to be different and the right to be creative belong to freedom. One cannot believe in freedom and be cynical about the potentialities of individual men or of human societies. The very essence of the ideal of freedom is the assumption that "potentially, human beings and human groups have something unique to contribute to the totality of life."[29] As Dr. Kaplan rises to the peak of his social ethics, the mantle of the cultural relativist falls away, and is replaced by a prophetic fervor and a Kantian intensity. Whatever prevents the free development of potential uniqueness into actual creativity is slavery! "When a man is made to subserve a purpose of which he is unaware or in which he is not interested, he is a slave."[30]

Clearly we have moved to a deeper level than that of the merely political freedom with which we started. We have, in fact, moved with Dr. Kaplan to that inner freedom, or freedom of the spirit, which must sustain political freedom. For "freedom must be conceived not only as a condition of society but also as a state of mind." Inner freedom is "the unyielding refusal to recognize the legitimacy of brute force, or to bow before its authority."[31] Dr. Kaplan describes three elements of which this freedom of the spirit is compounded: "the unreconciled heart," "the challenging mind," and "the fearless and cooperative will." The unreconciled heart refuses respect to mere size, denies that blind fate or inexorable necessity must triumph over human purposes and justice, and will not "make peace with fraud and violence, regardless of the success to which they lead, or the prestige achieved by means of them."[32] The challenging mind reinforces the unreconciled heart in the struggle against brute force by demanding that every tradition and every authority, every purpose, ideal, belief or standard must be able to justify itself to the reason. Tradition must be the servant of man in his slow and cumulative progress, not man the inert slave of tradition. Freedom of thought is an intrinsic element in the maintenance of the dignity of the individual.[33] The challenging mind demands the right to examine the dogmas of the present as well as those of the past. It refuses uncritical assent to the "tyranny of the multitude," to the conventionalism of the mass mind. It maintains the right to think in the face of the flood of propaganda which threatens to engulf all thought.

And yet, it is with one's contemporaries that one must live and strive to advance human welfare. This is "the crucial problem of freedom; how to guard our own individuality and the capacity to think for ourselves, and yet cooperate with those whose background, upbringing and whole outlook are different from our own. This is an art human beings are slow to learn. Democracy may well be conceived as the process of social experimentation by which men are seeking to learn that art, and to apply step by step the wisdom acquired as a result of this experimentation."[34] If the goals of democratic society are ever to be achieved, the defenders of democratic freedom must have not only a fearless will to live, but also a resolute will to live together. Freedom from fear and the achievement of a readiness to cooperate with our fellows — "the fearless and cooperative will" — are essential to the winning of inner freedom.

Just as the chief external mode of manifestation of freedom is in political organization, the chief external mode of manifestation of equality is in economic justice. Equality, in this economic sense or in any other, is not a natural endowment. Equality is an ideal end-product of society, not a gift of nature. It is "an essential social objective."[35] And yet, "Civilization has always tended to destroy equality, because it has favored the gravitation of control over things toward the few who happen to be stronger and more cunning."[36] On the one hand, Dr. Kaplan is Huxleyan in his insistence that the "struggle for existence" and the "survival of the fittest" of evolutionary theory cannot be translated into social and ethical ideals.[37] On the other, he follows Tawney in regarding what men in society call "property" as "improperty;" most-so-called "property rights" are, for Dr. Kaplan, "property wrongs." He asserts that "From the standpoint of equality, the most deplorable aspect of the present social and economic order is the inordinate striving to seize as much control as the law permits. And the law, being based on complete ignorance or disregard of the changed conditions which jeopardize the sacredness of human rights, is such as to sanction the deprivation of those rights."[38] If nature and society are regarded as the only possible sources of human equality, then equality is impossible of attainment.

Here, again, it is necessary to move inward; basically, the demand for equality is neither natural nor, in the narrow sense, social. It is ethical and religious. "The religious perception of the sacredness of the individual personality, i. e. of the importance of the individual as an end in himself and not merely as a means to another, is the only adequate rationale for democratic equality; it is the only safeguard against the tyranny of both mobs and state."[39] Further evolution of improperty wrongs will never lead to property rights. A radical shift of direction is necessary if the ideal of equality and justice is to be approached. "To change the social order so that it shall conform to the ethical demand for human equality involves nothing short of revolution . . . . The new order cannot be an outgrowth of the very principles that have produced the old."[40]

Fraternity as cooperation enters into the realization of equality even as it entered into the realization of freedom. The fundamental and essential revolutionary step which must be taken is to shift from competition to cooperation.

The reconstruction of our social institutions with a view to eliminating from them the competitive element involves recognizing that the time has come to put an end to the haphazard and planless character of our economic and political activities. The so-called ideal of "rugged individualism" in the world of business, and the policy of *laissez faire* in government, are merely attempts at institutionalizing combative selfishness. All this must now be replaced by intelligent planning on a scale of cooperation, which must ultimately embrace the whole of mankind.[41]

The democratic ideal must be universal; in no merely journalistic sense it must be a "one-world" ideal. Freedom, equality and cooperation must be for all mankind.

Soterics — The Religious Sanction for Democratic Values

It has often been pointed out, triumphantly, by opponents of democracy that liberty and equality are not compossible. An absolute liberty is destructive of equality; the maintenance of an absolute equality requires the restriction of liberty. Dr. Kaplan refers to this as "the paradox that the freedom of the individual is inconsistent with equality of all individuals."[42] Probably the most original and stimulating aspect of his theory of democracy involves his resolution of this paradox. Liberty and equality, on the level of this paradox, are empirical values. When they come into conflict, they hinder the achievement of human destiny; they become disvalues. It is possible for "the empirical values ... to which a democracy is dedicated ... to degenerate into disvalues, unless grounded in the super-empirical values which only religion can supply."[43] To avoid paradox on the empirical level, discussion of democracy must find a way to supply super-empirical sanction for our empirical values. Democratic ethics must be transformed into a religious ethics.

From what has been said earlier, it is apparent that Dr. Kaplan does not count too heavily upon the traditional religions for the support of democracy. He maintains that "the only agencies at present ready to provide those super-empirical values are the churches. But if they were permitted to do so, they would wreck our democracy by their rivalries and internecine conflicts."[44] Again we seem to have reached an *impasse*, yet again the way out is provided for in Dr. Kaplan's theory of culture. The effort to find a new principle of cultural integration along national lines, which we spoke of earlier, is interpreted by him not as "the will to live, but the will to live abundantly." This he calls the only universal frame of reference, the "will to salvation," where salvation is conceived not in other-worldly, but in this-worldly terms, as "maximum good or optimum which man expects to achieve with the aid of the culture in which he lives and has his being."[45] Every culture, and certainly the democratic cultures no less than the non-democratic cultures, is for its members a vehicle of salvation. The aim of "Soterics," conceived as the search for "a common universe of discourse for the various cultures which divide mankind into nations and for the various elements which threaten to fragmentize each culture or nation,"[46] is to substitute for the historic religious traditions in fostering awareness of kind. Soterics, rather than ethics or politics or economics, becomes, then, the central discipline for the study of human life.

Viewed from the perspective of Soterics, the empirical values and the super-empirical values are interrelated organically.

Only a society which recognizes the spiritual value of human personality will feel responsible for enabling the individual to realize his vital values. Only a society which realizes the spiritual value of human brotherhood will utilize the vital values in such a way as to have all human beings benefit from them. And only in a society in which cosmic values are realized, will individuals be inspired to sacrifice purely individualistic values for the achievement of social values as expressive of what life means to them.[47]

Freedom, in such a view, goes beyond political freedom, goes beyond even what we called earlier "inner freedom." It lies "at the very root of man's spiritual life, and is the prime condition of his self-fulfillment, or salvation."[48] Moreover, "equality would mean that all human beings are entitled to experience the dignity of selfhood or personality, the moral character of society, and the reality of God."[49] Thus all conflict between the ideals of freedom and equality is eliminated by the soterical emphasis of a religious ethic. The paradox of freedom is resolved by being transcended.

In the light of that ethic, freedom means the freedom of the individual to the maximum development of his powers in the pursuit of all interests that do not frustrate the co-operation of individuals for common ends necessary for the salvation of all. Equality then means the equal right of all individuals to pursue their own personal interests and to contribute in accordance with their ability, to the common purposes.[50]

The culmination of Kaplan's theory of Soterics is suggested by his belief that each culture is a way of salvation to its members. This is as much as to say that, implicitly at least, each culture *is* a religion. There is ready for the discovery a democratic religion, in which "the democratic empirical values would be sanctioned by the super-empirical values of individual responsibility, the sanctity of the person, and equality of opportunity as well as before the law."[51] Between this religion and the traditional faiths there would be no necessary conflict. Although each had its own definition of salvation, all alike would be ways to salvation. Such is the claim to exclusiveness of the various churches that this religion would probably be opposed by all the existing denominations. This opposition might be overcome in time. Democratic religion would be universal in its reference; however, in order to avoid being merely a congeries of "vague generalities," it would have to be based — for America — on "the particularity of the life, the strivings, the experience, the travails, the hopes and the ideals of the American people at its best."[52] The values of American democratic religion would be universal; its specific practices, rites and ceremonies, its *sancta*, would be particular.

Public buildings and public schools, offices of public trust and the officers who are entrusted with them, the symbols and the literature of American life, all find their place in the pattern of democratic religion. For "Democracy is virtually a doctrine of national salvation" and these various institutions of democratic life are "to all intents, religious institutions which attempt to utilize this doctrine of national salvation as a means of promulgating social solidarity and effective collaboration among the citizens of the nation."[53] "In that kind of American religion the empirical values based on 'the laws of nature' will be translated into a mode of national life that will deserve the blessing of 'nature's God.' "[54] For, after all, "Democracy is a faith; its validity is not scientifically demonstrable. It demands *a priori* acceptance of ideals which can be proved valid only by our committing ourselves to their realization. It is a scheme of salvation that implies belief in a Power that makes for salvation."[55]

NOTES

[1] "Towards a Philosophy of Cultural Integration," in Bryson *et al.*, eds., *Approaches to Group Understanding*, Harper & Bros., New York, 1947, p. 590.

[2] E. B. Tylor, *Primitive Culture*, Henry Holt & Co., New York, 1889, vol. I, p. 1.

[3] "The Cultural Approach to Sociology," in Calverton, ed., *The Making of Society*, Modern Library, New York, 1937, p. 694.

[4] Kaplan, "Towards a Philosophy of Cultural Integration," p. 590.

[5] *Ibid.*, p. 590.

[6] If documentation of this point is necessary, see Malcolm Hay, *The Foot of Pride*, Beacon Press, Boston, 1950.

[7] Kaplan, "Towards a Philosophy of Cultural Integration," p. 591.

[8] *Ibid.*, p. 595.

[9] See, for example, "Jewish Education for Democracy," *The Reconstructionist*, V, no. 15; "The Place of Religion in a Democracy", *Review of Religion*, XII, p. 184; and *The Future of the American Jew*, Macmillan, New York, 1948, pp. 18, 284, etc.

[10] "Towards a Philosophy of Cultural Integration," p. 596.

[11] *Ibid.*, p. 597.
[12] *Ibid.*, p. 598.
[13] "The Place of Religion in a Democracy," *Review of Religion*, XII, p. 179.
[14] "Jewish Education for Democracy," *The Reconstructionist*, V, no. 15.
[15] *The Reconstructionist*, XVI, no. 9. Italics in the original.
[16] "Jewish Education for Democracy."
[17] *Ibid.*
[18] *The Future of the American Jew*, p. 17.
[19] *The Reconstructionist*, XVI, no. 14.
[20] Kaplan, "Democracy and Zionism," in F. E. Johnson, ed., *Foundations of Democracy*, Harper & Bros., New York, 1947, p. 241.
[21] *The Future of the American Jew*, p. 325. Italics in the original.
[22] There is a detailed summary of Dr. Kaplan's proposals in *Judaism in Transition*, Behrman House, New York, 1941, "Appendix 1," pp. 301–306. *The Future of the American Jew*, pp. 106–122, published 1948, shows no essential modification of these earlier proposals. Compare above, Samuel Dinin, "Mordecai M. Kaplan's Concept of Organic Jewish Community," pp. 45–64.
[23] "Democracy and Zionism," p. 240.
[24] "The Place of Religion in a Democracy," p. 179.
[25] *The Future of the American Jew*, p. 293.
[26] *Ibid.*, pp. 283–284.
[27] Kaplan, "Religious Foundations of Democracy," *The Reconstructionist*, IX, no. 5.
[28] Kaplan, *The Meaning of God in Modern Jewish Religion*, Jewish Reconstructionist Foundation, New York, 1947, p. 273.
[29] *Ibid.*, p. 271.
[30] *Ibid.*, p. 276.
[31] *The Future of the American Jew*, p. 284.
[32] *Ibid.*, p. 288.
[33] Dr. Kaplan's own refusal to accept the catchwords of the day is admirably illustrated in the course of his discussion of the challenging mind: "It has become fashionable to ascribe to organized religions the principle of the dignity of the individual. That is not true. The organized traditional religions have always deprecated and frowned down the challenging mind. They have always treated it as dangerous and in need of suppression. In traditional religious circles, free thought is still regarded as synonymous with irreligion and anarchy." *The Future of the American Jew*, pp. 290–291.
[34] *Ibid.*, p. 293.
[35] *Ibid.*, p. 315.
[36] *The Meaning of God in Modern Jewish Religion*, p. 218.
[37] Compare, for example, *The Future of the American Jew*, p. 316, with Huxley's *Evolution and Ethics*.
[38] *The Meaning of God in Modern Jewish Religion*, pp. 222–223, following R. H. Tawney, *The Acquisitive Society*.
[39] *The Future of the American Jew*, p. 148.
[40] *The Meaning of God in Modern Jewish Religion*, p. 223.
[41] *Ibid.*, p. 241.

[42] "Towards a Philosophy of Cultural Integration," p. 622.
[43] "The Place of Religion in a Democracy," p. 182.
[44] *Ibid.*, p. 182.
[45] "Towards a Philosophy of Cultural Integration," p. 604.
[46] *Ibid.*, p. 625. Compare below, Harold Schulweis, "Mordecai M. Kaplan's Theory of Soterics," pp. 263–281.
[47] *Ibid.*, p. 620.
[48] *The Meaning of God in Modern Jewish Religion*, pp. 270–271.
[49] *The Future of the American Jew*, p. 324.
[50] "Towards a Philosophy of Cultural Integration," p. 622.
[51] "The Place of Religion in a Democracy," p. 192.
[52] *Ibid.*, p. 183. Compare *The Faith of America*, ed. Kaplan, Williams and Kohn, H. Schuman, N. Y., 1951.
[53] *The Future of the American Jew*, p. 516. I have generalized this statement, which in the original refers only to public schools.
[54] "The Place of Religion in a Democracy," p. 192.
[55] *The Future of the American Jew*, p. 511.

MORDECAI M. KAPLAN'S THEORY OF SOTERICS

By Harold Schulweis

The serious critics of Mordecai Kaplan's philosophic efforts have been persistent in their accusations of his purported neglect of metaphysics. Of what value, it is argued, is "an account of the psychological and ethical consequences" of affirming a theology without the metaphysical substructure which deals with "things as a whole," without the belief that there is "something ontological, some affirmation . . . concerning the ultimate nature of things."[1] A theology which does not offer God as "the only tenable explanation of the universe,"[2] which does not deal with the problems of theodicy, sin, resurrection, and proofs for the existence and attributes of the Deity cannot be considered a theology at all.

It remains the task of this article to analyze and expound Dr. Kaplan's philosophy of "Soterics" precisely as a metaphysical approach and the crux of his theology. Not that this metaphysical analysis concerns itself with Being qua Being, or with speculation over ultimate or first principles which are disclosed trans-experientially by methods differing from those employed by the empirical sciences. Nor does his position involve the traditional schoolman's preoccupation with the transcendental nature of God, freedom and immortality.

Rather we are confronted with an "empirical metaphysics", a philosophic anthropology, which employs concepts of maximum generality in searching for the pervasive traits of the natural world and of human nature upon which may be constructed a defensible ethics and theology. Its root metaphors will be biological and organic, not mechanistic or discrete; its method, scientific; its conclusions, probabilistic, heuristic, in principle verifiable. It may be expected, therefore, that this metaphysics will stress growth, creativity, process, and that the theology so intimately connected with it will be naturalistically, humanistically oriented.

Before analyzing the soterical approach itself, it must be set in its historical perspective; for it arose as a contemporary response to the insolubility of the traditional problem inherent in positing the existence and character of a supernatural God. This problem may be stated thus: if there exists an antecedent Being, wholly independent of man, of whom no spatio-temporal attributes may be legitimately predicated, and whose nature lies therefore outside the realm of human experience, in what sense can such a Reality be said to be known by men, in what sense meaningful to men? The very incomprehensibleness in human terms of such a supernatural God denies the conditions both for its confirmation and its rejection, and renders the concept logically meaningless as well. Thus the supernaturalist's claim becomes impregnable, by virtue not of its inherent, irresistible logic but of its "logically meaningless" formulation. That equally arbitrary alternate and even contradictory claims to a supernatural Being, each irreconcilable, yet each enjoying the same irrefutability because of their "in principle" unverifiable status, have co-existed in the same epochs, is well-known. The troublesome and often violent history of theological controversy testifies to the dubious victory of such inviolability.

At this point the religious naturalist enters the scene. He cannot accept the belief in a supernatural God on "faith", though he himself, if he is like Dr. Kaplan, may hold at least one unverifiable presupposition. The difference is that, while his assumptions will simply be heuristic principles or hypotheses, subject at all times to question and rejection should they prove unworkable or fruitless, the propositions of orthodox theologians have actual ontological referents, in which the Being referred to is given absolute existential status not subject to doubt.

Rather the religious naturalist is convinced that the source of all the meaningful attributes of God is nowhere but in the experiences man has with his fellow men and with the rest of the natural world, these experiences differing in content from group to group, from society to society, from place to place. Thus in the very search of mankind for God, because it involves the articulation of the most treasured values in human endeavor and aspiration, the religious naturalist will seek his clues as to the nature of the divine itself.

He may know that when men claim to have experienced a revelation of a supernatural Being, they are unconsciously confusing the reality of the experience with the experience of Reality. He may know that "the Ethiopians make their gods black and snub-nosed, while the Thracians give theirs red hair and blue eyes" (Xenophanes); but he dismisses none of it. For the religious naturalist also knows that the process of reifying man's characteristics, values and ideals, captures and zealously guards for each society its *sancta*, its aspiration levels, its success criteria, its ethical rationale.

It is through this type of naturalistic quest that Dr. Kaplan found a more fruitful and acceptable approach. His theological position is based on the conviction that "by shifting the orientation from the God-concept, a point intended to be outside human experience, to the idea of man, we are likely to make more headway with the problem of salvation"[3] and speak more intelligently of the meaning of God. He has decided to take Feuerbach seriously: "If we are to understand religion, we must take as subject what has been taken for predicate and vice-versa."[4] Man as an *animal symbolicum* speaks of God and thereby enters the world of possibility, oughts and should-be. In worship he extols those elements which better his life and he seeks strength to eliminate the evils which plague it. In his struggle to find himself in this symbolic dimension, man can become more truly human and, thereby, more divine.

The truly revolutionary character of Dr. Kaplan's soterical approach, however, is not in this general application of his humanistic focus but, more precisely, in his interpretation of what constitutes personal salvation for every individual. For any man to play at all a significant part in this quest for Divinity in the world at large, he must seek out within himself that which will better his own personal life. Only to the extent to which he consciously realizes every humanizing potentiality in himself, will he attain a measure of personal salvation. Soterics is the study of the nature and method of achieving this end.

Soterics and the Growth Imperative

It is Dr. Kaplan's belief that Soterics can be a framework for salvation for all people regardless of varying personal viewpoints, because it is based on two elemental and compulsive factors in human nature itself on which all can agree: the will to live, which is the more basic, generalized concept, and its corollary, the will to maximum life, understood more specifically as the principle of self-realization. This latter principle is centered in the development of the productive personality of the self on every level:

a. On the level of the vitalities, the self is an organism of biogenic needs (hunger, sex, etc.) and socio-genic needs (the socially acquired needs like belonging to a group, status etc.), which demand gratification. Those ascetic, celibate, other-worldly philosophies which entirely deny these primary and secondary needs are, from the point of view of Soterics, factors inimical to healthful growth and salvation.

b. On the level of reason and intelligence, the self functions as the mediator of conflicting interests in the effort to harmonize and channelize the variety of experiences impinging on it. Like the Aristotelian "mean" and the Platonic "sense of justice," the rational exercise allows each impulse the measure of gratification consistent with the total welfare. It is the crucial instrument in exploiting the innate potentialities of the self and in its enlargement.

c. On the level of morale, the self is said to "harbor the values of the spirit or holiness," "the kingdom of ends."[5] On this level, morale and courage are furnished, supplying that emotive charge which transforms man's ethical, intellectual commitments into action. Here the dramatization of the search for self-actualization is celebrated through ritual and prayer; here the realm of purposes is recognized, articulated and made conscious.

Soterics is thus to be considered a this-worldly "normative science of human life in all its aspects, from the standpoint of verifiable experience."[6] It is a form of Art in which the diverse levels of human living, as above described, are integrated and each dimension given weight in accordance with the desired goal of the total health, happiness and creativity of the individual. The religious personality is therefore conceived of as an artist molding his self into the highest form, impelled by the soteric imperative to: "Withdraw into your Self and look. And if you do not find yourself beautiful yet, act as does the creator of a statue that is to be made beautiful; he cuts away here, he smooths there, he makes this line lighter, this other purer, until a lovely face has grown upon his work. So do you also: cut away all that is excessive, straighten all that is crooked, bring light to all that is overcast, labor to make all one glow of beauty, and never cease carving your statue until there shall shine out on you from it the godlike splendor of virtue, until you shall see the perfect goodness established in the stainless shrine."[7]

In this conception of salvation in terms of the attainment of the maximum good, primarily through the development of the inherent possibilities or potentialities of the organism, Dr. Kaplan has been more influenced by the contributions of recent psychiatry than by the romantic, idealistic metaphysics of self-realization. An increasing number of philosophically oriented psychiatrists like Fromm, Horney, Sullivan, Goldstein, have leaned heavily on the self-realization urge in man, in many instances to justify the goal and direction of their therapy and, in their writing, appear to be more concerned with the re-education of the individual personality towards this end than with treatment aimed at simple adjustment to existing conditions.

Kurt Goldstein, a psychiatric pathologist, refers throughout his books to the observation that "an organism is governed by the tendency to actualize as much as possible the individual capacities," and argues that this tendency is "the only drive by which the life of the organism is determined."[8] Karen Horney, concurring, writes: "Man, by his very nature and of his own accord, strives toward self-realization, ... and his set of values evolves from such striving." And in other words Erich Fromm articulates the same concept when he states the aim of psychiatric therapy to be "the optimal development of a person's potentialities and the realization of his individuality,"[10] his justification being the belief that "all organisms have an inherent tendency to actualize their specific potentialities."[11]

This relationship between health and salvation (i. e. self-realization) is not peculiarly new in religious philosophy. It is perhaps no etymological accident that the term salvation in so many languages is integrally related to the idea of "healing."[12] The central idea of salvation as "making whole" or a "re-establishment of a whole thing that was broken, disrupted, disintegrated"[13] has, however, been given a naturalistic cast in Soterics. The integrated development of the self-productive personality is now understood in religious terms as the quintessential ingredient in spiritual growth and the realization of the divine principle in man.

At this point, certain questions with respect to this approach have perhaps begun to be raised:

a. If to try to realize the maximum life is inherent in the nature of man, why Dr. Kaplan's soterical imperative to bring it about? There should appear to be no special need to recommend any action in accordance with human nature, since it is something which apparently no one can avoid doing.

The answer lies in the understanding that the drive for "maximum life" or self-realization is a generalized one inherent in human nature, and comprises many specific levels of activity on the part of the self which may require mediation. As for all specific impulses, self-consciousness and the use of reason are necessary for two reasons: to learn the best and surest way to satisfy them, and to learn how to integrate the demands of any one impulse to the total welfare of the organism at any given time. Thus, for Dr. Kaplan, the degree to which the individual can succeed in attaining his salvation depends upon the extent to which he has both sensitivity and self-awareness. The need to possess these two traits is what persuades Dr. Kaplan to call for the "artistic dimension" in man to achieve his measure of the divine.

b. Is not the concept of self-realization too vague and ambiguous to be of value as a basis for Soterics? It would seem that, whether one acts one way or the other, some natural capacity will be realized; and to actualize all the latent capacities of man offers no methodological directive whereby to judge conflicting directions of fulfillment. As Henry Sidgwick, commenting on the self-realization theories of Green and Spencer put it: "The sinner realizes capabilities, in this broad sense (of self-realization) as much as the saint."[14]

It should be said in answer that the concept of maximum life or self-realization is not meant to be the sole characteristic of man, but represents rather that which is essentially human in man's nature. Salvation, therefore, does not depend on the fulfillment of any and every impulse indiscriminately, but the fulfillment of the potential of the organism in such a healthful fashion as will aid the individual in achieving the maximum good. How this maximum good is defined will depend on the individual's culture and its institutions at any given stage.

However, in a complex society such as ours, where differing criteria may co-exist, the problem of choosing from particular modes of behavior is aggravated. Horney, Fromm and the others previously mentioned frequently invoke "creativity," "spontaneity" or "productivity" as standards to distinguish between behavior leading to healthy development and that leading to stagnant or self-destructive conditions. Unfortunately, these terms (creativity, etc.) themselves seem to be defined as that which is self-fulfilling or that which leads to further growth and development. Clearly this is circular, and the need for clearly defined criteria is not therewith obviated.

Nevertheless, the proponents of the self-realization theory seem to have a pragmatic solution to this problem, implying experimentation and trial and error. While the positive characterization and criteria of self-realization remain ambiguous, the negative aspects (ill-health, anxiety phenomena etc.) are more precise. Significantly, they appear to make a presupposition which can be detected underlying their analyses, namely, that where self-realization is not in the direction of general health and well-being, the organism will manifest symptoms of disorder. Be it a subjective report of unhappiness, or a specialist's diagnosis of neurotic traits, or the appearance of psychosomatic ills, something will manifest itself. Thus, whether growth is healthful or inimical is not a matter of caprice, but is rooted in the constitutive demands of the organism.

Moreover, there is the further implication that there are such curative powers in the organism that when the proper corrective directives are applied, either by oneself or through a specialist, the organism will respond with well-being. Karen Horney expresses this belief that there are "curative forces inherent in the mind as well as the body, and that in cases of disorder of body or mind, the physician merely gives a helping hand to remove the harmful and to support the healing forces."[15] In the language of Dr. Kaplan, the "psychoanalyst and the artist have in common the giving of new form to what is by identifying in what is and eliciting from it that which can and ought to be."[16]

However, even if we establish a degree of internal consistency within the theory of self-realization, there is one further, crucial problem to be faced: the existence of an urge to self-realization is far from being accepted as a verified datum by the entire scientific world. The consequences of this doubtful status for Soterics will be more completely discussed (along with other problems held in common) in dealing with the more fundamental principle, the will to live.

The Will to Live

If the self-realization principle of Soterics is characteristic of the distinctively human species, it may be said that the will to live is common to all living forms. It must be noted at the outset, however, that the nature of this Spinozistic "endeavor to preserve one's own being" is not quite clear. The examples of its manifestations offered by Dr. Kaplan lead one to assume that it is intended by him to be an empirical datum; for example: "The healing of a wound, whether in a tree or in a living being, is a manifestation of an organic urge."[17] Moreover, since it is innate and, in its original form, "not meant to be conceived of as a conscious purpose of living beings,"[18] it would appear to take the form in human beings of a generalized instinct, understood as a complex, purposeful, motivating force, "a faculty of acting in such a way as to produce certain ends without previous education in their performance."[19]

It is of the essence for Dr. Kaplan to ground both the will to live as well as the will to maximum life (self-realization) in human nature, in the organism itself, for these data are intended to serve as the reliable, generic base for a normative universe of discourse among all mankind, regardless of the differing forms of specific societies. Thus, while given societies would supply varying norms in the achievement of salvation, the entire world would still be in a position to judge their efficacy.

However, as for the self-realization principle, agreement as to the existence of a general self-preservative urge in organisms is far from settled in psychological literature. Erich Fromm may state that "the desire to live is inherent in every organism and man cannot help wanting to live regardless of what he would like to think about."[20] But another eminent psychiatrist, Menninger, argues that "the best theory to account for all the presently known facts is Freud's hypothesis of a death instinct."[21] And Muzafer Sherif writes what might apply to both the preceding: "Such dramatic-sounding instincts as the instincts of death and destruction cannot be subjected to the check of controlled investigation."[22] It is clear therefore that, from an empirical point of view, considerable doubt is also cast upon the urge to self-preservation as the grounds for normative unity.

The difficulty with this latter "urge" seems to lie in making it a generalized designation of reactions to specifically bodily demands or deficits which, in fact, may only coincidentally have self-preservative value. To reify as motive that which may well be a contingent by-product is as unwarranted here as in the claim of a purposeful perpetuation of the species on the basis of a mating or sex instinct.

Further, the will to live, unqualified, may easily be perverted into a pathological drive, an unfettered egoism destructive of the nobler social values. It is in this respect that Kurt Goldstein views the self-preservative drive as "essentially characteristic of sick people," as symptomatic of "anomalous life, of the decay of life." While it may be that "sometimes the normal organism also tends primarily to avoid catastrophe ... this takes place under inadequate conditions and is not at all usual behavior."[23]

Anticipating such difficulties, Dr. Kaplan has sought to argue that the self which is being preserved includes the higher "ideal self" of social values as well as the self of the vitalities. "The truth is," he writes, "that the will to live is bi-polar. It is as given to self-spending as to self-preservation."[24] By thus subsuming the socially imposed nature of the self under the single category of the preservation of the self, Dr. Kaplan intends to avoid the embarrassment which confronted those Idealistic philosophers who formulated reasonably similar self-realization theories (Bosanquet, Green, Bradley, Royce). But at the same time, some strength is sapped from the effort to make self-preservation stem out of the original nature of the organism itself. There is undeniably a significant measure of truth in Mill's statement that "every respectable attribute of humanity is the result not of instinct but of the victory over instinct."[25]

However, even were there to be no question whatsoever as to the empirical status of these "urges," a serious gap in the position would exist all the same. For the mere universal agreement as to the empirically verified character of human nature in no way entails or guarantees universal agreement that human nature ought be fulfilled. It appears to be the case that in any normative system there is a logical priority of value to fact. Thus, even were it to be established that a death instinct does in fact operate, it is doubtful whether Dr. Kaplan would legitimate it as a normative base. That Dr. Kaplan assigns a telic significance to these two factors, (i. e. will to live and will to self-realization) namely, that their purpose lies in their fulfillment, does not make the leap from the descriptive to the normative any the less unwarranted.

Presuppositions of Soterics

Nevertheless, it would truly be regrettable were our difficulties with both the will to live and the will to maximum life to cause us to overlook the genuine contributions which Soterics can make as a "common hypothetical method of achieving salvation," as Dr. Kaplan puts it. Recognizing the problems, it appears reasonable to suggest the abandonment of these "wills" treated as verified data, and their acceptance as hypothetical outgrowths of a metaphysical substructure, the basic presuppositions of Dr. Kaplan's ethics and theology. This metaphysical substructure would contain at least three major presuppositions:

  a. There exist certain universal biological, psychological and social needs and interests in man.
  b. The integrated gratification of these needs and interests is a value;
  c. The world is so salvation-conditioned as to enable their gratification.

Such metaphysical presuppositions are, of course, not even subjects for verification in the scientific sense, not by virtue of their meaninglessness, but because the nature of these presuppositions has nothing to do with truth or falsity but rather with pragmatic efficacy. It must be carefully noted that these principles are unlike the unverifiable propositions of supernaturalism, for they make no claim whatsoever to existential or ontological status. Their use is regulative and heuristic, not substantive and constitutive; and they are themselves subject to rejection should they not prove fruitful.

Soterical presuppositions are vindicated on the same grounds as are, let us say, the principles of induction or of the uniformity of nature made by science itself. It has more than once been pointed out that "all knowledge which on a basis of experience tells us something about what is not experienced is based upon a belief (inductive principle) which experience cannot confirm or confute, yet which ... appears to be as firmly rooted in us as many facts of experience."[26]

The presuppositions themselves ought now to be more closely examined:

  a. Requisite to the construction of a universal ethics, "a kind of valuational Esperanto," is the recognition of certain universal needs (innate) and interests (acquired). This might well direct the attention of Soterics to such well-accepted but simpler biological drives as hunger, sex, thirst, among others, and to such social-psychological interests as status and role-taking. The generalized formulations of the will to live and the will to maximum life would be considered hypotheses subject to further study, and not so critically necessary to Soterics should they prove untenable.

Investigation in this direction should also lead to a clearer understanding of the nature of the self, a basic category in the Soterics of Dr. Kaplan; for the essence of value appears to be judged in terms of the activities and behavior contributory to the actualization of the self's natural tendencies. It is the self which experiences desires and impulses and seeks their satisfaction, and it is the self which, in a manner of speaking, is also experienced, becoming an object unto itself, in that it evaluates the consequences of its behavior and organizes its value system. The self might be said, then, to contain the material, formal, final and efficient causes of its being. This is a distinctively humanistic element in Soterics, portraying as it does the self as an active agent, an artist creating its salvation, in proper contrast with the quietistic, passive role of the self which merely awaits otherworldly salvation.

However, much study into this vital category is made necessary by Soterics, since the self is so complex and multifunctional in nature. A central problem remains as to the proper balance in the assignment of value to the varying aspects of the self as both an egoistic and a social entity.

b. The presupposition that the balanced and integrated gratification of human needs and interests is valuable appears as central to many naturalist theories of value. Certainly merely descriptive, inductively confirmable knowledge concerning means and ends never in itself entails normative conclusions. Taken together, however, the first and the second presuppositions make it sensible to argue on the basis of the predicted consequences of a given action in terms of the total health picture by assuring a common response from all rational men. Thus, the utilitarian's argument about pleasurable or painful consequences could not affect the agent who neither experiences nor sets a value on pleasure or pain. Nor could a contemporary argument against behavior leading to human destruction be successful against those who deny the desirability of the maintenance of the life of species *homo sapiens*.

Moreover, in stating that the source of value lies in the integrated satisfaction of the needs and interests of the organism, Dr. Kaplan, among other naturalists, is proposing an indissoluble relationship between salvation and health. Physical and mental hygiene and the religious ethics of Soterics are not related simply by analogy. What is healthful and what is moral are one and the same questions, employing the same criteria.

With the successful advent of psychiatric therapy, the relationship between mental and moral hygiene has been reinforced. Many an unethical act is understood as a manifestation of illness. We have begun to recognize this in our evaluation of compulsive gamblers, sadists, alchoholics, psychopathic murderers, kleptomaniacs and so on. The psychological names given to these "vices" have taken them out of the category of simple sin and put them into the psychiatric laboratories. Murder and theft certainly still are evil, but now understood not vaguely in terms of theology but in terms of the consequences for the total functioning of the organism.

There are, of course, certain ethical problems which, insofar as the individual is more remotely involved, are different from those previously mentioned; but the difference is one of kind rather than of degree. There is, to be sure, less likelihood for a patient to argue against the physician prescribing treatment than there is for the moral agent to argue against the ethicist on the relative merits of democracy, peace or war, slum clearance or the extension of social security. This is because the patient's pain is intense, personal and pressing; the results of the prescription are relatively immediate and often known to produce the desired relief, and the problem is more readily isolable and less complex.

To argue, however, that democracy is superior because it is more productive than totalitarianism, or to condemn war because it destroys potential forces of creativity and stability, requires an evaluation of remote consequences. These consequences, from the moral viewpoint, are no less important than immediate ones; but it requires the wisdom of foresight and an understanding of the nature of social and individual welfare.

In situations where the factors of intensity and propinquity are attenuated, education of the individual as to the inter-relatedness of events not directly affecting him and as to the far-reaching consequences of decision needs be planned more skillfully. The penetration of psychiatry, its methods and therapy into the field previously monopolized by abstract analyses or dogmatic theology is a good omen for Soterics. The soterical emphasis on total (mental, physical, and moral) health as the heart of personal salvation adumbrates the dominant theme of naturalist religion and theology.

c. The soterical presupposition of a salvation-conditioned universe so patterned as to contain the means of satisfying man's craving for self-realization is fundamental to its religious emphasis. It points to the distinguishable events in the universe which, as men, we recognize as contributory to human growth and to which we owe natural allegiance.

Appreciation of and natural piety towards such isolable powers for human salvation does not mean to eliminate the reality of evil. It serves to emphasize not that Reality is good, but that goodness is real.[27] The "given-ness" of societal and non-human environments which man "takes" as contributory to value is meant to deny as false the conviction of some that the universe is essentially hostile to human ends. In the same spirit as Dr. Kaplan, Van der Leeuw extols the universe experienced as good by pointing to "water and trees, the fruit of the fields and beasts in the forest (as) bringers of salvation; the force issuing from their power transforms the gloom of life into joy and happiness .... Culture too is 'salvation,' that is a deed which is willed or volitional."[28]

This particular presupposition was referred to by Dr. Kaplan himself as a soterical "inference," an acknowledged "willed faith," pragmatically understood. As the purposes of adequacy, intersubjectivity and consistency serve to vindicate the inductive principle, so the purposes of salvation alone justify the sentiment that "man's cosmos is *en rapport* with the human will to salvation."[29] The moral optimism of such a salvation principle is, like the principle of induction, motivational and directive. It offers man a structure of expectancies creating belief in the possibilities of human experience which inspire men to achieve that end.

This morale is not even intended to make men good, but specifically to keep them strong. In the language of the pragmatic maxim, Dr. Kaplan asserts that "insofar as the belief in God makes a difference in a person's life or in the life of a group, it must have consequences in the domain of effectiveness."[30] What working principle, which sustains human endeavor whether in science or religion, is not inclined to interpret reality as somehow amenable to the aspirations of men?

Morale in Reconstruction

John Stuart Mill stated unequivocally the problematic in the naturalist's reconstruction of traditional supernaturalism: "It needs be considered whether in order to obtain the effective morale resulting from supernaturalist faith, it is necessary to travel beyond the boundaries of the world which we inhabit; or whether the idealization of our earthly life, the cultivation of a high conception of what it may be made, is not capable of supplying a poetry, and in the best sense of the word a religion, equally fitted to exalt the feeling and, with the same aid from education, still better calculated to ennoble the conduct, than any belief respecting unseen powers."[31]

The problem is poignantly presented. Once a man is informed that faith in a salvational cosmos is an instrument which gains for us moral optimism and strengthens our hearts, does not his prayer become too self-conscious? Will anyone recite *geshem* (prayer for rain) knowing full well that no palpable favors will ensue, that it may only serve to direct his feelings of gratitude to an indispensable natural force?

The naturalist must recognize the problem as formidable. Still, it is too late for him to turn back and pretend that neither philosophy nor science has made its inroads. Those religious personalities committed to a naturalist position cannot afford the luxury of bemoaning the loss of a certain type of morale attendant on the supernaturalist's faith, the more since many other consequences of such belief are entirely disfunctional.

The reconstructing naturalist needs rather invade new areas of morale and plan new interpretations of symbols and rites so as to compensate for the loss of comfort and ease afforded by facile conformity to convention. The observation of the sociologist, Robert Merton, is of interest in this respect: "Those functionalists who ... attend only to the effects of such symbolic practices [rituals] upon the individual state of mind ... neglect the fact that these very practices may on occasion take the place of more effective alternatives. And those theorists who refer to the indispensability of standardized practices or prevailing institutions because of their observed function in reinforcing common sentiments must look first to functional substitutes before arriving at a conclusion, more often premature than confirmed."[32] It is in such a fruitful direction that Soterics impells us to explore.

In the midst of public religious apathy, in the sight of piece-meal emendations, false sentiments and half-truths, the religious naturalist needs base his morale on the wisdom of the past and the vision of a future. "The sun shines today also. There is more food and flax in the fields. There are new lands, new men, new thoughts. Let us demand our own works and laws and worship."[33]

---

[1] Milton Steinberg, "Theological Problems of the Hour", *Rabbinical Assembly Proceedings*, Rabbinical Assembly of America, New York, 1949, p. 378.

[2] Milton Steinberg, *The Common Sense of Religious Faith*, (pamphlet), Jewish Reconstructionist Foundation, Inc., New York, 1947, p. 12.

[3] From a manuscript as yet unpublished, *by M. M. Kaplan*, tentatively entitled *The Art of Being Human*.

[4] L. Feuerbach, quoted in H. Höffding, *History of Modern Philosophy*, Macmillan, London, 1915, vol. II, p. 277.

[5] *The Art of Being Human*, manuscript, p. 60a.

[6] *Ibid.*, p. 33.

[7] Plotinus, *The Essence of Plotinus*, MacKenna tr., Oxford University Press, New York, 1934, p. 49.

[8] Kurt Goldstein, *The Organism*, American Book Co., New York, 1939, p. 196.

[9] Karen Horney, *Neurosis and Human Growth*, W. W. Norton, New York, 1950, p. 15.

[10] Erich Fromm, *Psychoanalysis and Religion*, Yale University Press, New Haven, 1950, p. 74.

[11] *Ibid.*, p. 20.

[12] *Saos* in Greek; *salvus* in Latin; *Heil* in German. Interestingly, too, soteriology, in the study of hygiene, refers to the laws of health.

[13] Paul Tillich, *The Relation of Religion to Health*, paper presented at University Seminar on Religion, Columbia University, 1945–6, p. 349.

[14] *Lectures on the Ethics of T. H. Green, H. Spencer and J. Martineau*, Macmillan, London, 1902, p. 64.

[15] Karen Horney, *Neurosis and Human Growth*, p. 348.
[16] M. M. Kaplan, *The Art of Being Human*, p. 112.
[17] M. M. Kaplan, "Toward a Philosophy of Cultural Integration", in *Approaches to Group Understanding*, ed. Bryson et al., Harper & Bros., New York, 1947, p. 603.
[18] M. M. Kaplan, "The Need for Normative Unity in Higher Education" in *Goals for American Education*, ed. Bryson et al., Harper & Bros., New York, 1950, p. 308.
[19] William James, *Principles of Psychology*, Henry Holt, New York, 1931, vol. II, p. 383.
[20] E. Fromm, *Man For Himself*, Rinehart & Co., New York, 1947, p. 18.
[21] Karl Menninger, *Man Against Himself*, Harcourt, Brace & Co., New York, 1938, p. 13.
[22] Muzafer Sherif, *An Outline of Social Psychology*, Harper & Bros., New York, 1948, p. 20.
[23] Kurt Goldstein, *The Organism*, p. 197.
[24] M. M. Kaplan, *The Need for Normative Unity*, p. 312.
[25] John Stuart Mill, "Essay on Nature", in *Three Essays on Religion*, Henry Holt, New York, 1874, p. 46.
[26] Bertrand Russell, *Problems of Philosophy*, Oxford University Press, 1948, p. 69.
[27] All the more puzzling is Henry Wieman's claim that Dr. Kaplan identifies the universe with God or goodness and is thus "forced to defend his belief in the goodness of the universe against the facts of evil." *Review of Religion*, XIV, no. 1. [Prof. Wieman has apparently revised his views. Compare above, pp. 263–281.— Eds.]
[28] G. Van der Leeuw, *Religion in Essence and in Manifestation*, Allen and Unwin, London, 1938, pp. 101, 104.
[29] M. M. Kaplan, *The Future of the American Jew*, Macmillan, New York, 1948, p. 193.
[30] M. M. Kaplan, *The Art of Being Human*, p. 75.
[31] J. S. Mill, "The Utility of Religion", in *Three Essays on Religion*, p. 105.
[32] Robert Merton, *Social Theory and Social Structure*, Free Press, Glencoe, Ill., 1949, p. 37.
[33] Ralph Waldo Emerson, quoted in Morris R. Cohen's *A Dreamer's Journey*, Beacon Press, Boston, 1949, p. 180.

THE WAY I HAVE COME

By Mordecai M. Kaplan

My heartfelt thanks go out to my friends and colleagues for their contributions to this book. I deeply appreciate the difficulty of the task which each of them generously undertook. In all my theorizing I am obsessed by the principle that nothing can mean anything except in a context. In all my planning my main endeavor is to see life "steadily and whole." Only their friendship for me could have led them to accept the invitation to discuss me in the fragmentized form necessitated by a cooperative tribute of this kind. The word which the Talmud has for such a difficult undertaking is: "Break the flask, but be sure not to spill the wine." The best way, therefore, for me to express my appreciation of their efforts is to supply the context in which the various elements in my thinking and phases of my activity originated and took shape.

The Most Important Thing about a Man

William James quotes with great glee Chesterton's statement that the most important thing about a man is his view of the universe. For a landlady considering a lodger, we are told, it is more important to know his philosophy than his income, and for a general fighting an enemy, to know the enemy's philosophy than to know his numbers. If, as this quotation implies, one's philosophy is to be understood as synonymous with one's view of the universe, what Prof. Henry N. Wieman[1] identifies as my idea of God would be the most important thing about me, since one's idea of God necessarily reflects one's idea of the universe or cosmos. It is, therefore, indeed a source of satisfaction to me to find myself seeing eye to eye with so eminent a religious thinker as Prof. Wieman, with regard to what men like James and Chesterton considered the most important thing about a man.

I am grateful to Prof. Wieman for having taken the trouble to set forth his own conception of God. His statement proves how remarkably parallel, though independently, our lines of thinking have run. He is entirely correct in stressing that my view of the universe is by no means pantheistic, since I consistently adhere to the principle that Godhood is only a particular aspect of the universe, that aspect of it which makes for man's salvation. I am especially thankful for his having taken up the cudgels in defense of the concept of "process." That concept is in keeping with the scientific approach. It approximates more clearly the ontological character of God than the traditional concept of a being. To conceive of fire as a process of rapid oxidation is scientifically and ontologically nearer the truth than to believe that it was snatched by Prometheus from the gods on Olympus and brought down to earth, or that it is one of the four elements of the universe, or that it is a substance called "phlogiston." The average mind will undoubtedly have to undergo a long habituation in scientific thinking to experience process as the form in which reality presents itself to us, whether it be sensate, like the visible and tangible objects about us, or invisible like personality, parenthood, or one's nation.

However, if one's view of the universe and of God is as important as James and Chesterton contend it is, that importance, in my opinion, derives not from the character of the view itself. No idea as such, not even an idea of the cosmos, can exercise that potency over a man's conduct as to outweigh all other influences that go into the shaping of his life. For a view of the universe and of God to rate as of primary importance, it must be seen in the entire context of the experiences which have led up to it. In fact, any view whatever, whether it be scientific, political or theological, to be properly understood, should have as much of its ancestry known as possible. We should know what were the problems that led to its being arrived at or accepted. What experiences, or what other views, gave rise to those very problems? A view that is not a solution of a problem is like an unearned money draft that is not drawn upon, and which, therefore says nothing of the earning or spending capacity of the owner. A view of the universe or of God that is accepted uncritically as part of one's upbringing, and that is not tested in the crucible of experience is bound to remain inert. Far from being the most important thing about a man, it is apt to be the least important.

The importance, therefore, which attaches to anyone, by virtue of his idea of God, derives from the way that view is arrived at, from the road he has traveled, the difficulties he has overcome and the problems he has had to solve in order to get to his destination. The way I have come to *see* the cosmos is due to the *way* I have come to see the cosmos. That *way* has been one of arduous struggle with the problem of personal self-adjustment. I have had to find myself, and to make my place, in the world into which I was born. It was the only world in which I had any chance of achieving happiness and self-fulfillment. The significance, therefore, of my basic theology or philosophy of life resides, I believe, in the particular experiences and problems by which I came to it, and in demonstrating the general truth that a person's view of the universe is the most telling index of his character only when it has functioned as a means of helping him find his way in life.

The Earliest Memories — God in the Background or Being Jewish at the Age of Seven

The world into which I was born was the extremely circumscribed one of a small town in the Jewish Pale of nineteenth century Russia. It was the very year in which the Russian Government inaugurated the Pobyedonostzev policy of christianizing one third of the Jewish population, expelling another third, and killing off the rest. But, circumscribed as my world was in terms of contacts with the Great Society, economically, politically or socially, it was of great depth in time relations in that it was a Jewish world. My father was, as a youth, one of those precocious talmudists whom ambitious fathers-in-law would select for their daughters, and whom they would support for a number of years as a form of dowry. My grandfather died not long after Mother was married. Since she was the oldest child, and the only daughter, it was her turn to become the main support of the household, while Father continued his studies and waited for a suitable post as a rabbi.

As the only son in that kind of household, my future as a rabbi was cut out for me from the very start, and my Jewish training began the moment I began to speak. I recall sitting on Father's knee and being asked by him to spell out the Hebrew alphabet with the aid of matches. He had just returned from one of the talmudical academies where he had won additional laurels and rabbinic authorizations. My skill with the Hebrew alphabet was rewarded by a whistle in the form of a leaden bird. I must have been then about four years old. I recall another incident from those early years; I could not have been more than six. I found myself alone on a street far from my home. It was a summer day and a thunderstorm with heavy lightning broke out. I overcame my fears by reciting the appropriate benediction. When I got home, I described my adventure, taking care to mention the fact that I had looked around to see that the four ells in which I stood were free of dung before I recited the benediction. I do not recall the circumstances under which that law had been imparted to me.

I mention this and other instances of ritual observance, in order to point out what early habits gave the particular bent to my thinking in later years. These observances represented to me an obligatory way of life to which I had to conform, as a matter of course. Whether I was reciting the brief thanksgiving prayer on opening the eyes, or the prayers on going to bed, or various prayers and benedictions during the day, they all had one meaning for me — that of being a Jew. God was always in the background. He was never confronted. When at the age of five I began attending *heder*, my formal education consisted of nothing but learning to read the prayers. Before a year was over I began to read the Pentateuch and to translate it into Yiddish, the vernacular of all the Jews in town. The long hours at *heder* together with the meticulous observance of Sabbaths, feasts and fasts in the home, made being a Jew a whole day and a whole year affair. References to God were frequent, but only as part of general discourse. I recall particularly the use of a substitute expression for the word God, when He was referred to as "He (who may not be mentioned) because of unwashed hands." Such was my upbringing up to the beginning of my eighth year when I was taken by Mother to Paris, where I lived for about a year.

Self-Identification with the Jewish People

Ever since then I have been living in two civilizations, the Jewish and the non-Jewish. I do not recall being troubled in any way by the sudden transition in my mode of life. During the year at Paris I attended public school the greater part of the day, and a Jewish *heder* in the afternoon. The *heder* was located in a Jewish neighborhood where east-European Jews had recently settled. It was conducted alternately in Yiddish and in French. From the beginning of my ninth year, when I was brought to this country, until my twelfth year, my education consisted mainly of Jewish studies, with the addition of some formal courses in the three R's in the afternoon. I studied Bible with commentaries and Talmud in Yiddish; I picked up the English language from the street, as did my school mates. Speaking Yiddish meant to me being a Jew, so that when my schoolmates spoke English in the synagogue I resented it and told them so.

When I began attending public school in my twelfth year, I tried to get my parents to speak English at home. They, on the other hand, still planned to make a rabbi of me. There were times when I preferred playing with the boys in the street to studying the dialectics of the law of damages. Mother would then haul me back into the house, and when my reluctance persisted, Father would say to her, "Why do you force him to study? The worst that can happen to him is that he will have to sell newspapers for a living. If that's what he wants, let him be." That had more effect on me than Mother's insistence.

By the time I became *bar mitzvah*, I had already been attending the Seminary for a year. The address which I delivered in Yiddish at the *Bar Mitzvah* celebration deserves mentioning, because it reflects what being a Jew then meant to me. The address was not my original composition. Its main theme had been written out by my father; but instead of memorizing it, I paraphrased it and gave most of it in my own words. I had digested the thought and felt it to be one of the main ideas I would have occasion to expound, when I would be old enough to be a rabbi. The main theme was the survival power of the Jewish people, as due to its observance of the *mitzvot*. The basis for that theme was the talmudic story told in the treatise of *Shabbat* about an ancient sage who, during the Hadrianic persecutions, was about to be arrested by a Roman officer for wearing *tefilin*. When the officer grabbed him, a miracle occurred. The *tefilin* changed into the wings of a dove. Why were they changed into the wings of a dove? Because Israel is likened to a dove.

That little speech then spelled for me complete self-identification with the Jewish people and its struggle for survival. It also meant a vivid awareness of ritual observances as the *sine qua non* of its survival. Whatever I then knew about God had to do with that awareness. I was not troubled about the idea of God any more than I was about the idea of my own personality. It did not occur to me to ask what God looked like any more than to ask what my own soul, for which I thanked God every morning, looked like. I regarded as irrefutable proof of Divine Providence the argument in Psalm 94 which reads: "He that planteth the ear shall He not hear? He that formed the eye, shall He not see?" Having read that psalm as a morning prayer prescribed for Wednesdays, I could not help being reminded by it at least once a week that God took note of my behavior.

The Beginnings of Conflict

During my college years I pursued at the Seminary the studies of Biblical exegesis, Talmud and Jewish History. These studies had the effect of deepening my Jewish consciousness, but troubling my Jewish conscience. I began to experience the pangs of inner conflict. The study of the Jewish medieval philosophers, which was part of the Seminary curriculum, did not help to bridge the gap that divided the thought world of the Bible and the Talmud from the thought world I lived in. Medieval Jewish philosophy did not recognize any such gap as even thinkable. The Bible, as the word of God, could not, according to the medieval theologians, but speak an eternal language. All that we had to do was to acquire the key to that language. From first to last those theologians were devoid of any historical sense or of any conception of evolution in religion. How could they possibly satisfy me, when whatever I studied had to have for me its own intrinsic context in order to have meaning? I had to know just how the various books of the Bible came into being. This hunger for concrete information concerning the authorship, the dates and the historical circumstances pertaining to the writing of the texts was completely ignored at the Seminary. It was during those years that I came under the influence of Arnold B. Ehrlich, one of the greatest Jewish exegetes in modern times. He taught me to penetrate through the vast layers of traditional commentaries to the rock-bottom original intent of the biblical authors. In doing so, he undermined my belief in the Mosaic authorship of the Torah and in the historicity of the miracles.

My father, who wished to counteract the heretical influence of Ehrlich, had me study Maimonides' *Guide To The Perplexed*, with a Jewish philosopher and scientist, Joseph Sossnitz. I once asked Sossnitz: "How can we ascribe to Moses the authorship of a text like the following: 'And Moses was the humblest of all men?'" His reply was that Moses was so unselfconscious that he could write about himself in the third person. I cannot say that the answer satisfied me. Thus, wishing on the one hand to live up to the expectations of my parents and of the Seminary, and on the other hand being tossed about by doubts and questionings concerning the tradition which I would soon be expected to teach others, I had a hard time maintaining my inner equilibrium during those storm and stress years of my life. It was in that state of mind that I was graduated from the Seminary at the age of twenty-one, and, after continuing post-graduate studies, both general and Jewish, for an additional year, I accepted a call to an Orthodox pulpit.

Avoiding Theological Problems

How, it may be asked, was it possible for me in that turbulent state of mind to accept a pulpit and to organize educational courses for young and old? Two factors contributed to my being accepted by the Orthodox congregation and to my own ability to accept the situation. One was my conformity to Jewish ritual practice to which, despite my doubts and questionings, I strictly adhered. That was due, no doubt, to the pious home in which I had been brought up, and to the Seminary where I had by that time spent nine years. The other factor was the abundance of Jewish teaching and preaching material available which was informative and edifying, and which did not necessitate one's becoming involved in any of the basic theological problems.

Jewish education consisted then, and still does, in transmitting a reading knowledge of the traditional texts, which contained enough material for the lay person to master, without his coming upon the questions and doubts which agitated me. Preaching did not present a problem, because the principal theme of the traditional subject matter is not the nature of God but the Jewish people, its origin, its character, its hopes, its frustrations and its destiny as highlighted by the vicissitudes of its career. With struggle for survival as the perennial problem of the Jewish people, there is nothing that the Jew wants so much to hear about, if he is at all interested in being a Jew, as those very themes of Israel's career. The Bible and the Midrash are an inexhaustible source of texts on which to base ideas and opinions concerning the dangers that threaten Jewish existence or hinder the enhancement of Jewish life.

It is important for the reader to get the full significance of this fact about the type of Jewish subject matter that is taught in the schools and preached from the pulpits. He will then begin to understand how it is possible for religious schools and even for institutions of higher learning to conduct educational and religious activities without any dogmatic theology. How far that is still true may be gathered from the three typical sermons given recently by representative rabbis of the Reform, Orthodox and Conservative wings in Judaism before the "New York Board of Rabbis" as "The Most Important High Holy Day Message for the Year 5712." The Reform rabbi is quoted as having "treated of the moral crisis of our age" with specific reference to the Kefauver revelations. The Orthodox rabbi "interpreted the role of the Diaspora Jew in the national reawakening" and the Conservative rabbi spoke on "the universalist implications in the restoration of Israel." One does not have to subscribe to a single one of the thirteen principles of Maimonides' creed to preach any one of those three sermons. One of them concerned itself with the social and political corruption which the Kefauver report revealed, and the other two with the implications of the establishment of the State of Israel. And those were topics for the three days of the year which traditionally are a call for a return to God.

I do not think it will be amiss to quote the substance of two typical sermons I delivered during those years in my ministry. They will demonstrate to what extent Judaism meant for me, as well as for my congregants, first and foremost the striving to keep the Jewish people alive and help it earn for itself great moral and spiritual prestige.

My trial sermon was based on the rabbinic interpretation of the text in Genesis which reads: "They (Joseph's brothers) said to one another, 'Behold, this dreamer cometh. Come now and let us slay him, and cast him into one of the pits, and we will say: "An evil beast hath devoured him; and we shall see what will become of his dreams."'" (Gen. 37:19-20) According to the Sages it was not Joseph's brothers who said "We shall see what will become of his dreams," but the *Shekinah*. Since the vicissitudes that befell Joseph may be interpreted as prefiguring the vicissitudes of the Jewish people, these words of the *Shekinah* may be taken as a challenge to the nations that seek to destroy the Jewish people. God challenges them: "Who will win in the end, the Jewish people with its dreams, or its enemies with their determination to destroy it?" That approach to the text gives the preacher occasion to refer to the dreams which the great prophets cherished concerning the Jewish people, to the incessant houndings to which it has been subjected and to the redemption that awaits it. In all this, God is a subject of discourse, but entirely in the capacity of Israel's Redeemer.

Another typical sermon which stands out in my mind was one based on a text from the Psalms which reads: "I shall not die but live, and declare the works of the Lord." That served as an occasion to characterize the three groups into which Jews who wished to remain Jews might be classified. The largest group, I said, consists of those who are satisfied with a minimum of Jewishness. They take part in some social or philanthropic activities, mainly for the purpose of warding off anti-Semitism. They may even say they are proud to be Jews, but they do nothing with that pride. A second and smaller group consists of those who are engaged in the upbuilding of

Israel's ancient land, and whose attachment to Jewish life is on the whole of a secular character. The third and the most promising group consists of maximum Jews who climax their Jewish interests with a sense of moral and religious purpose. Though in that kind of sermon the conception of God figures as a source of edification, the main emphasis is on the problem of Jewish survival. This time, however, it is the internal rather than the external aspect of that problem that is stressed.

But Not for Long

The moment, however, I ventured beyond the domain of edification and attempted to advocate some specific policy as to how one can and should live as a Jew in a modern environment, I got myself into trouble. I felt the need, for example, of taking a definite attitude toward the fact that the general economy in which we live at present makes it virtually impossible for the average Jew to refuse to work on the Sabbath. On a Yom Kippur that happened to fall on the Sabbath, I made a plea for at least a partial observance on Friday night, and for the cultivation of the Sabbath spirit in the home during the day following, on the principle of "save what you can." The more pious members of the congregation protested against that kind of preaching, as giving official sanction to the violation of the Sabbath. That convinced me that *as long as Jews adhered to the traditional conception of Torah as supernaturally revealed, they would not be amenable to any constructive adjustment of Judaism that was needed to render it viable in a non-Jewish environment.*

On the other hand, for Jews to be fully apprised of the fact that the dogma of *Torah min ha-shamayim* (supernatural origin of Torah) has become totally untenable, and not to have anything that might take the place of that dogma, I regarded as perhaps even more fatal a disaster than was the burning of the Temple and the destruction of the Second Commonwealth in the year 70. To me it then seemed that the House of Israel was afire, and that unless strenuous efforts were made to save it, it would be destroyed forever. I found myself in a tragic quandary. Here was I in my middle twenties, entrusted with the spiritual leadership of a large Orthodox congregation. The men and women of that congregation expected me to help them and their children live as Jews and have their lives made more meaningful by virtue of such a life. But they wanted it achieved on the basis of a religious dogma in which they believed blindly, and which I could not believe at all. By their believing blindly, I do not mean that they had implicit faith in it, but that they were afraid to approach it open-eyed and open-minded.

The only way my staying on in the Jewish ministry could make sense would be if I could find some tenable faith which would not be refuted by established facts. I did not have to know too much philosophy and metaphysics to realize that to live at all, particularly if we are to live intelligently, we must accept certain basic assumptions as ultimate. We must have implicit faith in the difference between reality and illusion, good and evil, right and wrong, truth and falsehood, the beautiful and the ugly. But faith in a specific tradition concerning miracles in contravention of laws of nature is no such foundation, and can never be so ultimate as to be exempted from the searching scrutiny of the mind. Dogmatists who resent such scrutiny have a habit of misrepresenting it as a cold and heartless rationalism which is bent on undermining faith. That is an unfair tactic to confuse the issue. No sane mind would ignore its own limitations to the point of refusing to take anything on faith. To use that fact, however, as it is used by dogmatists time and time again, as sufficient ground for the blind acceptance of *specific traditions* concerning supernatural miracles is unpardonable sophistry.

To question the assumptions of *Worlds in Collision*, or not to believe in the "flying saucers" does not necessarily mean to dispense with faith. One cannot find fault with Judah Halevi for naively accepting as irrefutable what he regarded as eye-witness testimony to substantiate the miracles in the desert.

Are we not told in the Pentateuch that they took place in the presence of the entire people of Israel? Did not the entire people of Israel witness the theophany at Sinai, and did they not all hear God's voice with their own ears? Nine hundred years ago such an argument was bound to carry weight. Even learned men had then but little knowledge of the universal tendency to treat fiction as fact. Herodotus, in his account of the battle of Salamis, relates that "a phantom in the form of a woman appeared to the Greeks, and, in a voice that was heard from end to end of the fleet, cheered them on to fight." Would any one today, on the strength of the numbers that are recorded as having heard and seen that vision, regard that miracle as historic?

Seeking a Substitute for the Dogma of Revelation

It is true that none of my congregants ever asked me point blank whether or not I really believed in the dogma of *Torah min ha-shamayim*. But I could not help feeling that they expected me to believe in it, and, what is worse, that they assumed that my being a rabbi and my pleading for the intensification of Jewish life stemmed from my acceptance of that dogma. That gave rise in me to a growing sense of sailing under false colors, and to a restless urge to find a way out of the ministry. I was considering various alternatives, like taking up insurance, going into business, or taking up law. But my deeper intuition dissuaded me from allowing a misconception, blindly and loosely held by an unsophisticated laity, to move me to take a step that would be tantamount to forfeiting the moral and material investment made in me by those who, prompted by the will to perpetuate Jewish life, had trained me for a position of spiritual leadership. To abandon my calling and to turn to some other in which I could escape the need of grappling with the problem of Jewish survival I felt would be to act irresponsibly and, therefore, unethically.

I concluded that the only ethical course for me to pursue was to treat the dogma of the supernatural origin of the Torah not as an end in itself, not as a truth for which we were to live as Jews, but as a means of stressing the supreme worth and authoritative character of the Torah. I needed that evaluation of the Torah, otherwise I would have been left without even the means of identifying the Jewish people, to say nothing, of attaching to it any distinction or merit. It was that which now troubled me, and not the dogma of the supernatural origin of the Torah. I had to look to other than Jewish sources for a convincing proof of the intrinsic worth of the Sacred Scriptures. That proof, to be convincing, had to be based on the assumption that the Sacred Scriptures were written and edited by fallible human beings and could not therefore be infallible. The study of medieval Jewish theology had taught me one very important truth, namely, that we can be good Jews and nevertheless learn from non-Jews some of the most fundamental truths in religion. The Jewish theologians learned their abhorrence of all anthropomorphic conceptions of God from Aristotle. So why should I feel inhibited from looking to non-Jewish sources for the truth about our Scriptures?

It was at this point in my self-education that I came upon the writings of Matthew Arnold that dealt with the problem which had agitated me. His *Literature and Dogma*, and his *God and the Bible* not only extricated me from the morass of doubt and questioning, but led me up to a mount of vision where new vistas were opened to me. Here at last I found a helpful "Guide for the Perplexed" of our day. I learned to appreciate the Bible for what constitutes its true worth, an expression of human nature at its best, the most articulate striving of man to achieve his salvation or self-fulfilment, and an expression of his most conscious recognition that only through righteousness can he achieve it. I began to see that no other writings, however they might excel the Bible in word artistry or philosophic depth, could compare with it in depth of passion for the one all-embracing purpose of all its teachings and ordinances, that of establishing God's Kingdom on earth. What makes the biblical writings even more remarkable is that, while the great ancient classics, which were the works of poets, seers and thinkers who on occasion rose to great heights of moral vision, remained mere literature, the writings that go to make up the Bible became the religion of the Jews.

Arnold is illuminating not only because he points out the uniqueness of the Bible in dealing with conduct, which is "three-fourths of life," but because his is perhaps the first frank attempt to free the Bible from the need of regarding it as supernatural and infallible as a prerequisite to appreciating its high worth. Arnold argues with the utmost clarity and objectivity to prove that it is not the purpose of the Bible to teach a metaphysically correct conception of God. Its purpose is rather to inculcate, by means of popular tales, laws and prophetic exhortations, that God is "a Power that makes for righteousness — not ourselves." All else is merely the fruit of the imagination and not to be treated as literal fact, least of all to be turned into religious dogma.

Matthew Arnold's alternative to the "God of miracles" and the "God of metaphysics" is the "God of experience." That third alternative rounded out the thought pattern which was then shaping itself in my mind, as I was recovering my faith in the Bible. It revived my confidence in the potentialities of the Jewish people which in the past had displayed great moral genius. Belief in the God of experience is an integral part of a naturalist world outlook like that of Arnold's, for brute nature by itself is too abounding in evil to permit man to pursue his goal of salvation without suffering occasional defeats and frustrations. Man needs the assurance, which only faith in God as the Power that makes for righteousness can give him, that his virtuous strivings are not in vain.

All this was a source of great relief to me, because it convinced me that, despite the chasm that divided my conception of God and the Bible from that of my congregants, I was in a position to imbue them with a love for both as a means of winning and holding their loyalty to the Jewish people. The notion of having them love God and the Bible as a means of saving their own souls did not even occur to me. Whatever individual salvation they were to achieve was always thought of by me as analogous to the sense of triumph the individual soldier enjoys when his battalion or regiment wins a battle. For being a Jew has always been associated in my mind with sharing the life of the Jewish people, just as being a soldier is inconceivable except as one is a member of an army.

Israel the Central Reality

But if Matthew Arnold supplied me with a conception of God and of the Bible which reawakened my faith in the latent possibilities of the Jewish people, I needed some evidence in contemporary Jewish life and thought to keep that faith alive. There were no signs on the American scene of a Jewish awakening, nor was there any contemporary thinker among American Jews who gave evidence that Jews could evolve the ideas needed for our day. For signs of Jewish awakening I had to turn to the Zionist movement, and for evidence that we had begun to adventure beyond the stereotypes of medieval philosophy, I had to turn to Ahad Ha-am with his version of spiritual Zionism. Through the impact of both Zionism and Ahad Ha-am's writings, I became fully aware of the essential character of the Jewish universe of discourse, of which, despite my having moved and having had my being in it, I was either unaware or had a wrong idea.

That impact effected in me nothing less than a Copernican revolution. I discovered that throughout Judaism's universe of discourse, the people of Israel was the central reality, and that the meaning of God and of Torah can be properly understood only in relation to that central reality. The main concern of Judaism was the Jewish people, its origin, its vicissitudes, its sins and repentance, and the laws it had to conform to in order to achieve its destiny. In the course of that concern, God played the role of father, king and redeemer, that is, of provider, ruler and savior. What God was, metaphysically or ontologically, mattered only to a few intellectuals now and then. But what God meant morally, socially, economically, politically mattered to all of Israel's spiritual leaders, beginning with Moses.

To find plausible this view, which is supported by an unbiased and preconceptionless survey of the Jewish heritage, I had to fit it into the general character of all human thought and behavior. Thus I arrived, by way of a clearer awareness of Judaism's universe of discourse, at what I soon recognized to be pragmatism, the philosophical method which insists upon rendering thought, if it is to be more than word-play, relevant to man's needs. Any idea, to have meaning, must be seen in a context of natural conditions and human relations. The function of the belief in God is to make us aware of the moral and spiritual context of our conduct, so that we come to move within the orbit of the "Power that makes for righteousness." Judaism uses the belief in God to make Jews aware of the natural conditions that have to be established and the human relations that have to be maintained for the Jewish people, if it is to achieve salvation collectively and individually.

When I arrived at this stage of my thinking, which I happened to expound in the presence of Solomon Schechter and my fellow-alumni of the Seminary, I found myself beyond the point where I could consistently serve my Orthodox congregation and retain my inward peace. I, therefore, gladly accepted the invitation to head the newly proposed teachers training department of the Seminary. That soon afforded me the opportunity of trying out on my students the feasibility of rendering the Jewish spiritual heritage religiously meaningful and appealing with the aid of the above defined pragmatic approach to the belief in God. I then developed that method of interpretation which Eugene Kohn explains in great detail and with great clarity.[2]

This pragmatic approach to the belief in God is an imperative to render it meaningful by making evident the difference it makes in conduct and character. By that time I was convinced that man has to be content with assuming the existence of a noumenal reality to which the belief in God refers, and to let it go at that, just as he does with the idea of gravitation or personality. But as a means to salvation that belief needs to be explored from the standpoint of its practical bearing on moral and spiritual aspects of our conduct. I began to realize that a belief in God, which is not translated into terms of social and psychological experience is an empty sentimentalism. On the other hand, social and psychological experience which does not reckon with the belief in God is blind and directionless.

How was I to learn which social and psychological experiences in Jewish life help to bring out the best in the Jew and to enhance the future of the Jewish people, and can therefore serve as the basis for articulating, as a Jew, the belief in God? The only way, it seemed to me, was to turn to the study of human nature in the group and in the individual, in order to find out what bearing the belief in God had on conduct and character in ancient and primitive civilizations.

The Individual and the Group

It was then that I found myself in need of relearning the meaning of personality. As little as God was to be conceived as a magnified man, so little was the personality to be conceived as the ghost-double of the individual body. Instead I have since acquired the habit of thinking of it as a process which takes place in the web of activities and relationships in which the individual body acts and is acted upon. The dialectic between the personality and its environment helped me to become aware of the meaninglessness of an isolated self, free from all social contact. That the individual is the product of his social environment, that he owes his very mind and personality to this interaction with the members of the group to which he belongs, impressed itself on my mind with the force of a revelation.

Fortunately, however, the individual did not dissolve for me into a complex of group relations. The strong sense of individual responsibility which had its roots in my religious upbringing, prevented me from being allured into the trap of reductionism into which psychologists and sociologists have a tendency to walk. Because of that trap religionists have avoided the disciplines of the human sciences; but they have also deprived themselves of indispensable understanding of human nature. I was saved from the reductionist fallacy of the social psychologists by holding on to the irreducible fact of individual responsibility. Though I could not explain responsibility either scientifically or metaphysically, I could no more treat it as an illusion than I could afford to treat as an illusion the cars on the street that I had to cross.

This belief in the objective character of responsibility has as its correlative the belief in God. Of this I became aware the more I delved into studies in social psychology and the psychology of religion, which proliferated during the first two decades of this century. Those studies threw new light on the integral relation of religion to the social, economic and political aspects of society. The place of religion, or of the belief in God, in the context of society began to emerge for me with growing clarity. It became clear to me that the belief in God has functioned principally as a means of fostering a sense of solidarity among the members of self-perpetuating groups, whether they be clans, tribes, nations or churches. In that capacity, a deity is to a group what the ego is to the individual. For a group to have a religion in common, its members must have other interests in common besides religion. The religion of the group, in becoming internalized in the individual, gives rise to a sense of responsibility, or conscience.

Most of my subsequent efforts in teaching Judaism and promulgating the furtherance of Jewish life are a conscious product of these three ideas: (1) the mutual dependence of the individual and the social, (2) the role of the belief in God in fostering group self-consciousness and (3) the indispensability of common secular interests as the matrix for that role of the belief in God. From that time it became clearer to me that Judaism was anything but a religion as defined by Whitehead, when he said that "a religion is what the individual does with his solitariness," except perhaps in the sense that the individual finds his solitariness so unbearable that he must seek some society to which to belong.

Just as it became impossible for me to think of an individual human being as human when abstracted from any group culture or civilization to supply him with a specific language and a universe of discourse, so I could no longer think of an individual Jew's living withdrawn from the Jewish people and detached from its tradition of habits and values. By the same token, I could no longer think of a people apart from the habits and values which helped to keep it united, which bound its members to one another by a sense of mutual responsibility, and which referred to some transcendent source as their sanction. I could not conceive the Jewish people as able, in the future any more than it was in the past, to maintain its solidarity without religion.

What Is Religion? What Is Jewish Religion?

A religion thus came to mean to me the sum of those habits and values which give a people the will to live in common, to perpetuate itself and to make the best use of its collective life. In achieving these results a people wins salvation. That was the light in which I saw the religion of all the authoritative writings, teachings, forms of worship and ritual practices. Whatever element of individualism they contained was but the life of the Jewish people internalized in the consciousness of the individual. God is always "our God," the God of Israel. The one call to which all who profess Jewish religion, no matter for what reason, readily respond with a religious thrill is, "Hear, O Israel, the Lord our God, the Lord is One." The principle of Jewish peoplehood, forcefully expounded in the chapter by Jack J. Cohen,[3] thus found its rationale in the socio-psychological studies I pursued during those years.

Does that mean that the Jews continue to worship a tribal, or ethnic deity? Such, indeed, is the assumption of many Christian theologians who both ignore the role of the Church in their own religion, and misinterpret the significance of the universal tendency to associate a deity with a particular human society. Human experience, as recorded in the histories and psychologies of religion, teaches that God is a correlative term, like "father" or "king." As "father" implies "child" and "king" implies "subjects," so God implies a "human society," whether it be a tribe, people, nation or church, in the relationship to which His godhood expresses itself. Insofar as God is addressed, or is the subject of address, He is bound to be the God whom men have come to know through the civilization of the society to which they belong. Each society regards its principal god as a universal god, and accounts for his special interest in itself on the ground of its being chosen by him or its being closely related to him in a physical sense. Tribal gods whose power and function are limited to a particular tribe there have always been, but these are generally the inferior gods in the pantheons of the primitive or pagan religions. The principal god in those religions is, as a rule, a universal god whose providence is centered upon the people that worships him. The God of Israel is no more tribal, because of the special providence He has been regarded as exercising over Israel, than the God of the Christians is a tribal deity because, according to Christian theology, He extends special grace only to the members of the Church.

But though Jewish religion can easily be absolved of the charge of being a limited ethnic religion, it cannot function in a vacuum. It requires a living Jewish people and the will of that people to perpetuate itself and to keep on growing in the things of the spirit, as a medium in which to function. Translated into terms of the individual, this means that to have Jewish religion, the individual Jew must be animated by an irrepressible will to belong to the Jewish people, and by such devotion to it as to utilize his ambition for the enhancement of the Jewish people as a very occasion for his own self-fulfillment. His sense of responsibility as a Jew must be mediated through the Jewish people. His conduct and character as a Jew must be such as to sanctify God's name and not profane it. Consequently, the problem of the Jewish religion cannot be solved apart from the problem of the continuance and growth of the Jewish people. Thus, what is at stake is not only the religion of the Jewish people, but its entire heritage or civilization.

That explains why the Reform movement in the nineteenth and the beginning of the twentieth century, despite its laudable efforts to vitalize the Jewish tradition, its recognition of the dynamic character of the Jewish heritage, and its modernization of Jewish worship, seemed to me incapable of keeping Judaism alive. Its fundamental mistake was to treat the national character of traditional Judaism as extraneous to its moral and religious teachings which have a universal significance. The early Reformers believed that not only would the incorporation of Jews into the body politic of the nations that granted them civic rights be facilitated, but that Judaism would finally achieve the status of a universal religion if it were freed from the shell of nationhood. They, therefore, interpreted the Jewish emancipation as the fulfillment of the Messianic hope, in that it finally released the Jews for the great mission for which they had been chosen by God, that of spreading the truth of ethical monotheism.

Reform at that time amounted to a formal demobilization of the Jewish people as an organic entity. It put in place of the Jewish people a loose group of individuals who subscribed to a platitudinous philosophy of life, which on a few days in the year would be expounded and glorified, but which no one would dare to translate into specific social, economic or political action. How long can such a philosophy be preached without becoming a source of boredom? And how long can a group dedicated to such a philosophy continue to exist? By eliminating from Judaism the hope of having Eretz Yisrael become once again the land where Jews could in freedom live their own civilization to the full, and by regarding every expression of Diaspora Jewish life outside worship as at best "extra-curricular" and irrelevant to the Jewish mission, early Reform undermined the very psychological and sociological basis of a normally functioning religion.

By then I was certain that, if Judaism was to survive, it had to be re-formed. But to re-form Judaism at the sacrifice of the Jewish people seemed to me to resemble the feat of the Cheshire cat in Alice's Wonderland which managed to vanish "beginning with the end of the tail and ending with the grin which remained some time after the rest of it had gone." Likewise while insisting that the Jewish people vanish, Reform stressed the doctrine that the Jewish people was divinely chosen.

Judaism As an Evolving Religious Civilization

To counteract the tendency of reducing that which united Jews and gave them group identity to a religion in the conventional sense, I found it necessary to introduce a modification in our Jewish semantics. The term Judaism was no longer to be a synonym for Jewish religion. It was to denote the entire civilization of the Jewish people. That is how I came to use the term Judaism in a sense analogous to that of Hellenism or Americanism. Only in that sense can it imply all that is involved in the present struggle of the Jewish people to survive and find meaning in its life. Judaism is more than the Jewish religion. It is the sum of *everything* about the Jewish people, past, present and future, that makes of the Jews a distinct and identifiable society. *Everything* that unites Jews among themselves and distinguishes them from the rest of the world is part of Judaism. Judaism embraces the entire cultural heritage of the Jews. It consists of language, literature, history, laws, mores, folkways, ethical norms and ideals, all of which have their roots in Eretz Yisrael and are related to the purpose of individual and collective salvation, thereby attaining religious significance.

Far from being static, Judaism has undergone a process of evolution which, viewed from the present, divides itself into three distinct stages. The first stage coincides with the era of the first Commonwealth which came to an end in 586 B. C. E., with the destruction of the first Temple. The second stage coincides with the era of the Second Commonwealth which came to an end with the destruction of the second Temple in 70 C. E. The third stage lasted throughout the centuries following, until about the end of the eighteenth century, when Jews began to be emancipated from the status of alienage and to be accorded civic equality with their non-Jewish neighbors.

The following problem which I had to solve at this point led to an important discovery in the dynamics of religion. Since the Jewish religion has already passed through a number of stages that differed so markedly from each other in their conception of God and in the religious practices associated with the worship of Him, what did the Jewish religion have in common throughout all these stages that enabled it to retain its unbroken continuity? It was important to answer this question not merely for the sake of understanding the past. It involves the current situation. In entering upon the new stage, the Jewish religion will have to undergo further changes. What will constitute its sameness or continuity?

The answer, which I derived from the relation of religion to group life, enabled me to discover what we really mean by a religion's maintaining its continuity, despite radical changes in its beliefs and practices. I became aware that, in every civilization or culture of a people, certain elements in it, principally persons, places, objects and texts are singled out as holy because of the power they are supposed to exert, from the standpoint of welfare and salvation. These are the *sancta* of a civilization. They are transmitted from generation to generation. As a result of changes which a people undergoes in the course of time, the power or holiness of these *sancta* is accounted for differently, in keeping with the changes in general outlook and conception of God. These *sancta*, however, in remaining the same from generation to generation, convey a feeling of group sameness and continuity to the generations that cherish or revere them. Consequently, so long as we Jews hold sacred the same persons, places, objects, relationships, texts, special days etc., as did our ancestors, though for reasons different from theirs, we live by the same religion as they did. Moses, Eretz Yisrael, a Torah scroll, the covenant between God and Israel, Sacred Scripture, Yom Kippur are such *sancta* in Jewish religion. That principle, while solving the problem of continuity in Jewish religion amid the changes which it is bound to undergo, also helps to emphasize the fact that belonging to the Jewish people is a basic prerequisite to professing Jewish religion.

The discovery of the role which the *sancta* of a civilization play in maintaining the continuity of a religion has helped me formulate the position we Jews should take toward the ritual observances in our own religion. Ritual observances consist in specific actions to be performed, or formulas to be recited, in association with the *sancta*. In tradition, the actions and the formulas are prescribed as matters of divine law, or *Halakhah*. The attitude of the Orthodox wing, and to a large extent also that of the Conservative wing in Judaism, with regard to ritual observance, has been that no changes should be made except in the spirit of *Halakhah*. Though that sounds plausible and feasible in theory, in practice no change of any significance has been promulgated in the spirit of *Halakhah* by either wing for the last one hundred years. The reason is not reluctance to make changes, but the inherent impossibility of doing so, without resorting to outright abrogation of, or amendment to, the law.

To allow the infeasibility of treating ritual observance as *Halakhah* to serve as an excuse for allowing such observance to fall into desuetude would be fatal to Jewish religion, because it would lead to the neglect of the Jewish *sancta*. We should feel free to revise traditional rites and observances, and to create new ones.[4] The criterion in dealing with them should be the twofold one, of making us aware of our Jewishness and more conscious of the meaning of God in human experience. We should not mind the lack of uniformity that is bound to result in our observances, though we should endeavor to reduce that lack to a minimum. The highlighting of the same *sancta* would counteract the consequences of what might be too much latitude in the manner of observance.

Strengthening the Will to Live as Jews

The awareness that Judaism has passed through different stages and has undergone such radical transformations as to amount to metamorphoses is indispensable, if we are not to be overwhelmed by the complexities of the situation in which we Jews find ourselves today. That awareness will, in the first place, enable us to see that situation as an inevitable transition stage, with all the evils that usually mark such a stage. Secondly, it will help us overcome the fear of meeting new conditions in new ways, since we would only be wasting time and energy if we were to look to the past for precedents to help us solve problems that could never have been imagined in ancient times. That awareness in itself is one of the unprecedented facts in our present situation. Every transition from one stage to the next was effected, in the Judaism of the past, without awareness that any real change was taking place in outlook and attitude. Hence those who lived then were spared the shock which comes with suddenly becoming aware of having to undergo transformation in order to go on living. This pain of awareness is the price which human beings have to pay for rapid changes in their modes of life and thought. Why should we Jews expect to be spared these growing pains?

It became apparent to me that Jewish life demanded something much more thoroughgoing than a revamping or refurbishing of the traditional ways and ideas. Our problem was more than a case of removing accumulated patina, modernizing the prayerbook, preaching in the vernacular, beautifying the synagogue, estheticizing the worship, and insinuating modern-sounding terminology into the interpretation of traditional texts and doctrines. These were merely ways of treating the symptoms of what ailed contemporary Judaism. They did nothing to get at the root of the ailment. They did not affect the rapid disintegration of the will to live as Jews, of the will to bring up one's children as Jews and to transmit to them the Jewish heritage in a way that would insure their taking it over and cultivating it for transmission to subsequent generations.

The pre-occupation with combating anti-Semitism and raising funds for the victims of anti-Semitism and for philanthropic purposes, which if neglected might lead to anti-Semitism, gives the illusion that Jews are interested in remaining Jews. To be sure, most congregations do concern themselves with the maintenance of Jewish spiritual and moral values, and the religious schools together with a few rabbinical and teacher training schools are struggling hard to have Judaism take root in this land. But, in the first place, there is great danger in the fact that at most only between thirty-five and forty percent of the Jewish population in this country have any religious affiliations, and that, even of these, scarcely more than ten percent are religiously active. The danger lies in the further fact that, with the general tendency of the American middle class to be other-directed rather than self- or inner-directed, the centrifugal and escapist influence of the vast majority of indifferent Jews, and particularly of their children, might prove even more difficult to withstand than that of the non-Jewish environment. If Jewish life is to survive in this country it will have to be rendered immune to the disintegrative influences that emanate from indifferent and assimilationist Jews even more than to those that emanate from the majority population.

It became clear to me that the most plausible reinterpretation of the traditional beliefs would not save Judaism. For on what could their plausibility rest, if not on their acceptability and their relevance to universal human experience? Suppose the story of Creation is made to sound plausible as the ancient way of expressing the idea that in the phenomenon of creativity, whether in nature or in man, we behold a manifestation of divinity. Does one have to be a Jew to accept that idea? Evidently no more than one has to be a Greek in order to accept Plato's and Aristotle's ideas, or to be inspired by them?

Even if the subject matter of Jewish education were entirely compatible with the best in modern thought, or perhaps by very reason of such compatibility, it could not motivate one to live as a Jew and to accept all the handicaps to which being a Jew subjects one. That fact, which is borne out by experience, is what a scientific study of religion leads one to expect. We now know that ritual precedes the reasons, in the form of myths and legends, given for its enactment. Hence, appreciation of the universal meaning of ritual observances is not enough. Something besides the communication of universal meanings and values is necessary to keep a religion alive. Action, based on an understandable or an intuitive grasp of psychological and social factors which operate in a religion, is far more likely to bring about a religious revival than the most rational kind of theology.

The mistake which is generally made is to treat psychological and social factors in religion merely as means, and extraneous to the religious results they are intended to achieve. Thus is set up an artificial barrier between religious and secular. That mistake was not made in the past. Mores, folkways and social institutions that entered into the fabric of Jewish life possessed as much of a religious character as prayer, worship, and faith. It was that which rendered the civilization of the Jewish people religious.

The Jewish Center

It therefore seemed to me that the only way to counteract the disintegrative influences within, as well as without, Jewish life was to create the *conditions* that would not only set in motion socially and psychologically constructive forces, but that would also make them forces for religion. What was needed, I then thought, was to transform the synagogue into a *bet am*, or a neighborhood Jewish Center. Instead of the primary purpose of congregational organizations being worship, it should be social togetherness. That togetherness should find an outlet in the utilization, to the fullest cultural, moral and spiritual advantage, of the leisure which modern machine civilization has made possible.

The history of the Synagogue, and of its beginnings during the second Commonwealth, is a striking illustration of the importance of creating new social agencies when new conditions arise that threaten the life of a people or of its religion. The integration of Jews into a non-Jewish civilization created such conditions. They, therefore, justified transforming the Synagogue into a new kind of social agent, to be known as a "Jewish Center."[5] The function of the Jewish Center would have to be the all-inclusive one of developing around the leisure interests a sense of social solidarity through face-to-face association and friendship. The workaday interests had long ceased to be a common meeting ground for Jews. It was, therefore, urgent to foster the leisure interests as a means to a common meeting ground. The cultivation of the arts, literature, drama, music and the dance, together with studies and discussions leading to the raising of ethical standards in the home life, and in the conduct of business and industry, and to the moral improvement of civic affairs, could provide enough occasion for a creative use of leisure. The pursuit of specifically Jewish studies and interests would then no longer have to be carried on in a vacuum, but would be made relevant to the other leisure activities.

The people, however, whom I succeeded in getting to establish the first Jewish Center were unable to grasp the significance of the new experiment in Jewish living. Even scholarly Jews, and those capable of appreciating a religious development after it has become a part of history, find it difficult to think of themselves or their contemporaries as inaugurating a new development in our day. The study of history is seldom conducive to the making of history. Consequently, the synagogue or communal center, instead of being seen by them as an expression of the Jewish will to live and to create the new social organs by which to sustain itself, was caricatured as intended to produce "muscular" and "swimming pool" Judaism. Since those who ought to know better could be so obtuse to the possibilities of the new type of Jewish institution, how could one expect the laity to be alive to those possibilities? Consequently, though Jewish centers have been established throughout the land as an inevitable result of the need of Jews to find facilities for social and leisure activities under Jewish auspices not provided by the traditional type of synagogue or temple, they are not conspicuous for having made any contribution to Jewish values. They may, in the larger cities, have kept many youngsters off the streets and out of mischief, but the main justification for their existence, that of motivating Jewish activities and interests, has so far been none too evident.

My own experience with the first Jewish Center in this country convinced me that while ideas, to have an effect on human life, must be incorporated in institutions, institutions that are devoid of ideas or based on the wrong ideas are bound to prove sterile. Simultaneously, therefore, with the effort to create for American Judaism the social organs or institutions which modern conditions of living have rendered necessary, attention must be given to the development of an ideology on which those organs or institutions would have to be based. In establishing the Society for the Advancement of Judaism, my purpose was to create a forum for the articulation of an ideology which called for nothing less than a complete rethinking of the principles on which Judaism must henceforth rest, for the reconstruction of the organizations and institutions through which Jews act collectively, and for the replenishment of Jewish cultural values in which present interests play a role.

New Criteria of Loyalty to Judaism

Perhaps nothing could be more indicative of the revolution which I felt had to be effected in the entire pattern of thinking and living as Jews than my formulation at that time of new criteria of loyalty to Judaism. So long as being a Jew meant belonging to the Jewish nation whose origin, early career, and destiny had been set forth in the Torah, and so long as the way of life and its goal, as embodied in definitive teachings in that same Torah, were a sufficient guide, the criterion of loyalty could well consist in subscribing to the principles underlying that Torah, that is, in a credo or series of beliefs. But now Judaism itself is in need of being recognized as a dynamic religious civilization. It is in a state of turbulent transition. If all will go well with it, it will enter upon a new stage in its development. In the Diaspora, Jews have to find a way of living in two civilizations and learning to integrate them in their own personalities.

Hence, what is most needed in our age to identify one as a Jew is a series of objectives which would help to turn one's efforts in the direction of the forthcoming stage in the evolution of Judaism. To accept those objectives, and to have them govern one's life as a Jew, is to entertain specific wants. These wants have to serve as criteria of Jewish loyalty. Such criteria of loyalty express the will to *live* as Jews, in contrast with the creedal criteria formulated by philosophers in the Middle Ages which expressed the will to *believe* as Jews. This means that what counts most in determining whether a Jew has it in him to help build a future for his people and his faith is the will to belong to the Jewish people, and the will to make of belonging to that people a commitment to live up to the best of which he is capable, and an incentive to improve the fortunes and the prestige of that people as a demonstration of God's providence in guiding its destiny. If that entire approach is, as some of the opponents of Reconstructionism contend, mere secularism or sociology, then I say of it what Patrick Henry said of his demand for liberty: "Make the most of it."

But meantime this will to live of the Jewish people, which, as experienced by the individual Jew, means his will to belong to that people, is daily growing weaker, due to social and economic pressures against which there is no counter-influence. Those to whom this fact has given concern have been divided as to what counter-influence is most likely to keep alive in the individual the will to remain a Jew, i. e. the will to identify himself with the Jewish people, to be one of them as the living cell is identified with the body of which it is a part. Anti-Semitism is often regarded as effective in arousing in the Jew the will to belong to his people. That is a mistake. If that will is lacking, anti-Semitism can only embitter the Jew to a point of hating himself and his fellow-Jews. Others have put their trust in Zionism as capable of fortifying the will to live as a Jew. Whether that is so depends upon what kind of Zionism we have in mind. Political Zionism, which is concerned merely with the firm establishment of a self-governing state, may very well be motivated by purely humanitarian considerations in which the destiny of Diaspora Jewry does not even figure.

The Unity of the Jewish People, in Israel and in the Diaspora

It is high time that those to whom the moral and spiritual future of Diaspora Jewry is a matter of concern begin to realize that it is impossible to omit from consideration what corresponds in Christianity to the aspect of polity. Polity refers to the social structure which must serve as the body or frame for a religion. A religious philosophy can exist without a polity or social structure, but not a religion. The Church functions as the social structure for Christendom. Those churches which possess some kind of visible polity are in a far stronger position than those which have been satisfied to become part of a so-called "Invisible Church." The latter are all too soon likely to become literally invisible. In Reform Judaism, prior to the 1937 Convention of its Rabbinical body in Columbus, Ohio, when it drew up a new set of "Guiding Principles," the Jewish people was teetering on the edge of invisibility. But so far, neither Reform nor Conservatism has taken any step to make provision for retrieving and reinstating the Jewish people as the visible body to which we might wish to be so bound as to have its life course into ours and our life into its life.

The need for making such provision has become all the more urgent since the establishment of the State of Israel. The difference between the full-blooded experiences which Jews in Israel share in common, in the course of their military struggles and of their efforts to absorb the new immigrants in the economy of the land, at the cost of tremendous sacrifices, on the one hand, and the thin and rather sterile experiences which Jews in the Diaspora share in common, on the other, is so great that an impassable chasm may divide the Jews of Israel from the Jews of the rest of the world. Certainly the diversity of religious beliefs and practices among all Jews is so pronounced as to reduce what was once the most cohesive solidarity in the world to a kind of human rubble. With all this, there is the troublesome fact that, ever since Jews began to be emancipated, their group status has been deteriorating to a point where it has become ambiguous and anonymous. Jews outside Israel know less today than ever what it is that should keep them Jews, or why they should foster the Jewish heritage. Arthur Koestler voices what is in the minds of many Jews when he says that Jewish parents "should stop to think whether they have the right to place the burden of the ominous knapsack, now void of contents, on their children who have not asked for it."[6]

Jews who wish to normalize their relationship to other Jews, whether in Israel or outside, cannot escape the necessity of having their bond of unity redefined, and their status as a people with a common history and a common destiny reaffirmed and sealed by a formal covenant. Some instrument — a kind of constitution, or a new *Mishneh Torah* — will have to be adopted that will outline the principal ways in which Jews should foster their unity through mutual help in time of need and through cooperation in the furtherance of Judaism as a religious civilization at all times. In all likelihood a long time will pass before the need for the enactment of such a covenant will be felt with a sufficient sense of urgency to consummate it. In the meantime, the idea of it should be promulgated by a ritual, on achieving maturity, analogous to the ritual of *bar mitzvah* on entering the teens.

A more immediate and more practical corollary of peoplehood as the newly recognized status of world Jewry is the establishment of local Jewish communities of an organic character. To be organic those communities would have to embrace all Jewish activities, particularly the religious and educational, and conduct those activities in such a way as to further, both directly and indirectly, a sense of Jewish peoplehood and the desire to strengthen it and to render it creative.

To Jews who are obsessed by the fear of being too conspicuously Jewish, or of being charged with Jewish isolationism or exclusionism, the very notion of an organic community is tabu. They hurl at everything they regard as too Jewish the epithet "ghettoism", and expect it to have the effect of a stink bomb. There is no arguing with those who are fear-obsessed. But for those who are amenable to reason, there is as much likeness between the organic community, which grows out of a clearly apprehended will to live as Jews, and the ghetto, into which our forebears were herded by their oppressors, as there is between a palace and a prison. Because a prison has walls within which it is misery to be compelled to live, we do not conclude that all living within walls is misery. The organic community, far from being a means of withdrawal from the world, should have the effect of enabling Jews to come to that world as co-partners and co-creators, instead of as passive parasites living off the cultural achievements of others. All this is ably set forth by Samuel Dinin in his chapter on "Community."[7]

To emphasize this expected outcome of Jewish organic community, I have had to articulate the principle that, in the Diaspora, it is henceforth the destiny of Jews to live in two civilizations. That cannot come about fortuitously. It has to be carefully thought through and planned in such a way as to result in integrated personality. That should be the chief business of the rabbis, educators, scholars, literati and all Jews of light and leading.

In the attempt to illustrate that principle in action, I have deemed it necessary to look to the American people and its civilization for moral and spiritual values with no less eagerness than to the Jewish people. The role which *sancta* play in a civilization in giving to that civilization a religion, a consciousness of its destiny, and an awareness of its having to be a means of salvation to those who live by it, affords us American Jews an opportunity to make an important contribution to American life. We should single out the heroes, the events, the texts, the relationships, the significant days, that help to fashion in the American people not only a common consciousness but also a common conscience, and interpret those American *sancta* from the standpoint of democracy as a way of life and as a means to salvation. What democracy, in this twofold capacity, can mean Joseph Blau has elaborated with climactic effect in his chapter in this book.[8] By stressing democracy in that spirit, we would contribute to the emergence of a religion for all Americans. American civilization would thus acquire a spiritual significance analogous for us Jews to that of Jewish civilization, and for Christians to that of Christian civilization. That it would do without in the least impugning either the Jewish or Christian social heritage.

This will at first not be an easy idea to digest. It runs counter to the conventional notion that a religion must insist on being the sole and exclusive holder of the key to salvation. To suggest the possibility of professing at the same time two religions, a Jewish or a Christian religion on the one hand, and an American religion, on the other, seems nothing less than ridiculous. On calmer consideration, however, the proposal calling for the accentuation of American *sancta*, and for placing them in a context of democracy raised to a religion and related to the belief in God will be seen as a much needed development in American life, and as an inescapable one, if democracy is to become a faith to live by as well as one to die for.

The question which was bound to force itself irresistibly on my mind at this point was the following: How is it possible for us Jews to accord to the events, persons, texts, places, which are highlighted in American life, a religious significance analogous to that of our own *sancta*, without giving up the claim to our being God's chosen people? As such a people, our religion can be the only true religion and the only means to salvation. What is true of us Jews is equally true of Christians who consider themselves the true Israel and the sole possessors of the key to salvation.

The fact, however, is that outside of classical Reform Judaism and traditional Orthodoxy, even believing Jews no longer take seriously the doctrine of the chosenness of the Jewish people. The Conservative group, in its recently published prayerbook, has played down that doctrine, by paraphrasing it in such a way as to take the teeth out of it. In the first place, the nations from among whom the Jewish people have been chosen are said to be only the heathen people, which are no longer in existence. From being a doctrine concerning the difference between the Jewish people and the *existing* nations, the chosen people idea has been transformed into a historical statement concerning the moral and religious superiority of the Jewish people to all ancient pagan peoples. An eminent theologian of the Conservative group has recently been quoted as saying that Christians and Mohammedans are also chosen peoples. In an environment which would bring us into contact with Hindus and Buddhists, they too would, no doubt, be accorded the title "chosen people." When every body is thus "chosen," chosenness loses its meaning. Reconstructionism, in its religious thinking, has merely advocated the disuse of the formula, "chosen people" and the substitution of the formula, "Thou hast brought us nearer to Thy service," which is free from invidious comparisons.

The obsolescence of the traditional doctrine of election is unquestionably one of the most striking phenomena in the evolution of Jewish religion. It is certain to remove the main obstacle which stands in the way of universalizing the method and the secret of Jewish religion. That method and secret consist in *utilizing the sancta in the life of a people as the frame of reference for its moral and spiritual values*. Such a frame of reference gives a sense of unity to a people, not only in space but also in time, and lifts its life to the level of cosmic significance. Since even religious Jews are beginning to give up the claim to having a monopoly on the method of salvation, we are in a position to apply that method to other civilizations without in the least impugning our own.

God the Power that Makes for Salvation

I have traveled a long distance from the point of departure at the beginning of this chapter, where I promised to have the *way* I came to see the universe account for the way I came to *see* the universe, particularly for what God has come to mean to me. In attempting to live up to the responsibility for which I had been intellectually and emotionally conditioned — that of helping my fellow-Jews to find their social and spiritual heritage worth cultivating, — my first achievement was to acquire a literary and inspirational, rather than a dogmatic and authoritative, understanding of the Bible. Next came the sense of immediacy with which I learned to experience the existential reality of the Jewish people, accompanied by a passionate drive to improve its position in the world and to raise its moral and spiritual prestige. From the various human sciences I gained a comprehension of human nature in the individual and in the group, and of the role of religion in the life of men and nations. Every one of these acquisitions was an answer to problems with which I was confronted in teaching, preaching and organizing men and women for the purpose of advancing Judaism in our American environment; each was tested in the crucible of theoretic and practical challenge.

The distillation of all that experience has come to be, in my case, a philosophy of life which, in the words of H. A. Overstreet, is "the totality of one's loyalties." Insofar as the belief in God, or loyalty to God, is an integral part of that philosophy, it necessarily finds expression in a theology. In view of the specific meaning given in that philosophy to the belief in God, the theology in which it is expounded is a humanist theology. The existential reality which constitutes its initial axiom or starting point is the universal urge in man, *qua* man, to transcend himself. Harold Schulweis rightly interprets this assumption or starting point as a pragmatic hypothesis by which to discover what is needed to render human life wholesome, meaningful and worthwhile.[9] It is this pragmatic hypothesis rather than either tradition, or the classical type of metaphysics, that has confirmed my belief in God as the Power that makes for salvation.

That hypothesis has led me to conclude that the way we come to know God is the correlative of the way we come to know that in us which we identify as personality and which reveals itself to the full in the drive to transcend itself. The civilizations and the religions of history are a record of man's striving for salvation. The Jewish people owes its continuity chiefly to its preoccupation with the urge to salvation. Due to that preoccupation, it has evolved a conception of God that has proved most capable of growing with the evolution of, and growth in, the understanding of salvation. By continuing to concern itself with the problem of what man must do and how he must live in order to transcend the subhuman heritage, the Jewish people is bound to achieve a new lease on life. Such concern will lead to a deepening of the meaning of God in human experience.

That is how I came to suggest the formulation of a new study to be known as Soterics, which should deal with salvation as a problem embracing the whole man. Though Soterics is necessarily grounded in certain scientific and metaphysical assumptions, in itself it is a third alternative to the scientific and the metaphysical approaches to the problem of salvation. That comes out with sufficient clarity in Harold Schulweis' discussion. Thus have I arrived, inductively, through trying to cope with the problem of the survival of the Jewish people, at a conception of God that virtually coincides with that held by Prof. Wieman, and which he arrived at inductively, no doubt, through an entirely different set of experiences. That fact encourages me to believe that the striving of the Jewish people to achieve a place for itself in the modern world is in keeping with the best in human nature, and holds out the possibilities of a new and much needed revelation of God in the world.

Notes

[1] Compare above, Henry N. Wieman, "Mordecai M. Kaplan's Idea of God," pp. 193–210.

[2] Compare above, Eugene Kohn, "Mordecai M. Kaplan As Exegete," pp. 137–154.

[3] Compare above, Jack J. Cohen, "Mordecai M. Kaplan's Concept of Peoplehood," pp. 27–44.

[4] Compare above, David Polish, "Mordecai M. Kaplan and Jewish Liturgy," pp. 211–221.

[5] Compare above, Louis Kraft, "Mordecai M. Kaplan's Contribution to the Jewish Center Movement," pp. 119–135.

[6] Arthur Koestler, *Promise and Fulfillment*, Macmillan, N. Y., 1949, p. 335.

[7] Compare above, Samuel Dinin, "Mordecai M. Kaplan's Concept of Organic Jewish Community," pp. 45–64.

[8] Compare above, Joseph L. Blau, "Mordecai M. Kaplan As a Philosopher of Democracy," pp. 243–261.

[9] Compare above, Harold Schulweis, "Mordecai M. Kaplan's Theory of Soterics," pp. 263–281.

CONTRIBUTORS TO THIS VOLUME

MORTIMER J. COHEN: Rabbi, Congregation Beth Sholom, Philadelphia, Pa.; President, Jewish Book Council of America.

IRA EISENSTEIN: Associate Chairman, Editorial Board, *The Reconstructionist*; Leader, Society for the Advancement of Judaism, New York.

JACK J. COHEN: Director, Jewish Reconstructionist Foundation; Educational Director, Society for the Advancement of Judaism, New York.

SAMUEL DININ: Executive Director, Bureau of Jewish Education, Los Angeles Jewish Community Council; Dean, School of Education, University of Judaism — West Coast Branch of the Jewish Theological Seminary of America.

SAMUEL C. KOHS: Field Secretary, Western States Section, National Jewish Welfare Board.

ISRAEL S. CHIPKIN: Editor, *Jewish Education*; Vice-President, Jewish Education Committee, New York; Vice-President, American Association for Jewish Education.

LOUIS KRAFT: General Secretary, National Council of the National Jewish Welfare Board; General Secretary, World Federation of Y. M. H. A.'s and Jewish Community Centers.

EUGENE KOHN: Managing Editor, *The Reconstructionist*.

HAROLD C. WEISBERG: Director of Field Activities, Jewish Reconstructionist Foundation.

Henry Nelson Wieman: Professor of Philosophy, Houston University; Emeritus Professor of Philosophy of Religion, University of Chicago.

David Polish: Rabbi, Beth Emet The Free Synagogue, Evanston, Illinois; Chairman, Reconstructionist Rabbinical Fellowship, Chicago, Illinois.

Alexander J. Burnstein: Rabbi, Adath Kelal Israel, New York; Instructor in Religion and Philosophy, Seminary School of Jewish Studies, Jewish Theological Seminary of America.

Roland B. Gittelsohn: Rabbi, Central Synagogue of Nassau County, Rockville Centre, L. I., N. Y.

Joseph L. Blau: Assistant Professor of Philosophy, Columbia University.

Harold Schulweis: Associate Rabbi, Temple Emanuel of Parkchester, New York; Instructor in Philosophy, College of the City of New York.